Taste of Home Farm to Table COOKBOOK

1610 N. 2nd St., Suite 102
Milwaukee, WI 53212-3906

Visit us at **tasteofhome.com**
for other Taste of Home books and products.

ISBN Trade Paperback: 978-1-62145-531-8
ISBN DTC Paperback: 978-1-62145-532-5
ISBN DTC Hardcover: 978-1-62145-726-8

Component Number DTC Paperback: 115800574S
Component Number DTC Hardcover:
116000502H
Library of Congress Control Number:
2020952307

Executive Editor: Mark Hagen
Senior Art Director: Raeann Thompson
Designer: Jazmin Delgado
Deputy Editor, Copy Desk: Dulcie Shoener
Copy Editors: Ann Walter, Kara Dennison

Cover
Photographer: Dan Roberts
Food Stylist: Josh Rink
Set Stylist: Melissa Franco

Pictured on front cover:
Avocado Salsa, p. 80
Grilled Onion & Skirt Steak Tacos, p. 119

Pictured on spine:
Herbed Grilled Corn on the Cob, p. 30

Pictured on back cover:
Tasty Marinated Tomatoes, p. 73;
Luscious Blueberry Jam, p. 294;
How to Make Salsa Roja, p. 71;
Refrigerator Jalapeno Dill Pickles, p. 301;
Best Ever Fresh Strawberry Pie, p. 217;
Carrot Soup with Orange & Tarragon, p. 108

Printed in USA
1 3 5 7 9 10 8 6 4 2

SAVOR THE GOODNESS

There's nothing quite like the unbeatable delight of juicy peaches, crisp cucumbers or vine-ripened tomatoes. That's why the editors at *Taste of Home* were so excited to gather their all-time favorite garden-fresh recipes, and put them into this mouthwatering collection.

With **Farm to Table Cookbook,** you'll discover 279 delicious ways to use up your garden bounty, take advantage of farmers market finds and relish the delight of fresh produce all year long.

From vibrant green beans and tender sweet corn to tart berries and succulent melon, this one-of-a-kind cookbook has recipes for all of your garden greats. In addition to recipes for these all-time classic fruits and veggies, you'll also find easy ideas for items such as elderberries, kohlrabi, leeks and others.

Enjoy frosty strawberry treats in the summer and hearty squash dishes in the fall. A section on leafy greens takes your salads to new heights, and an entire DIY chapter explains how simple it is to can, pickle and freeze your bounty so you can enjoy it whenever you'd like.

It's time to savor the goodness that only the freshest foods can deliver. Flip through the striking pages of **Farm to Table Cookbook,** and see just how easy (and delicious) it is to enjoy nature's best!

AT-A-GLANCE ICONS

Look for these icons for no-fuss meal planning. The clock icon represents dishes ready in 30 minutes or less. The 5-ingredient icon spotlights recipes that call for 5 ingredients or fewer (excluding water, salt, pepper, oils or optional items). The snowflake indicates which dishes freeze well, and the slow-cooker icon denotes recipes that simmer on their own.

MORE WAYS TO CONNECT WITH US: 

CONTENTS

A LITTLE KNOW-HOW GOES A LONG WAY WHEN HITTING THE MARKET

Mom was right when she told us to always eat our fruits and veggies. Supermarkets, specialty stores and farmers markets provide us with a wealth of options—from traditional vegetables we grew up with to adventurous heritage and exotic varieties. Here are a few things to keep in mind when selecting produce.

Why Do Organics Cost More?

- Organic foods take longer to grow. There are no chemicals or hormones to speed things up.
- Organic farms are typically smaller than traditional ones. That means they don't benefit from economies of volume and scale.
- Organic farming is more labor-intensive. Farmers rely on muscle to nurture crops and animals.

What's Does Your Produce Label Mean?

USDA Organic

USDA ORGANIC

This label signifies crops were grown without the use of pesticides or chemicals and without genetic modification. If you see this logo in green or black on the food's packaging, it's got the official stamp of approval from the U.S. Department of Agriculture, so you know it's legit.

GMO and Non-GMO

GMO stands for genetically modified organism. Produce labeled GMO has been engineered via DNA modification to be larger or more abundant, or to withstand drought or insect damage. Produce labeled non-GMO has not been modified in this way.

Natural

In theory, foods with this label are produced simply, without food additives, antibiotics, added colors or non-naturally occurring sweeteners. But buyer beware: The Food and Drug Administration has no official regulations regarding manufacturers' use of the "natural" label.

FARM-FRESH PICKIN'S

Here's what's best to buy according to season.

SPRING

Artichokes
Asparagus
Arugula
Avocados
Butter Lettuce
Chard
Green Beans
Mango
Morel
Mushrooms
Parsnips
Radishes
Rhubarb
Snap Peas
Spinach
Strawberries

SUMMER

Apricots
Baby Carrots
Cherries
Cucumbers
Bell Peppers
Blueberries
Boysenberries
Cantaloupe
Corn
Eggplant
Figs
Green Beans
Hearts of Palm
Key Limes
Lima Beans
Long Beans
Melon
Okra
Onions
Peaches
Pineapple
Raspberries
Snow Peas
Tomatoes
Watermelon
Zucchini

FALL

Acorn Squash
Apples
Beets
Broccoli
Cauliflower
Celery
Cranberries
Endive
Garlic
Ginger
Grapes
Jalapeno
Peppers
Kohlrabi
Mushrooms
Pears
Potatoes
Pumpkin
Quince
Sweet Potatoes

WINTER

Brussels Sprouts
Cabbage
Dates
Grapefruit
Horseradish
Kale
Mandarin
Oranges
Passion Fruit
Radicchio
Tangerines
Turnips
Winter Squash

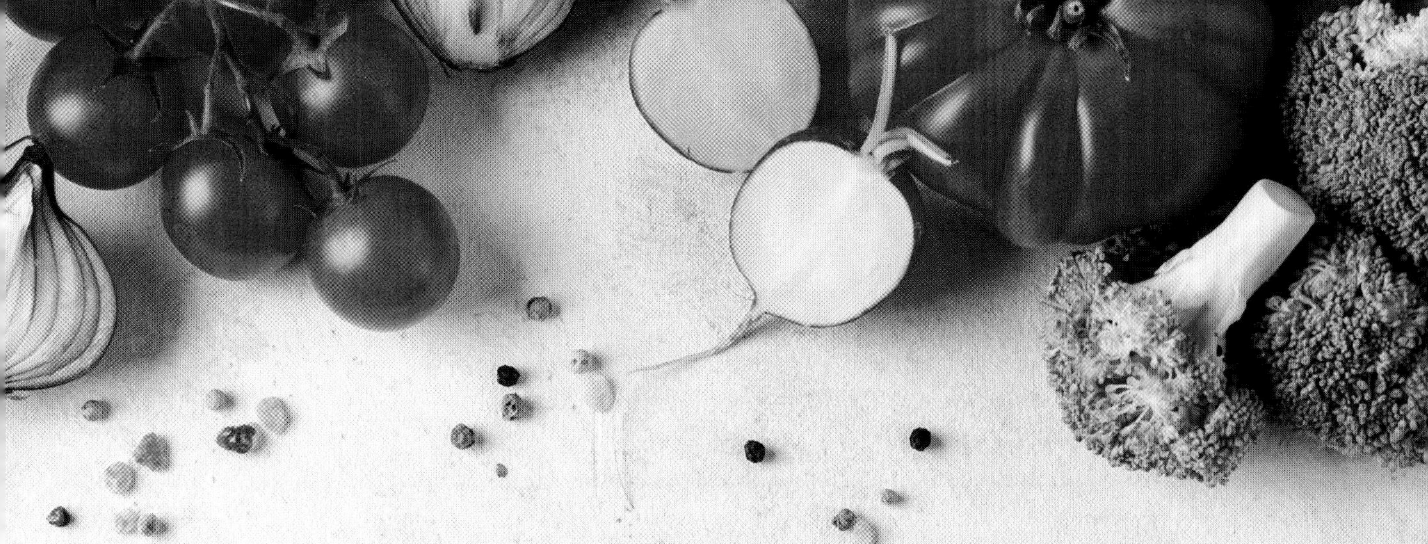

3 WAYS TO SPRUCE UP A SALAD

See page 164 for your basic greens, then add a few of the following ingredients.

Avocados
Most avocados have a buttery texture and a rich, slightly nutty flavor. The two most common avocados are Hass and Florida.

The Hass avocado is grown in California, weighs about half a pound, has a pebbly skin that changes from green to black as it ripens, and is available year-round.

The Florida avocado is grown in Florida, is larger than the Hass, and has a shiny medium green skin that doesn't change color as it ripens. It has more water and, ounce for ounce, less fat and fewer calories than the Hass. It is only available from early fall through winter.

Choose avocados that are heavy for their size and have no blemishes. If the avocado is hard, it will need to ripen before using. If it yields to gentle pressure, it is ready to slice. If the avocado has a small dent after pressing, it's too soft to slice but is suitable for mashing. If there is a large dent after pressing, it is overripe and the flesh is spoiled.

To ripen avocados, place them in a brown paper bag and leave at room temperature for a few days. To hasten ripening, add an apple or banana to the bag.

Store ripe avocados in the refrigerator for up to three days. Brush cut avocados with lemon or lime juice to help prevent the flesh from darkening. Place in an airtight container and eat within two days.

Cucumbers
The most popular cucumber is just classified as the common cucumber. It was bred to have a thicker skin than other cucumbers to protect it during shipping. This cucumber generally has a waxed coating on the skin to keep it fresher longer.

The Kirby cucumber is shorter and has bumpy skin. Originally used for pickling, it can be used in place of the common cucumber in recipes.

The English cucumber, also know as burpless or hothouse cucumber, is narrow and about 2 feet long. It's sold wrapped in plastic.

Select firm cucumbers with round ends. Avoid those with soft spots, bulging middles or withered ends. Store unwashed cucumbers in the refrigerator's crisper drawer for up to one week. Avoid cold areas of the refrigerator where the cucumber might freeze. Wash cucumbers before using. Peel waxed cucumbers and seed if desired.

Radishes
The most commonly available radish is the red radish, which is round or oval. Radishes have a peppery flavor that can range from mild to fiery.

White icicle radishes have a flavor similar to the red but are elongated and carrot-shaped. The Japanese daikon radishes are large white radishes that can weigh around 2 pounds.

Select firm, well-formed radishes. Avoid those that have cracks or blemishes. Store in the refrigerator crisper drawer for up to one week. Store daikon radishes for only three days. Wash or scrub with a vegetable brush before using.

BASIC COOKING METHODS

Get the most out of your veggies with these popular cooking techniques.

Blanching

Blanching means quickly dousing vegetables in boiling water to partially cook, remove skins or stop enzymatic action before freezing or canning. Blanched vegetables are also used in salads, stir-fries and as dippers for dips.

To blanch, bring a gallon of water to a full rolling boil for each pound of vegetables or half-pound of leafy vegetables.

Add vegetables to boiling water and start counting the blanching time as soon as the water returns to a boil. Cover and keep water boiling the entire time. If a recipe offers a range of blanching time, consider starting with the low end of the range for smaller pieces of food and the higher end for large pieces.

Drain and immediately immerse vegetables in ice water. This quickly stops the cooking process and helps the vegetables retain their color and texture. Drain and pat dry.

Boiling

Boiling requires at least 1-2 inches of water or, in some cases, water to cover the vegetables entirely. Broccoli requires only a shallow pot of water. Root vegetables such as carrots or parsnips, and tubers like potatoes are boiled completely covered with water.

To boil, wait for large bubbles to break on the water's surface. To simmer, reduce the heat to medium-low or low so that only tiny bubbles break the water's surface. To cook, reduce the heat to medium; the bubbles will be larger than a simmer but smaller than a boil.

Cooking time begins when the water returns to a boil, cook or simmer. If desired, add a little salt. If the vegetables are to be served in a sauce containing salt or with salty ingredients, it's best to omit the salt from the water.

Roasting and Baking

Roasting and baking are dry-heat methods of cooking that make the flavor of vegetables rich and sweet. Root vegetables, tubers, corn, onions, garlic, eggplant, winter squash and many other vegetables can be roasted.

Cut vegetables of similar density (such as carrots and potatoes) into uniform sizes for even cooking. For mixed vegetables of varying hardness, cut the denser vegetables into smaller pieces so they will cook for the same time as the softer vegetables.

Spread vegetables in a single layer in a baking pan with a 1-inch side; don't crowd the pan. If the pan is too small, the vegetables will steam and not get crisp.

Roast vegetables uncovered at 400° to 450°. Bake vegetables uncovered at 350° to 375°. Cook until the vegetables are tender. Stir occasionally.

Sauteing and Stir-Frying

Sauteing and stir-frying are high-heat cooking methods that quickly cook crisp-tender vegetables.

Cut vegetables into uniform sizes for even cooking. Pat them dry to avoid splattering when adding them to the hot oil.

Heat the oil over medium-high heat until it is hot or it has a shimmer. (Do not heat to smoking.)

Add the vegetables, making sure they are not crowded in the pan. If the pan is too small and the vegetables are crowded, they will steam and not crisp.

Add longer-cooking vegetables first, such as broccoli, then add the more delicate or watery types like mushrooms, tomatoes or zucchini.

Cook until the vegetables are crisp-tender, stirring constantly.

Steaming

Steaming uses the heat created from boiling water to cook the vegetables. Since the vegetables are not actually immersed in the water, more of their nutrients and flavors are preserved.

Place 1-2 inches of water in a saucepan. Place the vegetables in a steamer basket in the saucepan, making sure the water does not touch the bottom of the basket. Bring to a boil; cover and steam until vegetables are crisp-tender.

Cooking time begins when the water reaches a boil and creates steam.

COMMON CUTTING AND CHOPPING TECHNIQUES

Mincing and Chopping

Holding the handle of a chef's knife with one hand, rest the fingers of your other hand on the top of the blade near the tip. Using the handle to guide and apply pressure, move knife in an arc across the food with a rocking motion until pieces of food are the desired size. Mincing results in pieces no larger than ⅛ inch, and chopping produces ¼- to ½-inch pieces.

Dicing and Cubing

Using a utility knife, trim each side of the vegetable, squaring it off. Cut lengthwise into evenly spaced strips. The narrower the strips, the smaller the pieces will be. Stack the strips and cut lengthwise into uniformly sized strips. Arrange the square-shaped strips into a pile and cut widthwise into uniform cubes.

Making Bias or Diagonal Cuts

Holding a chef's knife at an angle to the length of the food, slice as thick or thin as desired. This technique is often used in stir-fry recipes.

Making Julienne Strips

Using a utility knife, cut a thin strip from one side of vegetable. Turn so flat side is down. Cut into 2-inch lengths, then cut each piece lengthwise into thin strips. Stack the strips and cut lengthwise into thinner strips.

Cutting Wedges

Using a chef's knife or serrated knife, cut the produce in half from stem end to the blossom end. Lay halves cut side down on a cutting board. Set knife at the center of one the halves and cut in half vertically. Repeat with other half.

Zesting

Pull a citrus zester across limes, lemons or oranges, being careful not to remove the bitter white pith. Chop zest strips into fine pieces if desired.

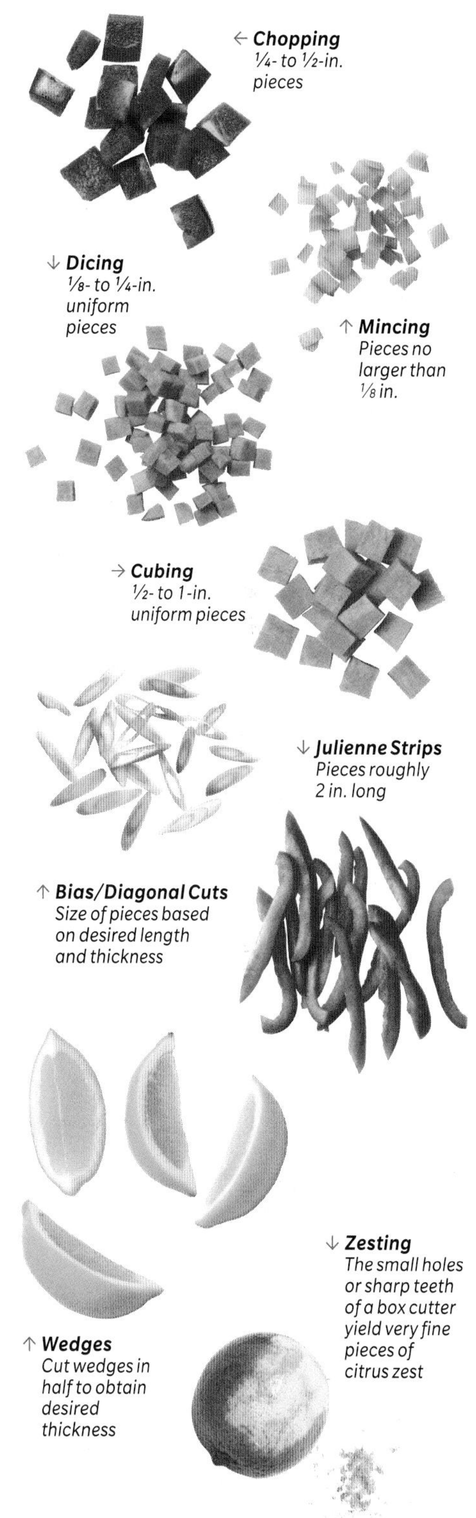

CHAPTER 1

GARDEN-FRESH CLASSICS

Tomatoes, peppers, rhubarb, corn...these are a few of the classics home cooks rely on to bring hearty yet wholesome dishes to the table. Turn here for new ways to enjoy the most popular garden greats.

SLOW-COOKER BEEF & BROCCOLI

I love introducing my kids to all kinds of flavors. This Asian-inspired slow-cooker meal is one of their favorites, so I serve it often.

—Brandy Stansbury, Edna, TX

PREP: 20 MIN. • **COOK:** 6½ HOURS • **MAKES:** 4 SERVINGS

- **2 cups beef broth**
- **½ cup reduced-sodium soy sauce**
- **⅓ cup packed brown sugar**
- **1½ tsp. sesame oil**
- **1 garlic cloves, minced**
- **1 beef top sirloin steak (1½ lbs.), cut into ½-in.-thick strips**
- **2 Tbsp. cornstarch**
- **¼ cup cold water**
- **4 cups fresh broccoli florets**
- **Hot cooked rice**
- **Optional: Sesame seeds and thinly sliced green onions**

1. In a 5-qt. slow cooker, combine the first 5 ingredients. Add beef; stir to coat. Cover and cook on low until tender, about 6 hours.

2. In a small bowl, whisk cornstarch and cold water until smooth; stir into slow cooker. Cover and cook on high until thickened, about 30 minutes. Meanwhile, in a large saucepan, place a steamer basket over 1 in. of water. Place broccoli in basket. Bring water to a boil. Reduce heat to maintain a simmer; steam, covered, until crisp-tender, 3-4 minutes. Stir broccoli into slow cooker. Serve over rice. If desired, garnish with optional ingredients.

1 cup: 366 cal., 9g fat (3g sat. fat), 69mg chol., 1696mg sod., 28g carb. (19g sugars, 2g fiber), 42g pro.

LEMON PEPPER ROASTED BROCCOLI

Fresh green broccoli turns tangy and tasty when roasted with lemon juice and pepper. A sprinkle of almonds adds crunch.

—Liz Bellville, Tonasket, WA

TAKES: 25 MIN. • **MAKES:** 8 SERVINGS

- **1½ lbs. fresh broccoli florets (about 12 cups)**
- **2 Tbsp. olive oil**
- **½ tsp. lemon juice**
- **¼ tsp. salt**
- **¼ tsp. coarsely ground pepper, divided**
- **¼ cup chopped almonds**
- **2 tsp. grated lemon zest**

1. Preheat oven to 450°. Place broccoli in a large bowl. Whisk oil, lemon juice, salt and ⅛ tsp. pepper until blended; drizzle over broccoli and toss to coat. Transfer to a 15x10x1-in. baking pan.

2. Roast 10-15 minutes or until tender. Transfer to a serving dish. Sprinkle with almonds, lemon zest and the remaining pepper; toss to combine.

1 cup: 84 cal., 6g fat (1g sat. fat), 0 chol., 103mg sod., 7g carb. (0 sugars, 4g fiber), 4g pro. **Diabetic exchanges:** 1 vegetable, 1 fat.

SLOW-COOKER
BEEF & BROCCOLI

BROCCOLI SALAD SUPREME

BROCCOLI SALAD SUPREME

People can't get enough of the sweet grapes and crunchy broccoli in this colorful salad. I appreciate its make-ahead convenience.

—Terri Twyman, Bonanza, OR

PREP: 10 MIN. + CHILLING • **MAKES:** ABOUT 20 SERVINGS

- 10 cups broccoli florets (about 3½ lbs.)
- 6 cups seedless red grapes (about 3 lbs.)
- 1 cup sliced celery
- 6 green onions, sliced
- 2 cups mayonnaise
- ⅔ cup sugar
- 2 Tbsp. cider vinegar
- 1 lb. sliced bacon, cooked and crumbled
- 1⅓ cups slivered almonds, toasted

1. In a large salad bowl, combine the broccoli, grapes, celery and onions. In a small bowl, combine the mayonnaise, sugar and vinegar. Pour over broccoli mixture and toss to coat.

2. Cover and refrigerate for at least 4 hours or overnight. Just before serving, gently stir in bacon and almonds.

1 cup: 344 cal., 26g fat (4g sat. fat), 14mg chol., 268mg sod., 25g carb. (20g sugars, 4g fiber), 7g pro.

GARLIC CHICKEN & BROCCOLI

This simple riff on Chinese chicken proves you can savor the takeout taste you crave while still eating right.

—Connie Krupp, Racine, WI

PREP: 15 MIN. • **COOK:** 3 HOURS • **MAKES:** 8 SERVINGS

- 2 lbs. boneless skinless chicken breasts, cut into 1-in. pieces
- 4 cups fresh broccoli florets
- 4 medium carrots, julienned
- 1 can (8 oz.) sliced water chestnuts, drained
- 6 garlic cloves, minced
- 3 cups reduced-sodium chicken broth
- ¼ cup reduced-sodium soy sauce
- 2 Tbsp. brown sugar
- 2 Tbsp. sesame oil
- 2 Tbsp. rice vinegar
- ½ tsp. salt
- ½ tsp. pepper
- ⅓ cup cornstarch
- ⅓ cup water
- Hot cooked rice

1. In a 4- or 5-qt. slow cooker, combine the chicken, broccoli, carrots, water chestnuts and garlic. In a large bowl, mix the next 7 ingredients; pour over chicken mixture. Cook, covered, on low until the chicken and broccoli are tender, 3-4 hours.

2. Remove the chicken and vegetables; keep warm. Strain cooking juices into a small saucepan; skim fat. Bring juices to a boil. In a small bowl, mix cornstarch and water until smooth; stir into cooking juices. Return to a boil; cook and stir until thickened, 1-2 minutes. Serve with the chicken, vegetables and hot cooked rice.

Freeze option: Place chicken and vegetables in freezer containers; top with sauce. Cool and freeze. To use, partially thaw in refrigerator overnight. Microwave, covered, on high in a microwave-safe dish until heated through, stirring occasionally; add water if necessary.

1¼ cups: 241 cal., 6g fat (1g sat. fat), 63mg chol., 798mg sod., 19g carb. (8g sugars, 3g fiber), 26g pro. **Diabetic exchanges:** 3 lean meat, 1 vegetable, ½ starch, ½ fat.

CHEESY BROCCOLI SOUP IN A BREAD BOWL

This creamy, cheesy broccoli soup tastes just like it came from a popular restaurant chain. My family requests it all the time. You can even make your own homemade bread bowls with the recipe on my blog, Yammie's Noshery.

—Rachel Preus, Marshall, MI

PREP: 15 MIN. • COOK: 30 MIN. • MAKES: 6 SERVINGS

- **¼ cup butter, cubed**
- **½ cup chopped onion**
- **2 garlic cloves, minced**
- **4 cups fresh broccoli florets (about 8 oz.)**
- **1 large carrot, finely chopped**
- **3 cups chicken stock**
- **2 cups half-and-half cream**
- **2 bay leaves**
- **½ tsp. salt**
- **¼ tsp. ground nutmeg**
- **¼ tsp. pepper**
- **¼ cup cornstarch**
- **¼ cup water or additional chicken stock**
- **2½ cups shredded cheddar cheese**
- **6 small round bread loaves (about 8 oz. each), optional**
- **Optional toppings: Crumbled cooked bacon, additional shredded cheddar cheese, ground nutmeg and pepper**

1. In a 6-qt. stockpot, heat butter over medium heat; saute onion and garlic until tender, 6-8 minutes. Stir in broccoli, carrot, stock, cream and seasonings; bring to a boil. Simmer, uncovered, until vegetables are tender, 10-12 minutes.

2. Mix cornstarch and water until smooth; stir into soup. Bring to a boil, stirring occasionally; cook and stir until thickened, 1-2 minutes. Remove bay leaves. Stir in cheese until melted.

3. If using bread bowls, cut a slice off the top of each bread loaf; hollow out bottoms, leaving ¼-in.-thick shells (save removed bread for another use). Fill with soup just before serving.

4. If desired, serve soup with toppings.

1 cup: 422 cal., 32g fat (19g sat. fat), 107mg chol., 904mg sod., 15g carb. (5g sugars, 2g fiber), 17g pro.

Test Kitchen Tip: Remove larger leaves and tough ends of lower stalks; wash. If using whole spears, cut lengthwise into 1-in.-wide pieces; stalks may also be peeled for more even cooking. If using florets, cut ¼-½ in. below heads; discard stalks.

FARMERS MARKET FIND

Select firm but tender stalks of broccoli with compact, dark green or slightly purplish florets. Store unwashed broccoli in an open bag in the refrigerator crisper drawer up to 4 days.

"MY FAMILY LOVED IT! WE ALL AGREED IT WAS VERY SIMILAR TO PANERA BREAD. I WILL NEED TO DOUBLE OR TRIPLE THIS RECIPE THE NEXT TIME I MAKE IT. DEFINITELY A KEEPER."

—JUSTDUCKY76, TASTEOFHOME.COM

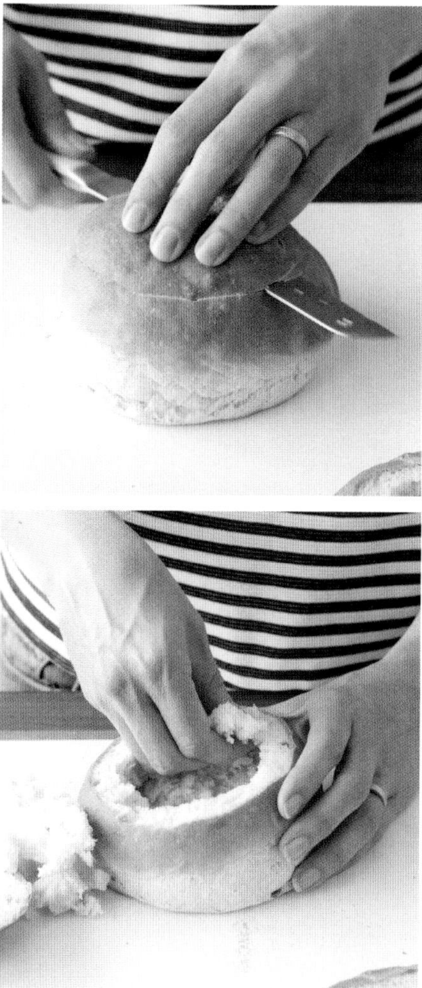

CHEESY BROCCOLI SOUP IN A BREAD BOWL

HOW-TO

Raid the Silverware Drawer

If you have a grapefruit knife, use its double-serrated blade to make quick work of carving out a bread bowl.

Make a Bread Bowl

- Carefully cut a thin slice off the top of the bread loaf.
- Hollow out the bottom of the loaf, leaving a ¼-in.-thick shell. Save the bread for another use. Add soup, stew or chili immediately before serving.

FAUX
POTATO SALAD

FAUX POTATO SALAD

Cauliflower in potato salad? You bet, along with carrots, olives and other yummy surprises.

—Mike Schulz, Tawas City, MI

TAKES: 30 MIN. • MAKES: 8 SERVINGS

- **1 medium head cauliflower, broken into florets**
- **1 medium carrot, chopped**
- **2 hard-boiled large eggs, chopped**
- **4 green onions, chopped**
- **1 celery rib, chopped**
- **¼ cup pitted green olives, halved lengthwise**
- **¼ cup thinly sliced radishes**
- **¼ cup chopped dill pickle**
- **¼ cup fat-free mayonnaise**
- **1 Tbsp. Dijon mustard**
- **¼ tsp. salt**
- **⅛ tsp. pepper**

1. In a large saucepan, bring 1 in. of water to a boil. Add cauliflower florets; cook, covered, 4-7 minutes or until crisp-tender. Drain and rinse in cold water. Pat dry and place in a large bowl. Add carrot, eggs, green onions, celery, olives, radishes and chopped pickle.

2. In a small bowl, mix the remaining ingredients. Add to cauliflower mixture; toss to coat. Refrigerate until serving.

¾ cup: 61 cal., 2g fat (0 sat. fat), 54mg chol., 375mg sod., 7g carb. (3g sugars, 3g fiber), 3g pro. **Diabetic exchanges:** 1 vegetable, ½ starch.

CAULIFLOWER WITH ROASTED ALMOND DIP

Make cauliflower sing with this sauce, rich in both color and flavor. The sauce takes some time but is well worth it.

—Lauren McAnelly, Des Moines, IA

PREP: 40 MIN. • BAKE: 35 MIN. • MAKES: 10 SERVINGS (2¼ CUPS DIP)

- **10 cups water**
- **1 cup olive oil, divided**
- **¾ cup sherry or red wine vinegar, divided**
- **3 Tbsp. salt**
- **1 bay leaf**
- **1 Tbsp. crushed red pepper flakes**
- **1 large head cauliflower**
- **½ cup whole almonds, toasted**
- **½ cup soft whole wheat or white bread crumbs, toasted**
- **½ cup fire-roasted crushed tomatoes**
- **1 jar (8 oz.) roasted sweet red peppers, drained**
- **2 Tbsp. minced fresh parsley**
- **2 garlic cloves**
- **1 tsp. sweet paprika**
- **½ tsp. salt**
- **¼ tsp. freshly ground pepper**

1. In a 6-qt. stockpot, bring the water, ½ cup oil, ½ cup sherry, salt, bay leaf and pepper flake to a boil. Add cauliflower. Reduce the heat; simmer, uncovered, until a knife easily inserts into the center, 15-20 minutes, turning halfway through cooking. Remove with a slotted spoon; drain well on paper towels.

2. Preheat oven to 450°. Place the cauliflower on a greased wire rack in a 15x10x1-in. baking pan. Bake on a lower oven rack until dark golden, 35-40 minutes.

3. Meanwhile, place almonds, bread crumbs, tomatoes, roasted peppers, parsley, garlic, paprika, salt and pepper in a food processor; pulse until finely chopped. Add remaining sherry; process until blended. Continue processing while gradually adding remaining oil in a steady stream. Serve with cauliflower.

1 serving: 194 cal., 16g fat (2g sat. fat), 0 chol., 470mg sod., 9g carb. (3g sugars, 3g fiber), 4g pro.

CAULIFLOWER & TOFU CURRY

Cauliflower, garbanzo beans and tofu are subtle on their own, but together they make an awesome base for curry. We have this recipe weekly because one of us is always craving it.

—Patrick McGilvray, Cincinnati, OH

TAKES: 30 MIN. • MAKES: 6 SERVINGS

1 Tbsp. olive oil
2 medium carrots, sliced
1 medium onion, chopped
3 tsp. curry powder
¼ tsp. salt
¼ tsp. pepper
1 small head cauliflower, broken into florets (about 3 cups)
1 can (14½ oz.) fire-roasted crushed tomatoes
1 pkg. (14 oz.) extra-firm tofu, drained and cut into ½-in. cubes
1 cup vegetable broth
1 can (15 oz.) garbanzo beans or chickpeas, rinsed and drained
1 can (13.66 oz.) coconut milk
1 cup frozen peas
Hot cooked rice
Chopped fresh cilantro

1. In a 6-qt. stockpot, heat oil over medium-high heat. Add carrots and onion; cook and stir until onion is tender, 4-5 minutes. Stir in seasonings.

2. Add cauliflower, tomatoes, tofu and broth; bring to a boil. Reduce heat; simmer, covered, 10 minutes. Stir in garbanzo beans, coconut milk and peas; return to a boil. Reduce heat to medium; cook, uncovered, stirring occasionally, until slightly thickened and cauliflower is tender, 5-7 minutes.

3. Serve with rice. Sprinkle with cilantro.

1⅓ cups: 338 cal., 21g fat (13g sat. fat), 0 chol., 528mg sod., 29g carb. (9g sugars, 7g fiber), 13g pro.

ROASTED BUFFALO CAULIFLOWER BITES

Try these savory bites for a kickin' appetizer that's healthy, too. It also makes a wonderful change-of-pace side dish!

—Emily Tyra, Traverse City, MI

TAKES: 25 MIN. • MAKES: 8 SERVINGS

1 medium head cauliflower (about 2¼ lbs.), cut into florets
1 Tbsp. canola oil
½ cup Buffalo wing sauce
Blue cheese salad dressing

1. Preheat oven to 400°. Toss cauliflower with oil; spread in a 15x10x1-in. pan. Roast until tender and lightly browned, 20-25 minutes, stirring once.

2. Transfer cauliflower to a bowl; toss with wing sauce. Serve with dressing.

⅓ cup: 39 cal., 2g fat (0 sat. fat), 0 chol., 474mg sod., 5g carb. (2g sugars, 2g fiber), 2g pro.

CAULIFLOWER &
TOFU CURRY

FARMERS MARKET FIND

When purchasing white cauliflower, look for heads that are pale without any brown or dark spots. The heads should be compact and free of any soft spots.

HOW-TO

Make It a Cauliflower Mash

- When chopping cauliflower, keep each piece the same size for even cooking.
- After returning the cooked cauliflower to the pan, move the pan to very low heat for a minute to evaporate any excess water.
- For a chunky mash, use a basic hand masher until the cauliflower reaches desired consistency. For a smoother texture, grab your hand mixer or try a food processor.

CAULIFLOWER MASH

CAULIFLOWER MASH

This quick and easy mashed cauliflower is a delicious alternative to same-old mashed spuds, and it's healthier, too!

—Nick Iverson, Denver, CO

TAKES: 20 MIN. • MAKES: 6 SERVINGS

- 1 large head cauliflower, chopped (about 6 cups)
- ½ cup chicken broth
- 2 garlic cloves, crushed
- 1 tsp. whole peppercorns
- 1 bay leaf
- ½ tsp. salt

1. Place cauliflower in a large saucepan; add water to cover. Bring to a boil. Reduce heat. Simmer, covered, until tender, 10-12 minutes. Drain; return to pan.

2. Meanwhile, combine remaining ingredients in a small saucepan. Bring to a boil. Immediately remove from heat and strain; discard garlic, peppercorns and bay leaf. Add broth to cauliflower. Mash to reach desired consistency.

⅔ cup: 26 cal., 0 fat (0 sat. fat), 0 chol., 308mg sod., 5g carb. (2g sugars, 2g fiber), 2g pro. **Diabetic exchanges:** 1 vegetable.

CHEESY CAULIFLOWER BREADSTICKS

These grain-free breadsticks are made with cauliflower instead of flour. Serve with your favorite marinara sauce.

—Nick Iverson, Denver, CO

PREP: 20 MIN. • BAKE: 30 MIN. • MAKES: 12 SERVINGS

- 1 medium head cauliflower, cut into 1-in. florets (about 6 cups)
- ½ cup shredded part-skim mozzarella cheese
- ½ cup grated Parmesan cheese
- ½ cup shredded cheddar cheese
- 1 large egg, room temperature
- ¼ cup chopped fresh basil
- ¼ cup chopped fresh parsley
- 1 garlic clove, minced
- 1 tsp. salt
- ½ tsp. pepper
- Marinara sauce, optional

1. Preheat oven to 425°. Process the cauliflower in batches in a food processor until finely ground. Microwave, covered, in a microwave-safe bowl on high until tender, about 8 minutes. When cauliflower is cool enough to handle, wrap in a clean kitchen towel and squeeze dry. Return to bowl.

2. Meanwhile, in another bowl, mix cheeses together. Stir half of cheese mixture into cauliflower, reserving remainder. Combine next 6 ingredients; stir into cauliflower.

3. On a baking sheet lined with parchment, shape cauliflower mixture into an 11x9-in. rectangle. Bake until edges are golden brown, 20-25 minutes. Top with the reserved cheese; bake until melted and bubbly, 10-12 minutes. Cut into 12 breadsticks. If desired, serve with marinara sauce.

1 breadstick: 66 cal., 4g fat (2g sat. fat), 26mg chol., 340mg sod., 4g carb. (1g sugars, 1g fiber), 5g pro. **Diabetic exchanges:** 1 vegetable, 1 medium-fat meat.

BOURBON CHICKEN TACOS WITH CORN

I wanted to try a different take on taco night and decided on barbecue for the theme. Even my father enjoyed this casual dinner, and he normally doesn't care for tacos.

—LaDale Hymer, Cleveland, OK

PREP: 30 MIN. • COOK: 3 HOURS • MAKES: 8 SERVINGS

- 1 cup ketchup
- 1 small red onion, finely chopped
- ¼ cup packed brown sugar
- 2 Tbsp. Worcestershire sauce
- 2 Tbsp. maple syrup
- 2 Tbsp. cider vinegar
- 1 Tbsp. chopped fresh parsley
- 2 garlic cloves, minced
- ¼ tsp. pepper
- 3 Tbsp. bourbon, divided
- 1½ lbs. boneless skinless chicken breasts

SALSA

- 2 cups fresh or thawed frozen corn
- 1 cup chopped sweet red pepper
- ½ cup finely chopped red onion
- 2 medium limes, zested and juiced
- ⅛ tsp. hot pepper sauce
- ½ tsp. salt
- ¼ tsp. pepper
- 8 flour tortillas (8 in.)
- Minced cilantro, optional

1. In a 3-qt. slow cooker, combine the first 9 ingredients and 2 Tbsp. bourbon. Add chicken; turn to coat. Cook, covered, on low until a thermometer reads 165°, 3-4 hours. Remove chicken; shred with 2 forks. Return to slow cooker; stir in remaining bourbon. Heat through.

2. Meanwhile, for salsa, combine corn, red pepper, onion, lime zest, lime juice, hot sauce, salt and pepper in a bowl. Serve chicken in tortillas with salsa. If desired, top with cilantro.

1 taco: 387 cal., 6g fat (2g sat. fat), 47mg chol., 855mg sod., 58g carb. (22g sugars, 4g fiber), 23g pro.

FREEZER SWEET CORN

People ask me how to freeze corn on the cob because my frozen corn tastes as good as fresh! This way it stays crisp-tender and now I can have fresh corn any time of the year.

—Judy Oudekerk, St. Michael, MN

PREP: 30 MIN. • COOK: 15 MIN. • MAKES: 3 QT.

- 4 qt. fresh corn (cut from about 20 ears)
- 1 qt. hot water
- ⅔ cup sugar
- ½ cup butter, cubed
- 2 tsp. salt

In a stockpot, combine all of the ingredients; bring to a boil. Reduce heat; simmer, uncovered, 5-7 minutes, stirring occasionally. Transfer to large shallow containers to cool quickly, stirring occasionally. Freeze in airtight containers, allowing headspace for expansion.

½ cup: 113 cal., 5g fat (2g sat. fat), 10mg chol., 245mg sod., 18g carb. (9g sugars, 2g fiber), 2g pro.

Test Kitchen Tip: A fluted tube cake pan is a well-known tool for catching kernels and milk from fresh-cut corn. If you don't have one—or you don't want to risk nicking its finish—use a small bowl inverted inside a larger one.

FREEZER
SWEET CORN

SWEET CORN & ZUCCHINI SOUFFLE

SWEET CORN & ZUCCHINI SOUFFLE

As novice gardeners, my husband and I sowed zucchini seeds—15 hills' worth! Happily, my family requests this side dish often, so it's a keeper.

—Carol Ellerbroek, Gladstone, IL

PREP: 40 MIN. + STANDING • **BAKE:** 45 MIN. • **MAKES:** 10 SERVINGS

- **2 medium zucchini (about 1½ lbs.), shredded**
- **2½ tsp. salt, divided**
- **6 large eggs**
- **2 medium ears sweet corn, husked**
- **6 Tbsp. butter**
- **2 green onions, chopped**
- **6 Tbsp. all-purpose flour**
- **¼ tsp. pepper**
- **1¼ cups 2% milk**
- **½ cup shredded Swiss cheese**

FARMERS MARKET FIND

Look for sweet corn with green husks and fresh silk. Pull the husk down slightly, checking for even rows of firm kernels that don't appear too milky.

1. Place zucchini in a colander over a plate; sprinkle with 1 tsp. salt and toss. Let stand 30 minutes. Rinse and drain well; blot dry with paper towels. Meanwhile, separate eggs; let stand at room temperature 30 minutes. Grease a 2½-qt. souffle dish; dust lightly with flour.

2. Preheat oven to 350°. Place corn in a large saucepan; add water to cover. Bring to a boil. Reduce heat; cook, covered, 3-5 minutes or until crisp-tender; drain. Cool slightly. Cut corn from cobs and place in a large bowl.

3. In a large skillet, heat butter over medium-high heat. Add green onions and zucchini; cook and stir until tender. Stir in flour, pepper and remaining salt until blended; gradually stir in milk. Bring to a boil, stirring constantly; cook and stir 1-2 minutes or until sauce is thickened. Add to corn; stir in cheese.

4. Stir a small amount of hot zucchini mixture into egg yolks; return all to bowl, stirring constantly. Cool slightly.

5. In a large bowl, beat egg whites on high speed until stiff but not dry. With a rubber spatula, gently stir a fourth of the egg whites into zucchini mixture. Fold in remaining egg whites. Transfer to prepared dish.

6. Bake 45-50 minutes or until top is puffed and center appears set. Serve immediately.

1 serving: 178 cal., 12g fat (7g sat. fat), 152mg chol., 599mg sod., 10g carb. (3g sugars, 1g fiber), 8g pro.

"LOVE THIS TWIST ON A SOUFFLE. IT HELPED ME USE UP SOME EXTRAS FROM MY GARDEN. I WILL BE MAKING THIS AGAIN."

—RANDCBRUNS, TASTEOFHOME.COM

SWEET CORN-TOMATO SALAD

I always make this for family events and parties. It reminds me of all the fun barbecues and picnics over the years. Fresh corn and basil make a huge difference in this recipe.

—Jessica Kleinbaum, Plant City, FL

PREP: 15 MIN. • **COOK:** 10 MIN. + CHILLING • **MAKES:** 10 SERVINGS

- **8 medium ears sweet corn, husked**
- **1 large sweet red pepper, chopped**
- **2 cups cherry tomatoes, halved**
- **1 small red onion, finely chopped**
- **¼ cup coarsely chopped fresh basil**

DRESSING

- **½ cup canola oil**
- **¼ cup rice vinegar**
- **2 Tbsp. lime juice**
- **1¼ tsp. salt**
- **½ to 1 tsp. hot pepper sauce**
- **½ tsp. garlic powder**
- **½ tsp. grated lime zest**
- **¼ tsp. pepper**

1. Place corn in a large stockpot; add water to cover. Bring to a boil. Cook, covered, until crisp-tender, 6-8 minutes; drain. Cool slightly. Cut corn from cobs and place in a large bowl. Stir in red pepper, tomatoes, onion and basil.

2. In a small bowl, whisk the dressing ingredients until blended. Pour over the corn mixture; toss to coat. Refrigerate, covered, at least 1 hour.

¾ cup: 192 cal., 12g fat (1g sat. fat), 0 chol., 407mg sod., 21g carb. (9g sugars, 3g fiber), 3g pro. **Diabetic exchanges:** 2 fat, 1 starch, 1 vegetable.

5i HERBED GRILLED CORN ON THE COB

I'd never grilled corn until last summer when my sister-in-law served it. Wow! What a treat! So simple yet delicious—grilled corn is now a must on my summer menus.

—Angela Leinenbach, Mechanicsville, VA

PREP: 20 MIN. + SOAKING • **GRILL:** 25 MIN. • **MAKES:** 8 SERVINGS

- **8 medium ears sweet corn**
- **½ cup butter, softened**
- **2 Tbsp. minced fresh basil**
- **2 Tbsp. minced fresh parsley**
- **½ tsp. salt**

1. Place corn in a stockpot; cover with cold water. Soak 20 minutes; drain. Carefully peel back corn husks to within 1 in. of bottoms; remove silk.

2. In a small bowl, mix remaining ingredients; spread over corn. Rewrap corn in husks; secure with kitchen string.

3. Grill corn; covered, over medium heat until tender, 25-30 minutes, turning often. Cut string and peel back husks.

1 ear of corn with 1 Tbsp. butter mixture: 178 cal., 12g fat (7g sat. fat), 31mg chol., 277mg sod., 17g carb. (5g sugars, 2g fiber), 3g pro.

HERBED GRILLED CORN ON THE COB

HOW-TO

How to Grill Corn

- Place whole unshucked ears of corn in a stockpot and cover with cold water. Soak for 30 minutes then drain.
- Place the ears directly over hot coals. Grill for 30 minutes, turning corn occasionally or until the husks are completely charred black.
- Remove from grill, peel back the husks and remove silk. Butter and season to taste.

JALAPENO POPPER
MEXICAN STREET CORN

"WOW! WHAT A NEAT WAY TO JAZZ UP CORN ON THE COB!"

—BEEMA, TASTEOFHOME.COM

JALAPENO POPPER MEXICAN STREET CORN

We love this summer staple. If you're really feeling wild, sprinkle these with a bit of cooked and crumbled bacon.
—Crystal Schlueter, Northglenn, CO

TAKES: 30 MIN. • MAKES: 4 SERVINGS

- **4 ears fresh sweet corn**
- **2 jalapeno peppers**
- **3 Tbsp. canola oil, divided**
- **¾ tsp. salt, divided**
- **¼ cup panko bread crumbs**
- **½ tsp. smoked paprika**
- **½ tsp. dried Mexican oregano**
- **4 oz. cream cheese, softened**
- **¼ cup media crema table cream or sour cream thinned with 1 tsp. 2% milk**
- **2 Tbsp. lime juice**
- **Ground chipotle pepper or chili powder**
- **Optional: Chopped fresh cilantro and lime wedges**

1. Husk corn. Rub corn and jalapenos with 2 Tbsp. canola oil. Grill, covered, on a greased grill rack over medium-high direct heat until lightly charred on all sides, 10-12 minutes. Remove from heat. When jalapenos are cool enough to handle, remove skin, seeds and membranes; chop finely. Set aside.

2. Sprinkle corn with ½ tsp. salt. In a small skillet, heat remaining oil over medium heat. Add panko; cook and stir until starting to brown. Add paprika and oregano; cook until crumbs are toasted and fragrant.

3. Meanwhile, combine the cream cheese, crema, lime juice and remaining salt; spread over corn. Sprinkle with the bread crumbs, jalapenos, chipotle pepper and, if desired, cilantro and lime wedges.

NOTE: Look for media crema table cream in the international foods section.

1 ear of corn: 339 cal., 26g fat (9g sat. fat), 39mg chol., 568mg sod., 25g carb. (8g sugars, 3g fiber), 6g pro.:

BAKED SWEET CORN CROQUETTES

My delicious corn croquettes are baked like muffins instead of fried.
They can be served with butter but my family prefers salsa as an accompaniment.
—Karen Kuebler, Dallas, TX

PREP: 30 MIN. • BAKE: 10 MIN./BATCH • MAKES: 5½ DOZEN

- **3 cups fresh corn, divided**
- **1 cup cornmeal**
- **1 cup 2% milk**
- **1 tsp. sugar**
- **¼ tsp. ground cinnamon, optional**
- **4 oz. cream cheese, softened**
- **¼ cup butter, softened**
- **2 large eggs, room temperature**
- **3 cups shredded cheddar cheese**
- **Sour cream and minced chives**

1. Preheat oven to 350°. Place 2 cups corn kernels in a food processor; process until pureed. Transfer the pureed corn to a large bowl; whisk in the cornmeal, milk, sugar, remaining corn and, if desired, cinnamon until blended. In another bowl, beat cream cheese, butter and eggs until pale yellow and slightly thickened, about 10 minutes. Fold in cheddar cheese. Stir in the corn mixture.

2. Fill greased mini-muffin cups three-fourths full. Bake until a toothpick inserted in center comes out clean, 8-10 minutes. Serve warm; top with sour cream and chives.

1 appetizer: 52 cal., 3g fat (2g sat. fat), 15mg chol., 50mg sod., 4g carb. (1g sugars, 0 fiber), 2g pro.

CRISP CUCUMBER SALSA

Here's a fantastic way to use cucumbers. You'll love the creamy and crunchy texture and super fresh flavors.

—Charlene Skjerven, Hoople, ND

TAKES: 20 MIN. • MAKES: 2½ CUPS

- **2 cups finely chopped cucumber, peeled and seeded**
- **½ cup finely chopped seeded tomato**
- **¼ cup chopped red onion**
- **2 Tbsp. minced fresh parsley**
- **1 jalapeno pepper, seeded and chopped**
- **4½ tsp. minced fresh cilantro**
- **1 garlic clove, minced**
- **¼ cup reduced-fat sour cream**
- **1½ tsp. lemon juice**
- **1½ tsp. lime juice**
- **¼ tsp. ground cumin**
- **¼ tsp. seasoned salt**
- **Baked tortilla chip scoops**

In a small bowl, combine the first 7 ingredients. In another bowl, combine the sour cream, lemon juice, lime juice, cumin and seasoned salt. Pour over cucumber mixture and toss gently to coat. Serve immediately with chips.

¼ cup: 16 cal., 1g fat (0 sat. fat), 2mg chol., 44mg sod., 2g carb. (1g sugars, 0 fiber), 1g pro. **Diabetic exchanges:** 1 free food.

PENNSYLVANIA DUTCH CUCUMBERS

My mom's side of the family was German and Irish. Settling in Pennsylvania, they adopted some of the cooking and customs of the Pennsylvania Dutch. This is a Dutch dish Mom loved, and today it's my favorite garden salad. The blend of crisp cucumbers and homegrown tomatoes is wonderful!

—Shirley Joan Helfenbein, Lapeer, MI

PREP: 30 MIN. + CHILLING • MAKES: 6 SERVINGS

- **3 to 4 small cucumbers**
- **1 tsp. salt**
- **1 medium onion, thinly sliced into rings**
- **½ cup sour cream**
- **2 Tbsp. white vinegar**
- **1 Tbsp. minced chives**
- **½ tsp. dill seed**
- **¼ tsp. pepper**
- **Pinch sugar**
- **Optional: Lettuce leaves and tomato slices**

1. Peel cucumbers; slice paper-thin into a bowl. Sprinkle with salt; cover and refrigerate for 3-4 hours.

2. Rinse and drain cucumbers. Pat gently to press out excess liquid. In a large bowl, combine cucumbers and onion; set aside. In a small bowl, combine sour cream, vinegar, chives, dill seed, pepper and sugar.

3. Just before serving, add dressing to cucumbers; toss to coat. Arrange lettuce and tomatoes in a serving bowl if desired. Top with cucumbers.

1 cup: 61 cal., 3g fat (2g sat. fat), 13mg chol., 406mg sod., 5g carb. (2g sugars, 1g fiber), 2g pro.

PENNSYLVANIA DUTCH CUCUMBERS

CHICKEN-CUCUMBER GYROS

CHICKEN-CUCUMBER GYROS

I love reinventing classic recipes to fit our taste and healthy lifestyle. This recipe is quick to prepare and can be served with oven fries or on its own. You can add Greek olives, omit the onion or even use cubed pork tenderloin for a new taste.

—Kayla Douthitt, Elizabethtown, KY

PREP: 30 MIN. + MARINATING • COOK: 5 MIN. • MAKES: 6 SERVINGS

- **1½ lbs. boneless skinless chicken breasts, cut into ½-in. cubes**
- **½ cup salt-free lemon-pepper marinade**
- **3 Tbsp. minced fresh mint**

SAUCE

- **½ cup fat-free plain Greek yogurt**
- **2 Tbsp. lemon juice**
- **1 tsp. dill weed**
- **½ tsp. garlic powder**

ASSEMBLY

- **1 medium cucumber, seeded and chopped**
- **1 medium tomato, chopped**
- **¼ cup finely chopped onion**
- **6 whole wheat pita pocket halves, warmed**
- **⅓ cup crumbled feta cheese**

1. Place chicken, marinade and mint in a shallow dish and turn to coat. Cover and refrigerate up to 6 hours.

2. Drain chicken, discarding marinade. Place a large nonstick skillet over medium-high heat. Add chicken; cook and stir 4-6 minutes or until no longer pink.

3. In a small bowl, mix sauce ingredients. In another bowl, combine cucumber, tomato and onion. Serve chicken in pita pockets with sauce, vegetable mixture and cheese.

1 gyro: 248 cal., 4g fat (2g sat. fat), 66mg chol., 251mg sod., 22g carb. (4g sugars, 3g fiber), 30g pro. **Diabetic exchanges:** 3 lean meat, 1½ starch, ½ fat.

"YUMMY, FRESH AND HEALTHY. HIGHLY RECOMMENDED!"

—CAMI, TASTEOFHOME.COM

HOW-TO

Buy Cucumbers

Look for firm cucumbers that are uniformly dark green. They should feel heavier than they look. Avoid those that have withered ends or are beginning to wrinkle.

Store Cucumbers

You can store cucumbers in a plastic bag in the refrigerator for up to 1 week.

Prep Cucumbers

Scrub with soap under running water to remove the waxy substance that grocery stores apply.

SOUR CREAM CUCUMBERS

We have a tradition at our house to serve this dish with the other Hungarian specialties my mom learned to make from the women at church. It's especially good during the summer when the cucumbers are freshly picked from the garden.

—Pamela Eaton, Monclova, OH

PREP: 15 MIN. + CHILLING • MAKES: 8 SERVINGS

- **½ cup sour cream**
- **3 Tbsp. white vinegar**
- **1 Tbsp. sugar**
- **Pepper to taste**
- **4 medium cucumbers, peeled if desired and thinly sliced**
- **1 small sweet onion, thinly sliced and separated into rings**

In a large bowl, whisk sour cream, vinegar, sugar and pepper until blended. Add cucumbers and onion; toss to coat. Refrigerate, covered, at least 4 hours. Serve with a slotted spoon.

¾ cup: 62 cal., 3g fat (2g sat. fat), 10mg chol., 5mg sod., 7g carb. (5g sugars, 2g fiber), 2g pro. **Diabetic exchanges:** 1 vegetable, ½ fat.

SHRIMP & CUCUMBER CANAPES

These cute stacks really stand out on an appetizer buffet. Tasty, cool and crunchy, they come together in a snap.

—Ashley Nochlin, Port St. Lucie, FL

TAKES: 25 MIN. • MAKES: 2 DOZEN

- **½ cup ketchup**
- **4 tsp. Creole seasoning, divided**
- **1 Tbsp. finely chopped onion**
- **1 Tbsp. finely chopped green pepper**
- **1 Tbsp. finely chopped celery**
- **¼ tsp. hot pepper sauce**
- **1 pkg. (8 oz.) cream cheese, softened**
- **24 English cucumber slices**
- **24 peeled and deveined cooked medium shrimp**
- **2 Tbsp. minced fresh parsley**

1. For cocktail sauce, in a small bowl, combine the ketchup, 2 tsp. Creole seasoning, onion, green pepper, celery and pepper sauce. In another bowl, combine cream cheese and remaining Creole seasoning.

2. Spread or pipe cream cheese mixture onto cucumber slices. Top each with a shrimp and cocktail sauce. Sprinkle with parsley.

1 canape: 50 cal., 3g fat (2g sat. fat), 26mg chol., 218mg sod., 2g carb. (1g sugars, 0 fiber), 3g pro.

SHRIMP & CUCUMBER CANAPES

GINGER
GREEN BEANS

GINGER GREEN BEANS

The bright, gingery sauce on these green beans is delicious and so simple to whip together. It's perfection on either hot or cold beans, but I also really love it tossed with cooked shrimp.

—Marina CastleKelley, Canyon Country, CA

TAKES: 30 MINUTES • MAKES: 8 SERVINGS

- **1½ lbs. fresh green beans, trimmed**
- **1 tangerine, peeled, segmented, seeds removed**
- **¼ cup chopped green onions**
- **¼ cup soy sauce**
- **1 Tbsp. lemon juice**
- **1 Tbsp. olive oil**
- **1 Tbsp. minced fresh gingerroot**
- **1 garlic clove, peeled and halved**
- **1 tsp. packed brown sugar**
- **½ tsp. salt**
- **¼ tsp. pepper**
- **¼ tsp. white vinegar**

1. In a 6-qt. stockpot, bring 12 cups water to a boil. Add the green beans; cook, uncovered, 2-3 minutes or just until crisp-tender and bright green. Quickly remove and immediately drop into ice water. Drain and pat dry.

2. In a blender or food processor, combine remaining ingredients; process until well blended. Pour dressing mixture over beans; toss to coat. Refrigerate until serving.

¾ cup: 59 cal., 2g fat (0 sat. fat), 0 chol., 614mg sod., 9g carb. (4g sugars, 3g fiber), 3g pro. **Diabetic exchanges:** 1 vegetable, ½ fat.

GREEN BEAN BUNDLES

I found this recipe in a rural newspaper years ago and have made it often. The bean bundles are excellent with chicken or beef. Sometimes I'll arrange them around a mound of wild rice to make an eye-appealing dish.

—Virginia Stadler, Nokesville, VA

TAKES: 25 MIN. • MAKES: 8 SERVINGS

- **1 lb. fresh green beans, trimmed**
- **8 bacon strips, partially cooked**
- **1 Tbsp. finely chopped onion**
- **3 Tbsp. butter**
- **1 Tbsp. white wine vinegar**
- **1 Tbsp. sugar**
- **¼ tsp. salt**

1. Cook the beans until crisp-tender. Wrap 10 beans in each bacon strip; secure with a toothpick. Place on a foil-covered baking sheet. Bake at 400° until bacon is done, 10-15 minutes.

2. In a skillet, saute onion in butter until tender. Add vinegar, sugar and salt; heat through. Remove bundles to a serving bowl or platter; pour sauce over bundles and serve immediately.

1 bundle: 186 cal., 17g fat (7g sat. fat), 27mg chol., 286mg sod., 5g carb. (3g sugars, 2g fiber), 3g pro.

SHEET-PAN HONEY MUSTARD CHICKEN

This sheet-pan chicken is an easy gluten-free, low-carb meal ideal for busy weekdays. The chicken is tender, juicy and so delicious. It made the list of our favorite meals. You can substitute any low-carb vegetable for the green beans.

—Denise Browning, San Antonio, TX

PREP: 20 MIN. • BAKE: 40 MIN. • MAKES: 6 SERVINGS

- **6 bone-in chicken thighs (about 2¼ lbs.)**
- **¾ tsp. salt, divided**
- **½ tsp. pepper, divided**
- **2 medium lemons**
- **⅓ cup olive oil**
- **⅓ cup honey**
- **3 Tbsp. Dijon mustard**
- **4 garlic cloves, minced**
- **1 tsp. paprika**
- **½ cup water**
- **½ lb. fresh green beans, trimmed**
- **6 miniature sweet peppers, sliced into rings**
- **¼ cup pomegranate seeds, optional**

1. Preheat oven to 425°. Place chicken in a greased 15x10x1-in. baking pan. Sprinkle with the ½ tsp. salt and ¼ tsp. pepper. Thinly slice 1 lemon; place over chicken. Cut remaining lemon crosswise in half; squeeze juice into a small bowl. Whisk in oil, honey, mustard, garlic and paprika. Pour half the sauce over the chicken; reserve remaining for beans. Pour water into pan. Bake 25 minutes.

2. Meanwhile, combine beans, sweet peppers, and remaining sauce, ¼ tsp. salt and ¼ tsp. pepper; toss to coat. Arrange vegetables around chicken in pan. Bake until a thermometer inserted in chicken reads 170°-175° and beans are tender, 15-20 minutes. If desired, sprinkle with pomegranate seeds.

1 serving: 419 cal., 26g fat (6g sat. fat), 81mg chol., 548mg sod., 22g carb. (17g sugars, 2g fiber), 24g pro.

HOW-TO

Buy Green Beans

Look for beans that are uniform in color and size so they will cook consistently. Green beans should be firm and snap in half when bent.

Store Green Beans

Unwashed green beans keep well when stored in an airtight container in the refrigerator for up to 1 week.

Prep Green Beans

Trim beans by removing both ends. Wash the beans under cold running water. If you want to retain more of the sweet taste green beans have to offer, cook the washed beans whole and then trim off the ends.

BUTTERY ALMOND GREEN BEANS

Toasted almonds add crunch to this timeless treatment for fresh beans. They get extra flavor from onion soup mix and Parmesan cheese.

—Edna Hoffman, Hebron, IN

TAKES: 30 MIN. • MAKES: 8 SERVINGS

- **2 lbs. fresh green beans, trimmed**
- **2 cups water**
- **1 envelope onion soup mix**
- **⅔ cup slivered almonds, toasted**
- **2 Tbsp. grated Parmesan cheese**
- **1 tsp. paprika**
- **6 Tbsp. butter, melted**

1. In a large saucepan, combine the beans, water and soup mix. Bring to a boil. Reduce the heat; cover and simmer until beans are crisp-tender, 15-20 minutes.

2. In a small bowl, combine the almonds, cheese and paprika. Drain beans; drizzle with butter and sprinkle with almond mixture. Toss to coat.

¾ cup: 179 cal., 14g fat (6g sat. fat), 24mg chol., 407mg sod., 13g carb. (4g sugars, 5g fiber), 5g pro.

SWEET & TANGY SALMON WITH GREEN BEANS

I'm always up for new ways to cook salmon. In this dish, a sweet sauce gives the fish and green beans some down-home barbecue tang. Even our kids love it.

—Aliesha Caldwell, Robersonville, NC

PREP: 20 MIN. • BAKE: 15 MIN. • MAKES: 4 SERVINGS

- **4 salmon fillets (6 oz. each)**
- **1 Tbsp. butter**
- **2 Tbsp. brown sugar**
- **2 Tbsp. reduced-sodium soy sauce**
- **2 Tbsp. Dijon mustard**
- **1 Tbsp. olive oil**
- **½ tsp. pepper**
- **⅛ tsp. salt**
- **1 lb. fresh green beans, trimmed**

1. Preheat oven to 425°. Place fillets in a 15x10x1-in. baking pan coated with cooking spray. In a small skillet, melt butter; stir in brown sugar, soy sauce, mustard, oil, pepper and salt. Brush half of the mixture over salmon.

2. Place the green beans in a large bowl; drizzle with the remaining brown sugar mixture and toss to coat. Arrange green beans around fillets. Roast until fish just begins to flake easily with a fork and green beans are crisp-tender, 14-16 minutes.

1 fillet with ¾ cup green beans: 394 cal., 22g fat (5g sat. fat), 93mg chol., 661mg sod., 17g carb. (10g sugars, 4g fiber), 31g pro. **Diabetic exchanges:** 5 lean meat, 1½ fat, 1 vegetable, ½ starch.

Test Kitchen Tip: Craving Asian flavor? Add ½ tsp. minced fresh ginger to the sauce and use sesame oil instead of olive oil.

TWO-BEAN
TOMATO BAKE

TWO-BEAN TOMATO BAKE

Parmesan cheese, basil and garlic spice up this mouthwatering medley of beans, mushrooms, onion and tomato. It's even more flavorful when you use your garden harvest. We love the crumb topping because it adds a fantastic crunch.
—Dorothy Rieke, Julian, NE

PREP: 35 MIN. • **BAKE:** 35 MIN. • **MAKES:** 16 SERVINGS

- **1½ lbs. fresh green beans, cut into 2-in. pieces**
- **1½ lbs. fresh wax beans, cut into 2-in. pieces**
- **5 medium tomatoes, peeled and cubed**
- **½ lbs. fresh mushrooms, sliced**
- **1 medium sweet onion, chopped**
- **10 Tbsp. butter, divided**
- **1½ tsp. minced garlic, divided**
- **1½ tsp. dried basil, divided**
- **1½ tsp. dried oregano, divided**
- **1 tsp. salt**
- **1½ cups soft bread crumbs**
- **⅓ cup grated Parmesan cheese**

1. Place beans in a large saucepan and cover with water; bring to a boil. Cook, uncovered, for 8-10 minutes or until crisp-tender. Drain; add tomatoes and set aside.

2. In a large skillet, saute mushrooms and onion in 4 Tbsp. butter until crisp-tender. Add 1 tsp. garlic, 1 tsp. basil, 1 tsp. oregano and salt; cook 1 minute longer. Add to the bean mixture; toss to coat. Spoon into a greased 3-qt. baking dish.

3. Melt the remaining butter; toss with bread crumbs, cheese and remaining garlic, basil and oregano. Sprinkle over bean mixture.

4. Cover and bake at 400° for 20 minutes. Uncover; bake 15 minutes longer or until golden brown.

1 serving: 124 cal., 8g fat (5g sat. fat), 21mg chol., 283mg sod., 12g carb. (4g sugars, 4g fiber), 4g pro.

GREEN BEAN & POTATO SALAD

For family reunions, my mom would make everybody's favorite green bean and potato salad. Now I'm the one who makes and brings it.
—Connie Dicavoli, Shawnee, KS

PREP: 15 MIN. • **COOK:** 20 MIN. + CHILLING • **MAKES:** 10 SERVINGS

- **2 lbs. red potatoes (about 6 medium), cubed**
- **1 lb. fresh green beans, trimmed and halved**
- **1 small red onion, halved and thinly sliced**
- **¼ cup chopped fresh mint, optional**

DRESSING

- **½ cup canola oil**
- **¼ cup white vinegar**
- **2 Tbsp. lemon juice**
- **1 tsp. salt**
- **½ tsp. garlic powder**
- **¼ tsp. pepper**

1. Place potatoes in a 6-qt. stockpot; add water to cover. Bring to a boil. Reduce heat; cook, uncovered, 10-15 minutes or until tender, adding green beans during the last 4 minutes of cooking. Drain.

2. Transfer potatoes and green beans to a large bowl; add onion and, if desired, mint. In a small bowl, whisk dressing ingredients until blended. Pour over potato mixture; toss gently to coat. Refrigerate, covered, at least 2 hours before serving.

¾ cup: 183 cal., 11g fat (1g sat. fat), 0 chol., 245mg sod., 19g carb. (2g sugars, 3g fiber), 3g pro. **Diabetic exchanges:** 2½ fat, 1 starch.

PROSCIUTTO & PEAS PASTA TOSS

I love quick, simple pasta dishes, and this is one of my favorites. I prepare a tossed green salad while the pasta cooks and serve up a lovely light supper in minutes!

—Laura Murphy-Ogden, Charlotte, NC

TAKES: 20 MIN. • MAKES: 6 SERVINGS

- **1 pkg. (16 oz.) linguine**
- **½ cup fresh or frozen peas, thawed**
- **2 Tbsp. minced garlic**
- **1 Tbsp. Italian seasoning**
- **1 tsp. pepper**
- **¼ cup olive oil**
- **½ lb. thinly sliced prosciutto or deli ham, chopped**
- **¼ cup shredded Parmesan cheese**

1. Cook linguine according to package directions, adding peas during the last 3 minutes. Meanwhile, in a large cast-iron or other heavy skillet, saute garlic, Italian seasoning and pepper in oil until garlic is tender, about 1 minute. Stir in prosciutto.

2. Drain linguine; add to skillet and toss to coat. Sprinkle with cheese.

1⅓ cups: 461 cal., 16g fat (4g sat. fat), 36mg chol., 802mg sod., 58g carb. (3g sugars, 3g fiber), 22g pro.

PARMESAN SNAP PEA PASTA

This simple dish is always a hit, especially during the spring when sugar snap peas are the sweetest. To keep us from getting in a rut, I change up the flavors.

—Crystal Jo Bruns, Iliff, CO

TAKES: 30 MIN. • MAKES: 12 SERVINGS

- **1 lb. fresh sugar snap peas (about 5 cups), trimmed**
- **1 pkg. (16 oz.) angel hair pasta**
- **5 Tbsp. olive oil, divided**
- **1 medium red onion, finely chopped**
- **3 garlic cloves, minced**
- **½ tsp. salt**
- **¼ tsp. crushed red pepper flakes**
- **⅛ tsp. coarsely ground pepper**
- **1¼ cups grated Parmesan cheese, divided**

1. In a 6-qt. stockpot, bring 16 cups water to a boil. Add the peas; cook, uncovered for 3-4 minutes or just until crisp-tender. Using a strainer, remove peas from pot.

2. In the same pot, add the pasta to boiling water; cook according to package directions. Drain, reserving 1 cup cooking water; return to the pot. Toss with 3 Tbsp. oil.

3. In a large skillet, heat remaining oil over medium heat; saute onion until tender, 2-3 minutes. Add garlic and seasonings; cook and stir 1 minute. Stir in peas; heat through.

4. Toss with pasta, adding 1 cup cheese and reserved cooking water as desired. Sprinkle with the remaining Parmesan cheese.

¾ cup: 258 cal., 9g fat (2g sat. fat), 7mg chol., 254mg sod., 35g carb. (4g sugars, 3g fiber), 10g pro.

MINTY SUGAR SNAP PEAS

MINTY SUGAR SNAP PEAS

Fresh mint adds a lively touch to cooked sugar snap peas. It's also nice on green beans or carrots.

—Alice Kaldahl, Ray, ND

TAKES: 10 MIN. • MAKES: 4 SERVINGS

- **3 cups fresh sugar snap peas, trimmed**
- **¼ tsp. sugar**
- **2 to 3 Tbsp. minced fresh mint**
- **2 Tbsp. butter**

Place 1 in. of water in a large skillet. Add peas and sugar; bring to a boil. Reduce heat; simmer, covered, until peas are crisp-tender, 4-5 minutes; drain. Stir in mint and butter.

¾ cup: 102 cal., 6g fat (4g sat. fat), 15mg chol., 45mg sod., 9g carb. (4g sugars, 3g fiber), 4g pro. **Diabetic exchanges:** 2 vegetable, 1½ fat.

HOW-TO

Prep Sugar Snap Peas

The fibrous string that runs the length of the snap pea's casing should always be removed before cooking. To do this, grab the stem at one end, pinch slightly and pull across—the string will act as a "zipper" and can be removed with a gentle, continuous tug.

LEMONY SHRIMP
& SNOW PEA PASTA

LEMONY SHRIMP & SNOW PEA PASTA

This pretty pasta is a family favorite—the kids love the light lemony flavor and I love that they devour the fresh veggies. You can use other types of pasta noodles for variety, like bow ties or corkscrews.

—Jennifer Fisher, Austin, TX

TAKES: 30 MIN. • MAKES: 6 SERVINGS

- 1¾ cups uncooked gemelli or spiral pasta
- 2 Tbsp. olive oil, divided
- 2 cups fresh snow peas
- 1 lb. uncooked shrimp (26-30 per lb.), peeled and deveined
- 3 garlic cloves, minced
- ¾ tsp. salt, divided
- ¼ tsp. plus ⅛ tsp. pepper, divided
- 1 cup grape tomatoes, halved

DRESSING

- ¼ cup lemon juice
- 2 Tbsp. chopped fresh parsley
- 2 Tbsp. olive oil
- 2 garlic cloves, minced
- 2 tsp. grated lemon zest
- Optional: Additional grated lemon zest and chopped fresh parsley

1. Cook pasta according to package directions. Meanwhile, in a large cast-iron or other heavy skillet, heat 1 Tbsp. oil over medium heat. Add peas; cook and stir until crisp-tender, 2-3 minutes. Remove and keep warm.

2. In same pan, heat remaining oil over medium-high heat. Add shrimp; cook and stir until shrimp turn pink, 2-3 minutes. Add garlic, ½ tsp. salt and ¼ tsp. pepper; cook and stir 1 minute longer.

3. Drain pasta, reserving ½ cup pasta water. Add pasta to the shrimp mixture; stir in peas and tomatoes. In a small bowl, whisk lemon juice, parsley, oil, garlic, lemon zest and remaining salt and pepper until blended. Pour over shrimp mixture; toss to coat, adding enough reserved pasta water to moisten the pasta. If desired, sprinkle with additional lemon zest and parsley.

1⅓ cups: 279 cal., 11g fat (2g sat. fat), 92mg chol., 390mg sod., 28g carb. (3g sugars, 2g fiber), 18g pro. **Diabetic exchanges:** 3 lean meat, 2 starch, 1 fat.

SPRING PEA & RADISH SALAD

Winters can be very long here in New Hampshire. I always look forward to the first veggies of spring and making some lighter dishes like this fresh salad.

—Jolene Martinelli, Fremont, NH

TAKES: 20 MIN. • MAKES: 6 SERVINGS

- ½ lb. fresh wax or green beans
- ½ lb. fresh sugar snap peas
- 2 cups water
- 6 large radishes, thinly sliced
- 2 Tbsp. honey
- 1 tsp. dried tarragon
- ¼ tsp. kosher salt
- ¼ tsp. coarsely ground pepper

1. Snip ends off beans and sugar snap peas; remove strings from snap peas. In a large saucepan, bring water to a boil over high heat. Add beans and reduce heat; simmer, covered, 4-5 minutes. Add sugar snap peas; simmer, covered, until both beans and peas are crisp-tender, another 2-3 minutes. Drain.

2. Toss beans and peas with the radishes. In a small bowl, combine honey, tarragon, salt and pepper. Drizzle over vegetables.

⅔ cup: 50 cal., 0 fat (0 sat. fat), 0 chol., 86mg sod., 11g carb. (8g sugars, 2g fiber), 2g pro. **Diabetic exchanges:** 1 vegetable, ½ starch.

SPRING PEA SOUP

Truly a soup for the pea lover, this recipe originated with an idea in an old cookbook about eating better to live longer. Sauteed potatoes add body to an easy soup with a good texture and superb pea flavor.
—Denise Patterson, Bainbridge, OH

PREP: 10 MIN. • COOK: 30 MIN. • MAKES: 6 SERVINGS

- **2 cups cubed peeled potatoes**
- **2 Tbsp. butter**
- **6 cups chicken broth**
- **2 cups fresh or frozen peas, thawed**
- **2 Tbsp. minced chives**
- **Microgreens, optional**

1. In a large saucepan, saute potatoes in butter until lightly browned. Stir in the broth; bring to a boil. Reduce heat; cover and simmer until the potatoes are tender, 10-15 minutes. Add peas; cook until peas are tender, 5-8 minutes. Cool slightly.

2. In a blender, process soup in batches until smooth. Return all to the pan; heat through. Sprinkle with chives and, if desired, microgreens.

1 cup: 133 cal., 5g fat (2g sat. fat), 15mg chol., 1012mg sod., 18g carb. (4g sugars, 3g fiber), 5g pro.

"SUPER SIMPLE AND SIMPLY TASTY."

— JENNT1981, TASTEOFHOME.COM

HAM & PEA PASTA ALFREDO

When I want a filling meal that even the kids enjoy, I toss ham and sugar snap peas with Romano cream sauce and pasta.
—C.R. Monachino, Kenmore, NY

TAKES: 25 MIN. • MAKES: 8 SERVINGS

- **1 pkg. (16 oz.) fettuccine**
- **2 Tbsp. butter**
- **1½ lbs. sliced fully cooked ham, cut into strips (about 5 cups)**
- **2 cups fresh sugar snap peas**
- **2 cups heavy whipping cream**
- **½ cup grated Romano cheese**
- **¼ tsp. pepper**

1. Cook fettuccine according to package directions. Meanwhile, in a large skillet, heat butter over medium heat. Add ham and peas; cook and stir 5 minutes. Stir in the cream, cheese and pepper; bring to a boil. Reduce heat; simmer, uncovered, 1-2 minutes or until sauce is slightly thickened and peas are crisp-tender.

2. Drain fettuccine; add to skillet and toss to coat. Serve immediately.

1¼ cups: 582 cal., 32g fat (18g sat. fat), 151mg chol., 1032mg sod., 45g carb. (6g sugars, 3g fiber), 33g pro.

SPRING
PEA SOUP

STUFFED SWEET PEPPERS

STUFFED SWEET PEPPERS

Italian sausage and feta cheese give zest to the rice filling in these tender peppers I've prepared often over the years. When I was married in 1970, slow cookers were the rage. In our home, it's one appliance that's never gone out of style.

—Judy Earl, Sarasota, FL

PREP: 15 MIN. • COOK: 4 HOURS • MAKES: 5 SERVINGS

- **3 medium sweet red peppers**
- **2 medium sweet yellow peppers**
- **1 jar (14 oz.) spaghetti sauce, divided**
- **¾ lb. Italian turkey sausage links, casings removed**
- **¾ cup uncooked instant rice**
- **½ cup crumbled feta cheese**
- **½ cup chopped onion**
- **¼ cup chopped tomato**
- **¼ cup minced fresh parsley**
- **2 Tbsp. sliced ripe olives**
- **¼ to ½ tsp. garlic powder**
- **½ tsp. salt**
- **½ tsp. Italian seasoning**
- **½ tsp. crushed red pepper flakes**

1. Cut tops off peppers; chop tops and set aside. Discard stems and seeds; set pepper cups aside. Set aside ¾ cup spaghetti sauce; pour the remaining sauce into a 5-qt. slow cooker.

2. In a large bowl, combine the sausage, rice, cheese, onion, tomato, parsley, olives, garlic powder, salt, Italian seasoning, pepper flakes, and reserved chopped peppers and spaghetti sauce. Spoon into peppers.

3. Transfer peppers to slow cooker. Cover and cook on low for 4-5 hours or until sausage is no longer pink and peppers are tender.

1 stuffed pepper: 292 cal., 12g fat (3g sat. fat), 48mg chol., 1182mg sod., 30g carb. (10g sugars, 4g fiber), 17g pro.

JALAPENO POMEGRANATE COCKTAIL

Get your fix of jalapeno flavor sans the heat in this pretty, summery sipper. If you'd like some extra buzz, use a little less soda.

—Melissa Rodriguez, Van Nuys, CA

PREP: 10 MIN. + CHILLING • MAKES: 8 SERVINGS

- **2 jalapeno peppers, halved lengthwise and seeded**
- **1½ cups vodka**
- **6 to 8 cups ice cubes**
- **3 cups pomegranate juice**
- **3 cups Italian blood orange soda, chilled**
- **Lime wedges**

1. For jalapeno vodka, place jalapenos and vodka in a glass jar or container. Refrigerate, covered, 2-3 days to allow flavors to blend. Strain before using.

2. For each serving, fill cocktail shaker three-fourths full with ice. Add 3 oz. of pomegranate juice and 1½ oz. jalapeno vodka; cover and shake until condensation forms on the outside of the shaker, 10-15 seconds. Strain into a cocktail glass; top with 3 oz. soda. Serve with lime wedges.

1 cup: 184 cal., 0 fat (0 sat. fat), 0 chol., 12mg sod., 22g carb. (22g sugars, 0 fiber), 0 pro.

SPICY PEPPER HUSH PUPPIES

The crunchy exterior of these southern-style snacks is a nice contrast to the moist cornbread. Jalapeno peppers and hot sauce add a hint of heat.
—Taste of Home *Test Kitchen*

PREP: 15 MIN. • COOK: 5 MIN./BATCH • MAKES: 2½ DOZEN

- **1½ cups yellow cornmeal**
- **½ cup all-purpose flour**
- **1 tsp. baking powder**
- **1 tsp. salt**
- **2 large eggs, room temperature, lightly beaten**
- **¾ cup 2% milk**
- **2 jalapeno peppers, seeded and minced**
- **¼ cup finely chopped onion**
- **1 tsp. Louisiana-style hot sauce**
- **Oil for deep-fat frying**

1. In a large bowl, combine the cornmeal, flour, baking powder and salt. In another bowl, beat the eggs, milk, jalapenos, onion and hot sauce. Stir into dry ingredients just until combined.

2. In a cast-iron or other heavy skillet, heat oil to 375°. Drop tablespoonfuls of batter, a few at a time, into hot oil. Fry until golden brown on both sides. Drain on paper towels. Serve warm.

1 hush puppy: 56 cal., 3g fat (0 sat. fat), 14mg chol., 94mg sod., 7g carb. (0 sugars, 1g fiber), 1g pro.

5i SAUSAGE-STUFFED JALAPENOS

If you like foods that pack a little kick, you'll love these jalapenos filled with sausage and cheese. The recipe is one of my favorites for parties.
—Rachel Oswald, Greenville, MI

PREP: 20 MIN. • BAKE: 15 MIN. • MAKES: 44 APPETIZERS

- **1 lb. bulk pork sausage**
- **1 pkg. (8 oz.) cream cheese, softened**
- **1 cup shredded Parmesan cheese**
- **22 large jalapeno peppers, halved lengthwise and seeded**
- **Ranch salad dressing, optional**

1. In a large skillet, cook the sausage over medium heat until no longer pink; drain. In a small bowl, combine the cream cheese and Parmesan cheese; fold in sausage.

2. Spoon about 1 Tbsp. into each jalapeno half. Place in 2 ungreased 13x9-in. baking dishes. Bake, uncovered, at 425° until filling is lightly browned and bubbly, 15-20 minutes. Serve with ranch dressing if desired.

1 appetizer: 56 cal., 5g fat (2g sat. fat), 13mg chol., 123mg sod., 1g carb. (0 sugars, 0 fiber), 2g pro.

JALAPENO BURGERS WITH GORGONZOLA

On a whim, we mixed homemade jalapeno jam into ground beef patties, then topped the burgers with caramelized onions and tangy Gorgonzola cheese. Fabulous!

—Becky Mollenkamp, St. Louis, MO

TAKES: 30 MIN. • MAKES: 4 SERVINGS

- **1 Tbsp. canola oil**
- **1 tsp. butter**
- **1 medium onion, halved and thinly sliced**
- **Dash salt**
- **Dash sugar**

BURGERS

- **⅓ cup jalapeno pepper jelly**
- **½ tsp. salt**
- **¼ tsp. pepper**
- **1 lb. ground beef**
- **4 hamburger buns, split and toasted**
- **2 Tbsp. crumbled Gorgonzola cheese**
- **Thinly sliced jalapeno pepper, optional**

1. In a small skillet, heat oil and butter over medium heat. Add onion, salt and sugar; cook and stir until onion is softened, 3-4 minutes. Reduce the heat to medium-low; cook until deep golden brown, stirring occasionally, 4-6 minutes.

2. In a large bowl, mix jelly, salt and pepper. Add the beef; mix lightly but thoroughly. Gently shape into four ½-in. thick patties.

3. Grill the burgers, covered, over medium heat or broil 4 in. from heat 4-5 minutes on each side or until a thermometer reads 160°. Serve the burgers on buns with caramelized onion, cheese and, if desired, sliced jalapeno.

1 burger: 460 cal., 20g fat (7g sat. fat), 76mg chol., 669mg sod., 43g carb. (18g sugars, 2g fiber), 25g pro.

GRILLED JALAPENOS

When barbecuing for friends at home, I also use the grill to serve up hot appetizers. These crowd-pleasing stuffed peppers have a bit of bite. They were concocted by my son.

—Catherine Hollie, Cleveland, TX

TAKES: 25 MIN. • MAKES: 2 DOZEN

- **24 fresh jalapeno peppers**
- **¾ lb. bulk pork sausage**
- **12 bacon strips, halved**

1. Wash peppers. Cut a slit along 1 side of each pepper. Remove seeds; rinse and dry peppers.

2. In a skillet, cook sausage over medium heat until no longer pink; drain. Stuff peppers with sausage and wrap with bacon; secure with soaked toothpicks.

3. Grill peppers, uncovered, turning frequently, over medium heat until tender and bacon is crisp, about 15 minutes.

1 stuffed pepper: 97 cal., 9g fat (3g sat. fat), 17mg chol., 179mg sod., 1g carb. (1g sugars, 0 fiber), 3g pro.

ISRAELI PEPPER TOMATO SALAD

This Israeli salad, which is traditionally eaten at breakfast, lends itself to endless variety. Feel free to add ingredients such as olives, beets or potatoes for a change of pace. It's lovely alongside grilled main courses.

—Sandy Long, Lees Summit, MO

PREP: 25 MIN. + CHILLING • MAKES: 9 SERVINGS

- **6 medium tomatoes, seeded and chopped**
- **1 each medium green, sweet red and yellow peppers, chopped**
- **1 medium cucumber, seeded and chopped**
- **1 medium carrot, chopped**
- **3 green onions, thinly sliced**
- **1 jalapeno pepper, seeded and chopped**
- **2 Tbsp. each minced fresh cilantro, parsley, dill and mint**
- **¼ cup lemon juice**
- **2 Tbsp. olive oil**
- **3 garlic cloves, minced**
- **½ tsp. salt**
- **¼ tsp. pepper**

In a large bowl, combine the tomatoes, peppers, cucumber, carrot, green onions, jalapeno and herbs. In a small bowl, whisk together the remaining ingredients. Pour over the tomato mixture; toss to coat evenly. Cover and refrigerate for at least 1 hour. Serve with a slotted spoon.

1 cup: 64 cal., 3g fat (0 sat. fat), 0 chol., 143mg sod., 8g carb. (5g sugars, 3g fiber), 2g pro. **Diabetic exchanges:** 1 vegetable, ½ fat.

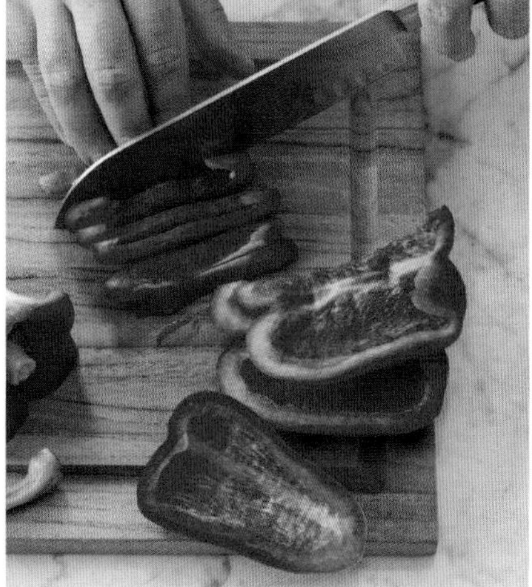

HOW-TO

Slice or Chop a Sweet Pepper

- Cut top and bottom off pepper and discard. Cut each side from pepper by slicing close to the center and then down. Scrape out seeds and discard.
- Cut away any ribs. Place cut side down on work surface and flatten slightly with your hand. Cut lengthwise into strips, then widthwise into pieces if desired.

ISRAELI PEPPER TOMATO SALAD

RHUBARB TORTE

Each year when Grandmother asked what kind of birthday cake I'd like, I always said I wanted this lovely rhubarb torte.

—Lois Heintz, Holmen, WI

PREP: 20 MIN. • BAKE: 1 HOUR • MAKES: 16 SERVINGS

- **1¾ cups all-purpose flour**
- **1 tsp. baking powder**
- **2 large egg yolks**
- **½ cup shortening**
- **2 Tbsp. sugar**
- **½ cup chopped walnuts**

FILLING

- **4 cups chopped fresh or frozen rhubarb**
- **2 cups sugar**
- **2 large egg yolks, room temperature**
- **¼ cup all-purpose flour**

MERINGUE

- **4 large egg whites, room temperature**
- **½ cup sugar**
- **1 tsp. vanilla extract**

Combine the first 6 ingredients with a fork until crumbly. Press into a greased 13x9-in. baking dish. Combine filling ingredients; mix well. Pour over crust. Bake at 350° for 50-60 minutes. In a bowl, beat egg whites until stiff. Gradually add sugar and vanilla, beating well. Spread or pipe over hot filling. Return to the oven until lightly browned, 10-15 minutes longer.

1 piece: 289 cal., 10g fat (2g sat. fat), 53mg chol., 42mg sod., 47g carb. (33g sugars, 1g fiber), 4g pro.

RHUBARB SCONES

Every year, my grandfather grows rhubarb and gives us a large supply. The tartness is similar to a cranberry, making it perfect for tossing into a scone. What a delicious treat alongside coffee!

—Danielle Lee, West Palm Beach, FL

PREP: 30 MIN. • BAKE: 20 MIN. • MAKES: 16 SERVINGS

- **1¼ cups whole wheat pastry flour**
- **1¼ cups all-purpose flour**
- **½ cup sugar**
- **1 Tbsp. baking powder**
- **1 tsp. ground cardamom**
- **½ tsp. salt**
- **½ cup cold unsalted butter, cubed**
- **1½ cups finely chopped fresh or frozen rhubarb, thawed (3-4 stalks)**
- **½ cup heavy whipping cream**
- **¼ cup fat-free milk**
- **1 tsp. vanilla extract**
- **Coarse sugar**

1. Preheat oven to 400°. In a large bowl, whisk the first 6 ingredients. Cut in butter until mixture resembles coarse crumbs. Add rhubarb; toss to coat.

2. In another bowl, whisk the cream, milk and vanilla; stir into crumb mixture just until moistened.

3. Turn onto a floured surface; knead gently 4-5 times. Divide dough in half; pat into two 6-in. circles. Cut each into 8 wedges. Place wedges on parchment-lined baking sheets; sprinkle with coarse sugar. Bake 18-22 minutes or until golden brown. Serve scones warm.

1 scone: 166 cal., 9g fat (5g sat. fat), 25mg chol., 155mg sod., 20g carb. (7g sugars, 1g fiber), 2g pro.

RHUBARB TORTE

RHUBARB-APRICOT BARBECUED CHICKEN

RHUBARB-APRICOT BARBECUED CHICKEN

Springtime brings back memories of the rhubarb that grew beside my childhood home. When I found ruby red stalks in the store, I created this recipe for them. My family gives this a big thumbs up.

—Laurie Hudson, Westville, FL

PREP: 30 MIN. • GRILL: 30 MIN. • MAKES: 6 SERVINGS

- **1 Tbsp. olive oil**
- **1 cup finely chopped sweet onion**
- **1 garlic clove, minced**
- **2 cups chopped fresh or frozen rhubarb**
- **¾ cup ketchup**
- **⅔ cup water**
- **⅓ cup apricot preserves**
- **¼ cup cider vinegar**
- **¼ cup molasses**
- **1 Tbsp. honey Dijon mustard**
- **2 tsp. finely chopped chipotle pepper in adobo sauce**
- **5 tsp. barbecue seasoning, divided**
- **1¼ tsp. salt, divided**
- **¾ tsp. pepper, divided**
- **12 chicken drumsticks (about 4 lbs.)**

1. In a large saucepan, heat oil over medium heat. Add onion; cook and stir until tender, 4-6 minutes. Add garlic; cook 1 minute longer. Stir in rhubarb, ketchup, water, preserves, vinegar, molasses, mustard, chipotle pepper, 1 tsp. barbecue seasoning, ¼ tsp. salt and ¼ tsp. pepper. Bring to a boil. Reduce heat; simmer, uncovered, until rhubarb is tender, 8-10 minutes. Puree rhubarb mixture using an immersion blender, or cool slightly and puree in a blender. Reserve 2 cups sauce for serving.

2. Meanwhile, in a small bowl, mix the remaining barbecue seasoning, salt and pepper; sprinkle over the chicken. On a lightly oiled grill rack, grill chicken, covered, over indirect medium heat for 15 minutes. Turn; grill until a thermometer reads 170°-175°, 15-20 minutes longer, brushing occasionally with remaining sauce. Serve with the reserved sauce.

2 chicken drumsticks with ⅓ cup sauce: 469 cal., 19g fat (5g sat. fat), 126mg chol., 1801mg sod., 35g carb. (28g sugars, 1g fiber), 39g pro.

TANGY RHUBARB FOOL

I came up with this recipe because I love mousse, and because it's an easy way to enjoy rhubarb in a dessert that's light and refreshing.

—Alan Mortensen, Dwight, IL

PREP: 30 MIN. + CHILLING • MAKES: 5 SERVINGS

- **4 cups plain yogurt**
- **3 cups chopped fresh or frozen rhubarb**
- **¾ cup sugar, divided**
- **2 Tbsp. water**
- **1 tsp. white balsamic vinegar**
- **Dash salt**
- **1 cup heavy whipping cream**
- **⅛ tsp. vanilla extract**

1. Line a strainer with 4 layers of cheesecloth; place over a bowl. Add yogurt to the strainer; cover yogurt with edges of cheesecloth. Refrigerate for 8 hours or overnight.

2. In a large saucepan, combine the rhubarb, ½ cup sugar, water, vinegar and salt; cook over medium heat for 12-15 minutes or until sugar is dissolved and rhubarb is tender. Transfer to a bowl; cover and refrigerate until chilled.

3. In a large bowl, beat cream until it begins to thicken. Add vanilla and remaining sugar; beat until stiff peaks form. Transfer the yogurt from cheesecloth to a bowl (discard liquid from first bowl). Gradually fold cream mixture into yogurt.

4. Fold yogurt mixture into rhubarb mixture. Spoon into dessert dishes. Cover and refrigerate for at least 1 hour before serving.

1 cup: 416 cal., 24g fat (15g sat. fat), 91mg chol., 141mg sod., 44g carb. (40g sugars, 1g fiber), 8g pro.

RHUBARBECUE

This simmered sauce has a wonderful blend of complex flavors that goes with any meat.

—Rd Stendel-Freels, Albuquerque, NM

PREP: 45 MIN. • BAKE: 2½ HOURS • MAKES: 8 SERVINGS

- **1½ tsp. salt**
- **1½ tsp. paprika**
- **1 tsp. coarsely ground pepper**
- **3 to 4 lbs. boneless country-style pork ribs**

SAUCE

- **3 cups sliced fresh or frozen rhubarb (about 7 stalks)**
- **2 cups fresh strawberries, halved**
- **2 to 3 Tbsp. olive oil**
- **1 medium onion, chopped**
- **1 cup packed brown sugar**
- **¾ cup ketchup**
- **½ cup red wine vinegar**
- **½ cup bourbon**
- **¼ cup reduced-sodium soy sauce**
- **¼ cup honey**
- **2 Tbsp. Worcestershire sauce**
- **2 tsp. garlic powder**
- **1 tsp. crushed red pepper flakes**
- **1 tsp. coarsely ground pepper**

1. Preheat oven to 325°. Mix the salt, paprika and pepper; sprinkle over the ribs. Refrigerate, covered, while preparing the sauce.

2. In a large saucepan, combine the rhubarb and strawberries; add water to cover. Bring to a boil. Cook, uncovered, until the rhubarb is tender, 8-10 minutes. Drain; return to pan. Mash until blended.

3. In a Dutch oven, heat 1 Tbsp. oil over medium heat. Brown the ribs in batches, adding more oil as needed. Remove the ribs from pan.

4. Add onion to same pan; cook and stir until tender, 4-6 minutes. Add remaining ingredients; stir in the rhubarb mixture. Return ribs to pan, turning to coat. Bring to a boil. Cover and bake until ribs are tender, about 2 hours. Bake, uncovered, until the sauce is slightly thickened, 30-35 minutes.

4 oz. cooked pork with ⅓ cup sauce: 533 cal., 19g fat (6g sat. fat), 98mg chol., 1158mg sod., 52g carb. (45g sugars, 2g fiber), 31g pro.

HOW-TO

Buy Rhubarb

Look for thin stalks that are red or pink in color. Thicker stalks impart an especially sour taste, as do the greener variety. Look for a smooth texture, and avoid stalks that are rough or pitted, as well as those with wilted leaves.

Store Rhubarb

Fresh rhubarb stalks don't last long, but sealing them in an airtight container will help them retain their moisture. They'll last 3 to 5 days in the refrigerator's vegetable drawer. You can also freeze them for up to a year. Cut stalks into 1-inch chunks for the best results when thawed.

Prep Rhubarb

Thoroughly wash rhubarb under cold running water. Then, cut off the ends near the root base, and remove the leaves by cutting off the tops of the stalks.

WINNIE'S MINI RHUBARB & STRAWBERRY PIES

Every spring, we had strawberries and rhubarb on our farm outside Seattle. These fruity hand pies remind me of those times and of my Grandma Winnie's baking.

—Shawn Carleton, San Diego, CA

PREP: 25 MIN. + CHILLING • **BAKE:** 15 MIN. • **MAKES:** 18 SERVINGS

- **3 Tbsp. quick-cooking tapioca**
- **4 cups sliced fresh strawberries**
- **2 cups sliced fresh rhubarb**
- **¾ cup sugar**
- **1 tsp. grated orange zest**
- **1 tsp. vanilla extract**
- **¼ tsp. salt**
- **¼ tsp. ground cinnamon**
- **3 drops red food coloring, optional**
- **Pastry for double-crust pie**
- **Sweetened whipped cream, optional**

1. Place the tapioca in a small food processor or spice grinder; process until finely ground.

2. In a large saucepan, combine the strawberries, rhubarb, sugar, orange zest, vanilla, salt, cinnamon, tapioca and, if desired, food coloring; bring to a boil. Reduce heat; simmer, covered, until the strawberries are tender, stirring occasionally, 15-20 minutes. Transfer to a large bowl; cover and refrigerate overnight.

3. Preheat oven to 425°. On a lightly floured surface, roll half of the dough out to an 18-in. circle. Cut 12 circles with a 4-in. biscuit cutter, rerolling scraps as necessary; press crust onto bottom and up sides of ungreased muffin cups. Cut 6 more circles with remaining crust. Spoon strawberry mixture into muffin cups.

4. Bake until filling is bubbly and crust golden brown, 12-15 minutes. Cool in pan 5 minutes; remove to wire racks to cool. If desired, serve with whipped cream.

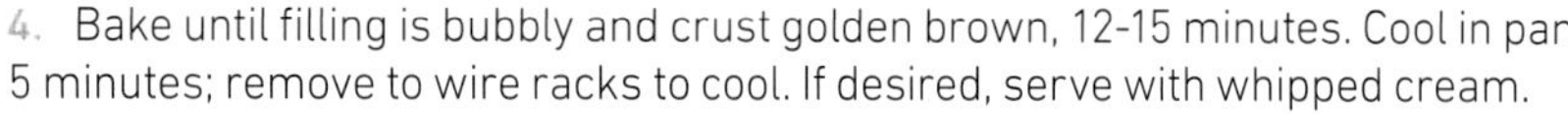

1 mini pie: 207 cal., 10g fat (6g sat. fat), 27mg chol., 171mg sod., 27g carb. (11g sugars, 1g fiber), 2g pro.

Pastry for double-crust pie (9 in.): Combine 2½ cups all-purpose flour and ½ tsp. salt; cut in 1 cup cold butter until crumbly. Gradually add ⅓ to ⅔ cup ice water, tossing with a fork until dough holds together when pressed. Divide dough in half. Shape each half into a disk; wrap. Refrigerate 1 hour or overnight.

MACAROON-TOPPED
RHUBARB COBBLER

MACAROON-TOPPED RHUBARB COBBLER

Crumbled macaroons are a unique addition to this cobbler's topping. Serve hearty helpings alone or with vanilla ice cream.
—Taste of Home *Test Kitchen*

TAKES: 30 MIN. • MAKES: 4 SERVINGS

4 cups sliced fresh or frozen rhubarb (1-in. pieces)
1 large apple, peeled and sliced
½ cup packed brown sugar
½ tsp. ground cinnamon, divided
1 Tbsp. cornstarch
2 Tbsp. cold water
8 macaroons, crumbled
1 Tbsp. butter, melted
2 Tbsp. sugar
Vanilla ice cream, optional

1. In a large cast-iron or other ovenproof skillet, combine the rhubarb, apple, brown sugar and ¼ tsp. cinnamon; bring to a boil. Reduce heat; cover and simmer until rhubarb is very tender, 10-13 minutes. Combine cornstarch and water until smooth; gradually add to the fruit mixture. Bring to a boil; cook and stir until thickened, about 2 minutes.

2. In a small bowl, combine the crumbled cookies, butter, sugar and remaining cinnamon. Sprinkle over fruit mixture.

3. Broil 4 in. from the heat until lightly browned, 3-5 minutes. If desired, serve warm with ice cream.

1 serving: 368 cal., 12g fat (7g sat. fat), 8mg chol., 45mg sod., 62g carb. (55g sugars, 5g fiber), 3g pro.

SPARKLING RHUBARB SPRITZER

Folks with a rhubarb plant or two will love this recipe.
It's a nice change from the usual lemonade.
—Sue Rebers, Campbellsport, WI

PREP: 5 MIN. • COOK: 15 MIN. + CHILLING • MAKES: 14 SERVINGS (3½ QT.)

12 cups chopped fresh or frozen rhubarb
4 cups water
2½ to 3 cups sugar
1 cup pineapple juice
2 liters lemon-lime soda, chilled

In a Dutch oven, bring rhubarb and water to a boil. Boil for 15 minutes. Cool for 10 minutes; strain and reserve juice. Discard pulp. Add sugar and pineapple juice to reserved juice; stir until sugar is dissolved. Chill thoroughly. Just before serving, add soda and ice cubes.

1 cup: 230 cal., 0 fat (0 sat. fat), 0 chol., 21mg sod., 58g carb. (55g sugars, 2g fiber), 1g pro.

TOMATO, AVOCADO & GRILLED CORN SALAD

With ripe tomatoes, fresh basil and grilled corn, this sunny salad tastes just like summertime!

—Angela Spengler, Niceville, FL

PREP: 20 MIN. • GRILL: 10 MIN. + COOLING • MAKES: 8 SERVINGS

- **1 medium ear sweet corn, husks removed**
- **3 large red tomatoes, sliced**
- **3 large yellow tomatoes, sliced**
- **¾ tsp. kosher salt, divided**
- **½ tsp. pepper, divided**
- **2 medium ripe avocados, peeled and sliced**
- **¼ cup olive oil**
- **2 Tbsp. red wine vinegar**
- **1 Tbsp. minced fresh basil, plus more for garnish**
- **⅓ cup crumbled feta cheese**

1. Grill corn, covered, over medium heat 10-12 minutes or until lightly browned and tender, turning occasionally. Cool slightly. Cut corn from cob.

2. Arrange tomato slices on a large serving platter. Sprinkle with ½ tsp. salt and ¼ tsp. pepper. Top with avocado slices. Whisk together the oil, vinegar, basil and remaining salt and pepper; drizzle half over the tomatoes and avocado. Top with grilled corn and feta; drizzle remaining dressing over top. Garnish with additional chopped basil.

1 serving: 164 cal., 13g fat (2g sat. fat), 3mg chol., 237mg sod., 11g carb. (4g sugars, 4g fiber), 3g pro. **Diabetic exchanges:** 2 fat, 1 vegetable, ½ starch.

Test Kitchen Tip: This dish is spectacular with fresh heirloom tomatoes. The amped-up flavor means you can cut back on the salt.

FIRE & ICE TOMATOES

You won't miss the salt in this refreshing tomato salad! It's well-seasoned with cayenne pepper, mustard seed and vinegar, but not the least bit spicy. This dish is always a hit at potlucks.

—Nan Rickey, Yuma, AZ

PREP: 10 MIN. • COOK: 5 MIN. + CHILLING • MAKES: 8 SERVINGS

- **5 large tomatoes, cut into wedges**
- **1 medium onion, sliced**
- **¾ cup white vinegar**
- **6 Tbsp. sugar**
- **¼ cup water**
- **3 tsp. mustard seed**
- **¼ tsp. cayenne pepper**
- **1 large cucumber, sliced**

1. Place tomatoes and onion in a large heatproof nonreactive bowl. In a small saucepan, combine vinegar, sugar, water, mustard seed and cayenne; bring to a boil. Cook 1 minute, stirring to dissolve sugar; pour carefully over tomato mixture. Cool completely.

2. Stir in cucumber. Refrigerate, covered, overnight.

¾ cup: 72 cal., 1g fat (0 sat. fat), 0 chol., 7mg sod., 17g carb. (14g sugars, 2g fiber), 2g pro. **Diabetic exchanges:** 1 vegetable, ½ starch.

TOMATO, AVOCADO & GRILLED CORN SALAD

HEIRLOOM TOMATO PIE

HEIRLOOM TOMATO PIE

My green-thumb neighbors like to share produce with me. I return the delicious favor by baking tomato pies for all.

—Angela Benedict, Dunbar, WV

PREP: 45 MIN. • BAKE: 35 MIN. + COOLING • MAKES: 8 SERVINGS

- **1¼ lbs. heirloom tomatoes (about 4 medium), cut into ¼-in. slices**
- **¾ tsp. salt, divided**
- **1½ cups shredded extra-sharp cheddar cheese**
- **¾ cup all-purpose flour**
- **¼ cup cold butter, cubed**
- **1 to 2 Tbsp. half-and-half cream**
- **5 bacon strips, cooked and crumbled**

FILLING

- **1 pkg. (8 oz.) cream cheese, softened**
- **½ cup loosely packed basil leaves, thinly sliced**
- **2 Tbsp. minced fresh marjoram**
- **1½ tsp. minced fresh thyme**
- **½ tsp. garlic powder**
- **⅛ tsp. coarsely ground pepper**

1. Preheat oven to 350°. Place tomato slices in a single layer on paper towels; sprinkle with ½ tsp. salt. Let stand 45 minutes. Pat dry.

2. Meanwhile, place cheese, flour and remaining salt in a food processor; pulse until blended. Add butter; pulse until butter is the size of peas. While pulsing, add just enough cream to form moist crumbs. Press dough onto bottom and up sides of an ungreased 9-in. fluted tart pan with removable bottom. Gently press bacon into dough. Bake 20-22 minutes or until light brown. Cool on a wire rack.

3. In a large bowl, beat the cream cheese, herbs and garlic powder until blended. Spread over crust. Top with the tomato slices; sprinkle with pepper. Bake until the edge is golden brown and tomatoes are softened, 35-40 minutes longer. Cool on a wire rack. Refrigerate any leftovers.

1 slice: 320 cal., 25g fat (14g sat. fat), 74mg chol., 603mg sod., 14g carb. (3g sugars, 1g fiber), 11g pro.

Test Kitchen Tip: Heirlooms are colorful tomatoes that are pricier than regular tomatoes, and for a reason. True heirloom tomatoes are open-pollinated varieties, and their seeds have been handed down for at least three generations. Bred for juiciness, color, shape and size, they have not been scientifically modified.

HOW-TO

Buy Tomatoes

Look for deep, consistent coloring. If the tomatoes have lighter patches, that means they weren't ripened on the vine and may offer less flavor. A tomato should feel heavier than it looks and be firm with little give.

Store Tomatoes

Storing tomatoes in the refrigerator makes them lose their flavor. Instead, place them on a counter away from direct sunlight, allowing them to ripen.

Prep Tomatoes

Tomatoes are particularly susceptible to pesticides, so if you're not going with organic, wash them with a bit of soap and running water.

ROASTED TOMATO SALSA

This recipe is the reason we grow a huge garden every summer. It's our family's all-time favorite salsa. We make gallons of it to share with our neighbors. You might find yourself eating it right out of the bowl with a spoon.

—Donna Kelly, Draper, UT

PREP: 25 MIN. + STANDING • MAKES: 24 SERVINGS (8 CUPS)

- **12 large tomatoes, halved and seeded, divided**
- **2 Tbsp. olive oil, divided**
- **1 bunch fresh cilantro, trimmed**
- **¼ cup lime juice**
- **4 garlic cloves, peeled**
- **2 tsp. grated lime zest**
- **1 large sweet yellow pepper, finely chopped**
- **6 jalapeno peppers, minced**
- **12 green onions, thinly sliced**
- **1 Tbsp. ground cumin**
- **1 Tbsp. smoked paprika**
- **1 Tbsp. ground chipotle pepper**
- **2 tsp. salt**
- **¼ tsp. Louisiana-style hot sauce**
- **Tortilla chips**

1. Arrange 6 tomatoes cut side down on a 15x10x1-in. baking pan; drizzle with 1 Tbsp. oil. Broil 4 in. from the heat until skin blisters, about 4 minutes. Cool slightly; drain well.

2. In a food processor, process uncooked and roasted tomatoes in batches until chunky. Transfer all to a large bowl.

3. Place cilantro, lime juice, garlic, lime zest and remaining oil in the food processor. Cover and process until blended; add to tomatoes. Stir in the peppers, onions, cumin, paprika, chipotle pepper, salt and hot sauce. Let stand 1 hour to allow the flavors to blend. Serve with chips.

¼ cup: 27 cal., 1g fat (0 sat. fat), 0 chol., 155mg sod., 4g carb. (2g sugars, 1g fiber), 1g pro. **Diabetic exchanges:** 1 vegetable.

5i ❄ OVEN-ROASTED TOMATOES

I love tomatoes, as they're both healthy and versatile. You can use these roasted tomatoes in sandwiches or omelets, or try them on top of broiled chicken.

—Julie Tilney (Gomez), Downey, CA

PREP: 20 MIN. • BAKE: 3 HOURS + COOLING • MAKES: 16 SERVINGS (4 CUPS)

- **20 plum tomatoes (about 5 lbs.)**
- **¼ cup olive oil**
- **5 tsp. Italian seasoning**
- **2½ tsp. salt**

1. Cut tomatoes into ½-in. slices. Brush with oil; sprinkle with Italian seasoning and salt.

2. Place on racks coated with cooking spray in foil-lined 15x10x1-in. baking pans. Bake, uncovered, at 325° for 3-3½ hours or until the tomatoes start to turn dark brown around edges and are shriveled. Cool 10-15 minutes. Serve warm or at room temperature.

3. Store in an airtight container in the refrigerator for up to 1 week.

Freeze option: Place in airtight freezer container; freeze for up to 3 months. Bring tomatoes to room temperature before using.

¼ cup: 45 cal., 4g fat (0 sat. fat), 0 chol., 373mg sod., 3g carb. (2g sugars, 1g fiber), 1g pro.

ROASTED TOMATO SALSA

DID YOU KNOW?

Roja or Verde?

Salsa roja, or red sauce, is most often served as a condiment with tortilla chips. It's made from tomatoes, onions, peppers, garlic and cilantro. Salsa verde is a green sauce made from tomatillos, lime juice and roasted green chiles. It's often served over cooked meats and dishes like enchiladas.

TURKEY MEDALLIONS WITH TOMATO SALAD

In this quick meal, turkey medallions with a crisp coating are enhanced by the bright, summery flavors of a garden tomato salad.

—Gilda Lester, Millsboro, DE

PREP: 30 MIN. • COOK: 15 MIN. • MAKES: 6 SERVINGS

- **2 Tbsp. olive oil**
- **1 Tbsp. red wine vinegar**
- **½ tsp. sugar**
- **¼ tsp. dried oregano**
- **¼ tsp. salt**
- **1 medium green pepper, coarsely chopped**
- **1 celery rib, coarsely chopped**
- **¼ cup chopped red onion**
- **1 Tbsp. thinly sliced fresh basil**
- **3 medium tomatoes**

TURKEY

- **1 large egg**
- **2 Tbsp. lemon juice**
- **1 cup panko bread crumbs**
- **½ cup grated Parmesan cheese**
- **½ cup finely chopped walnuts**
- **1 tsp. lemon-pepper seasoning**
- **1 pkg. (20 oz.) turkey breast tenderloins**
- **¼ tsp. salt**
- **¼ tsp. pepper**
- **3 Tbsp. olive oil**
- **Additional fresh basil**

1. Whisk together first 5 ingredients. Stir in green pepper, celery, onion and basil. Cut tomatoes into wedges; cut wedges in half. Stir into pepper mixture.

2. In a shallow bowl, whisk together egg and lemon juice. In another shallow bowl, toss bread crumbs with cheese, walnuts and lemon pepper.

3. Cut tenderloins crosswise into 1-in. slices; flatten slices with a meat mallet to ½-in. thickness. Sprinkle with salt and pepper. Dip in egg mixture, then in crumb mixture, patting to adhere.

4. In a large skillet, heat 1 Tbsp. oil over medium-high heat. Add a third of the turkey; cook 2-3 minutes per side or until golden brown. Repeat twice with the remaining oil and turkey. Serve with tomato mixture; sprinkle with basil.

1 serving: 351 cal., 21g fat (3g sat. fat), 68mg chol., 458mg sod., 13g carb. (4g sugars, 2g fiber), 29g pro.

Test Kitchen Tip: At just 13 grams of carbohydrates per serving, this is a hearty option for anyone looking to cut carbs.

RUSTIC TOMATO PIE

Perk up your plate with this humble tomato pie. We like to use fresh-from-the-garden tomatoes and herbs, but store-bought produce will work in a pinch.

—Taste of Home *Test Kitchen*

PREP: 15 MIN. BAKE: 30 MIN. • MAKES: 8 SERVINGS

- **Pastry for single-crust pie**
- **1¾ lbs. mixed tomatoes, cut into ½-in. slices, seeded**
- **¼ cup thinly sliced green onions**
- **½ cup mayonnaise**
- **½ cup shredded cheddar cheese**
- **2 Tbsp. minced fresh basil**
- **¼ tsp. salt**
- **¼ tsp. pepper**
- **2 bacon strips, cooked and crumbled**
- **2 Tbsp. grated Parmesan cheese**

1. Preheat oven to 400°. On a lightly floured surface, roll dough to a ⅛-in.-thick circle; transfer to a 9-in. pie plate. Trim crust to ½ in. beyond rim of plate.

2. Place half of the tomatoes and half of the onions in crust. Combine mayonnaise, cheddar cheese, basil, salt and pepper; spread over tomatoes. Top with remaining onions and tomatoes. Fold the crust edge over filling, pleating as you go and leaving an 8-in. opening in the center. Sprinkle with the bacon and Parmesan cheese. Bake on a lower oven rack until until crust is golden and filling is bubbly, 30-35 minutes. Transfer pie to a wire rack to cool. If desired, sprinkle with additional basil.

1 piece: 325 cal., 25g fat (11g sat. fat), 41mg chol., 409mg sod., 19g carb. (3g sugars, 2g fiber), 6g pro.

TASTY MARINATED TOMATOES

My niece introduced me to this colorful recipe some time ago. I now make it when I have buffets or large gatherings because it can be prepared hours ahead. This is a tasty way to use a bumper crop of tomatoes.

—*Myrtle Matthews, Marietta, GA*

PREP: 10 MIN. + MARINATING • MAKES: 8 SERVINGS

- **3 large or 5 medium fresh tomatoes, thickly sliced**
- **⅓ cup olive oil**
- **¼ cup red wine vinegar**
- **1 tsp. salt, optional**
- **¼ tsp. pepper**
- **½ garlic clove, minced**
- **2 Tbsp. chopped onion**
- **1 Tbsp. minced fresh parsley**
- **1 Tbsp. minced fresh basil or 1 tsp. dried basil**

Arrange tomatoes in a large shallow dish. Combine remaining ingredients in a jar; cover tightly and shake well. Pour over tomato slices. Cover and refrigerate for several hours.

2 slices: 91 cal., 9g fat (0 sat. fat), 0 chol., 6mg sod., 3g carb. (0 sugars, 0 fiber), 1g pro.

CHAPTER 2

SPECIAL FARMERS MARKET FINDS

From asparagus and avocados to sweet potatoes and leeks, you never know what gems you'll discover at the local market. Turn here for new ideas for some of these farm-fresh staples.

ASPARAGUS WITH FRESH BASIL SAUCE

Add zip to your appetizer platter with a super-easy asparagus dip. The bonus? It doubles as a tasty sandwich spread.

—Janie Colle, Hutchinson, KS

TAKES: 15 MIN. • **MAKES:** 12 SERVINGS

- **¾ cup reduced-fat mayonnaise**
- **2 Tbsp. prepared pesto**
- **1 Tbsp. grated Parmesan cheese**
- **1 Tbsp. minced fresh basil**
- **1 tsp. lemon juice**
- **1 garlic clove, minced**
- **1½ lbs. fresh asparagus, trimmed**

1. In a small bowl, mix the first 6 ingredients until blended; refrigerate until serving.

2. In a Dutch oven, bring 12 cups water to a boil. Add asparagus in batches; cook, uncovered, until crisp-tender, 2-3 minutes. Remove and immediately drop into ice water. Drain and pat dry. Serve with sauce.

1 serving: 72 cal., 6g fat (1g sat. fat), 6mg chol., 149mg sod., 3g carb. (1g sugars, 1g fiber), 1g pro. **Diabetic exchanges:** 1½ fat.

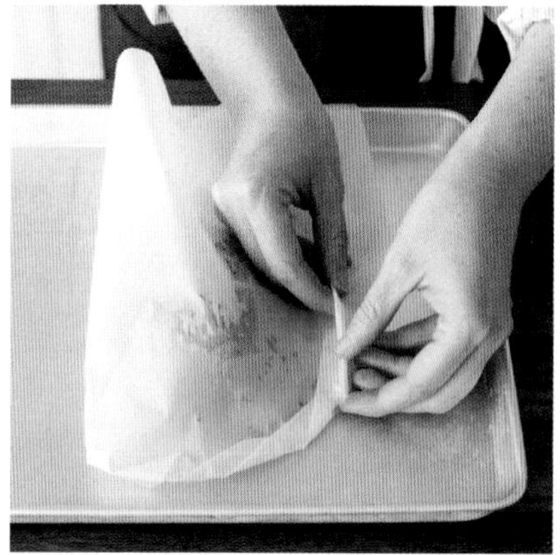

HOW-TO

Cook In Parchment Paper

Cooking food in parchment (en papillote) is an easy method in which the food is put inside a folded pouch of parchment and then baked. The paper holds in moisture to steam the food, which infuses it with flavor from citrus or other seasonings. This method is most often used for fish or vegetables, but works for poultry and lamb, too.

CITRUS SALMON WITH ASPARAGUS

This salmon dish is so simple to make yet so delicious, elegant and impressive. Baking in a parchment or foil pouch seals in the flavor.

—Dahlia Abrams, Detroit, MI

PREP: 20 MIN. • **BAKE:** 15 MIN. • **MAKES:** 6 SERVINGS

- **6 orange slices**
- **6 lime slices**
- **6 salmon fillets (4 oz. each)**
- **1 lb. fresh asparagus, trimmed and halved**
- **Olive oil-flavored cooking spray**
- **½ tsp. salt**
- **¼ tsp. pepper**
- **2 Tbsp. minced fresh parsley**
- **3 Tbsp. lemon juice**

1. Preheat oven to 425°. Cut parchment or heavy-duty foil into six 15x10-in. pieces; fold in half. Arrange the citrus slices on 1 side of each piece. Top with fish and asparagus. Spritz with cooking spray. Sprinkle with salt, pepper and parsley. Drizzle with lemon juice.

2. Fold parchment over fish; draw the edges together and crimp with fingers to form tightly sealed packets. Place in baking pans.

3. Bake packets until the fish flakes easily with a fork, 12-15 minutes. Open the packets carefully to allow the steam to escape.

1 packet: 224 cal., 13g fat (2g sat. fat), 57mg chol., 261mg sod., 6g carb. (3g sugars, 1g fiber), 20g pro. **Diabetic exchanges:** 3 lean meat, 1 vegetable.

FARMERS MARKET FIND

Look for asparagus with bright green or violet-tinged spears with firm (not limp) stems. Make sure the tips are closed and compact. When the bunch is squeezed, it should squeak.

CITRUS SALMON WITH ASPARAGUS

"WOWWY WOW WOW!"

—HILLY11, TASTEOFHOME.COM

ASPARAGUS, BACON & HERBED CHEESE PIZZA

ASPARAGUS, BACON & HERBED CHEESE PIZZA

Pizza night gets a refreshing and delicious makeover with tender spring asparagus.

—Dahlia Abrams, Detroit, MI

TAKES: 30 MIN. • MAKES: 6 SERVINGS

- **1 prebaked 12-in. pizza crust**
- **6 tsp. olive oil, divided**
- **1 cup shredded part-skim mozzarella cheese**
- **2¼ cups cut fresh asparagus (1-in. pieces)**
- **8 bacon strips, cooked and crumbled**
- **½ cup garlic-herb spreadable cheese**
- **¼ tsp. crushed red pepper flakes**

1. Preheat oven to 450°. Place crust on an ungreased 12-in. pizza pan or baking sheet; brush top with 4 tsp. oil. Top with mozzarella cheese, asparagus and bacon. Drop spreadable cheese by teaspoonfuls over pizza. Sprinkle with pepper flakes; drizzle with remaining oil.

2. Bake 12-15 minutes or until the cheese is lightly browned.

1 slice: 407 cal., 24g fat (11g sat. fat), 45mg chol., 748mg sod., 32g carb. (3g sugars, 2g fiber), 18g pro.

HONEY-LEMON ASPARAGUS

Everyone wants a second helping of these glazed spears, so I often double the recipe. For another option, try using a root vegetable like turnip or parsnip.

—Lorraine Caland, Shuniah, ON

TAKES: 15 MIN. • MAKES: 8 SERVINGS

- **2 lbs. fresh asparagus, trimmed**
- **¼ cup honey**
- **2 Tbsp. butter**
- **2 Tbsp. lemon juice**
- **1 tsp. sea salt**
- **1 tsp. balsamic vinegar**
- **1 tsp. Worcestershire sauce**
- **Additional sea salt, optional**

1. In a large saucepan, bring 8 cups water to a boil. Add the asparagus in batches; cook, uncovered, just until crisp-tender, 1-2 minutes. Drain and pat dry.

2. Meanwhile, in a small saucepan, combine the remaining ingredients. Bring to a boil. Reduce the heat; simmer, uncovered, 2 minutes or until slightly thickened.

3. Transfer asparagus to a large bowl; drizzle with glaze and toss gently to coat. If desired, sprinkle with additional sea salt.

1 serving: 73 cal., 3g fat (2g sat. fat), 8mg chol., 276mg sod., 12g carb. (10g sugars, 1g fiber), 2g pro. **Diabetic exchanges:** 1 vegetable, ½ starch, ½ fat.

HOW-TO

Prep Asparagus

- Rinse asparagus stalks well in cold water. The tender stalk should easily break from the tough white portion when gently bent. If not, cut off the white portion.
- If the tips are particularly large, use a knife to scrape off some of the scales.
- If the stalks are large, use a vegetable peeler to gently remove the tough area of the stalk.

AVOCADO SALSA

I first served this at a party—what a hit! The chunky mix of garlic, corn and avocado kept guests coming back for more.

—Susan Vandermeer, Ogden, UT

PREP: 20 MIN. + CHILLING • MAKES: 28 SERVINGS (7 CUPS)

- **1⅔ cups (about 8¼ oz.) frozen corn, thawed**
- **2 cans (2¼ oz. each) sliced ripe olives, drained**
- **1 medium sweet red pepper, chopped**
- **1 small onion, chopped**
- **5 garlic cloves, minced**
- **⅓ cup olive oil**
- **¼ cup lemon juice**
- **3 Tbsp. cider vinegar**
- **1 tsp. dried oregano**
- **½ tsp. salt**
- **½ tsp. pepper**
- **4 medium ripe avocados, peeled**
- **Tortilla chips**

1. Combine the corn, olives, red pepper and onion. In another bowl, mix the next 7 ingredients. Pour over corn mixture; toss to coat. Refrigerate, covered, overnight.

2. Just before serving, chop avocados; stir into salsa. Serve with tortilla chips.

¼ cup: 82 cal., 7g fat (1g sat. fat), 0 chol., 85mg sod., 5g carb. (1g sugars, 2g fiber), 1g pro. **Diabetic exchanges:** 1½ fat.

FARMERS MARKET FIND

If you're buying avocados to use right when you get home, choose those that yield a bit to the touch. Cup the avocado in your hand and give a gentle squeeze. If it gives a little, it's ripe and ready to use.

FRESH SHRIMP & AVOCADO NACHOS

I'm a fan of shrimp, and my family's big on nachos. When I combined those foods, our household had a new favorite.

—Teri Rasey, Cadillac, MI

PREP: 30 MIN. + CHILLING • MAKES: 10 SERVINGS

- **4 plum tomatoes, chopped**
- **3 tomatillos, husked and chopped**
- **4 jalapeno peppers, seeded and finely chopped**
- **1 small onion, chopped**
- **2 garlic cloves, minced**
- **¼ cup minced fresh cilantro**
- **3 Tbsp. olive oil**
- **2 Tbsp. seasoned rice vinegar**
- **1 Tbsp. lime juice**
- **1½ tsp. sea salt**
- **½ tsp. dried oregano**
- **1 lb. peeled and deveined cooked shrimp (31-40 per lb.), coarsely chopped**

TOPPING

- **2 medium ripe avocados, peeled and pitted, divided**
- **½ cup sour cream**
- **2 Tbsp. lime juice**
- **8 cups tortilla chips**
- **1 cup shredded lettuce**

1. In a large bowl, combine the first 11 ingredients. Cover and refrigerate until chilled, at least 30 minutes. Stir in shrimp.

2. For avocado cream, mash 1 avocado with sour cream and 1 Tbsp. lime juice until smooth. Cube remaining avocado and toss with remaining lime juice.

3. To serve, arrange chips on a large platter. Top with shrimp mixture, cubed avocado, lettuce and avocado cream; serve immediately.

1 serving: 264 cal., 16g fat (3g sat. fat), 72mg chol., 542mg sod., 20g carb. (3g sugars, 3g fiber), 12g pro.

Test Kitchen Tip: Seasoned rice vinegar is different from regular rice vinegar; it has added sugar and salt.

AVOCADO SALSA

HOW-TO

Peel Avocados

- Wash the avocado. Carefully cut into the ripe avocado stem to stern until you hit the pit. Repeat to cut the avocado into quarters.
- Gently twist the avocado to separate.
- Pull the skin back like a banana peel.

CHIPOTLE LIME AVOCADO SALAD

CHIPOTLE LIME AVOCADO SALAD

I'm a real believer in clean eating and a healthy lifestyle, which includes eating plenty of veggies. This salad is loaded with the summer's best, plus a little bit of heat.

—Letef Vita, Denver, CO

TAKES: 15 MIN. • MAKES: 4 SERVINGS

- **¼ cup lime juice**
- **¼ cup maple syrup**
- **½ tsp. ground chipotle pepper**
- **¼ tsp. cayenne pepper, optional**
- **2 medium ripe avocados, peeled and sliced**
- **½ medium cucumber, peeled and chopped**
- **1 Tbsp. minced fresh chives**
- **2 large tomatoes, cut into ½-in. slices**

In a small bowl, whisk lime juice, maple syrup, chipotle pepper and, if desired, cayenne until blended. In another bowl, combine avocados, cucumber and chives. Drizzle with dressing; toss gently to coat. Serve over tomatoes.

1 serving: 191 cal., 11g fat (1g sat. fat), 0 chol., 26mg sod., 25g carb. (17g sugars, 6g fiber), 3g pro.

AVOCADO CRAB BOATS

With a side of beans or rice, these boats are wonderful straight from the oven. You can also cover them, pack them on ice and take them to a picnic or potluck. Hot or cold, they're delicious!

—Frances Benthin, Scio, OR

TAKES: 20 MIN. • MAKES: 8 SERVINGS

- **5 medium ripe avocados, peeled and halved**
- **½ cup mayonnaise**
- **2 Tbsp. lemon juice**
- **2 cans (6 oz. each) lump crabmeat, drained**
- **4 Tbsp. chopped fresh cilantro, divided**
- **2 Tbsp. minced chives**
- **1 serrano pepper, seeded and minced**
- **1 Tbsp. capers, drained**
- **¼ tsp. pepper**
- **1 cup shredded pepper jack cheese**
- **½ tsp. paprika**
- **Lemon wedges**

1. Preheat broiler. Place 2 avocado halves in a large bowl; mash lightly with a fork. Add the mayonnaise and lemon juice; mix until well blended. Stir in crab, 3 Tbsp. cilantro, chives, serrano pepper, capers and pepper. Spoon into remaining avocado halves.

2. Transfer to a 15x10x1-in. baking pan. Sprinkle with cheese and paprika. Broil 4-5 in. from heat until cheese is melted, 3-5 minutes. Sprinkle with remaining cilantro; serve with lemon wedges.

1 filled avocado half: 325 cal., 28g fat (6g sat. fat), 57mg chol., 427mg sod., 8g carb. (0 sugars, 6g fiber), 13g pro.

Test Kitchen Tip: Ripe avocados can be stored in the refrigerator for up to 5 days to slow the ripening process. To speed it up, store hard avocados in a paper bag on the kitchen counter. Check often to see how they're coming along.

BRUSSELS SPROUTS IN ROSEMARY CREAM SAUCE

Brussels sprouts in an herb cream sauce? You've never had them like this—and you may never want them any other way!

—Liz Koschoreck, Berea, KY

TAKES: 30 MIN. • MAKES: 6 SERVINGS

- **1 lb. fresh Brussels sprouts (about 4 cups)**
- **¼ cup butter, cubed**
- **1 Tbsp. all-purpose flour**
- **1 cup heavy whipping cream**
- **1 Tbsp. coarsely chopped fresh rosemary**
- **2 garlic cloves, minced**
- **¾ tsp. salt**
- **¼ cup shredded Parmigiano-Reggiano cheese**
- **Freshly ground pepper**

1. Trim Brussels sprout stems; using a paring knife, cut an "X" in the bottom of each. Place sprouts in a large saucepan; add water to cover. Bring to a boil. Reduce heat; simmer, covered, 6-8 minutes or until almost tender. Drain.

2. Meanwhile, in a large saucepan, melt butter over medium heat. Stir in flour until smooth; gradually whisk in cream. Bring to a boil, stirring constantly; cook and stir 1-2 minutes or until thickened. Stir in rosemary and garlic. Add sprouts and salt; heat through, stirring to combine. Sprinkle with cheese and pepper.

⅔ cup: 256 cal., 24g fat (15g sat. fat), 78mg chol., 445mg sod., 9g carb. (3g sugars, 3g fiber), 5g pro.

GRILLED BRUSSELS SPROUTS

When we were on a beach vacation and I was trying to cook our entire meal on the grill, I turned our not-so-simple veggie choice into an easy grilled side. For spicier sprouts, season with red pepper flakes.

—Tiffany Ihle, Bronx, NY

TAKES: 30 MIN. • MAKES: 4 SERVINGS

- **16 fresh Brussels sprouts (about 1½-in. diameter), trimmed**
- **1 medium sweet red pepper**
- **1 medium onion**
- **½ tsp. salt**
- **½ tsp. garlic powder**
- **¼ tsp. coarsely ground pepper**
- **1 Tbsp. olive oil**

1. In a large saucepan, place a steamer basket over 1 in. of water. Bring water to a boil. Place sprouts in basket. Reduce the heat to maintain a simmer; steam, covered, until crisp-tender, 4-6 minutes. Cool slightly; cut each sprout in half.

2. Cut the red pepper and onion into 1½-in. pieces. On 4 metal or soaked wooden skewers, alternately thread the sprouts, red pepper and onion. Mix the salt, garlic powder and pepper. Brush vegetables with oil; sprinkle with salt mixture. Grill, covered, over medium heat or broil 4 in. from the heat until vegetables are tender, 10-12 minutes, turning occasionally.

1 skewer: 84 cal., 4g fat (1g sat. fat), 0 chol., 316mg sod., 11g carb. (4g sugars, 4g fiber), 3g pro. **Diabetic exchanges:** 1 vegetable, ½ fat.

BRUSSELS SPROUTS IN ROSEMARY CREAM SAUCE

Salt Eggplant

Salting eggplant draws out some of the liquid that carries bitter flavors. To salt, place slices, cubes or strips of eggplant in a colander over a plate; sprinkle the eggplant with salt and toss. Let stand about 30 minutes. Rinse, drain well and pat dry with paper towels.

LIME & SESAME GRILLED EGGPLANT

LIME & SESAME GRILLED EGGPLANT

When I lived in Greece, I fell in love with eggplant. My recipe's seasonings have an Asian theme, but the dish still makes me think of Greece.

—Allyson Meyler, Greensboro, NC

TAKES: 20 MIN. • MAKES: 6 SERVINGS

- **3 Tbsp. lime juice**
- **1 Tbsp. sesame oil**
- **1½ tsp. reduced-sodium soy sauce**
- **1 garlic clove, minced**
- **½ tsp. grated fresh gingerroot or ¼ tsp. ground ginger**
- **½ tsp. salt**
- **⅛ tsp. pepper**
- **1 medium eggplant (1¼ lbs.), cut lengthwise into ½-in. slices**
- **2 tsp. honey**
- **⅛ tsp. crushed red pepper flakes**
- **Thinly sliced green onion and sesame seeds**

1. In a small bowl, whisk the first 7 ingredients until blended; brush 2 Tbsp. juice mixture over both sides of eggplant slices. Grill, covered, over medium heat until tender, 4-6 minutes on each side.

2. Transfer eggplant to a serving plate. Stir honey and pepper flakes into remaining juice mixture; drizzle over eggplant. Sprinkle with green onion and sesame seeds.

1 serving: 50 cal., 2g fat (0 sat. fat), 0 chol., 246mg sod., 7g carb. (4g sugars, 2g fiber), 1g pro. **Diabetic exchanges:** 1 vegetable, ½ fat.

Test Kitchen Tip: Select a firm, round or pear-shaped, heavy eggplant with a uniformly smooth color and glossy, taut skin. The eggplant should be free from blemishes and rust spots with intact green caps and mold-free stems.

EGGPLANT FLATBREAD PIZZAS

I began making these delightfully different pies back when I was cooking only at home. Now I'm a chef!

—Christine Wendland, Browns Mills, NJ

TAKES: 30 MIN. • MAKES: 4 SERVINGS

- **3 Tbsp. olive oil, divided**
- **2½ cups cubed eggplant (½ in.)**
- **1 small onion, halved and thinly sliced**
- **½ tsp. salt**
- **⅛ tsp. pepper**
- **1 garlic clove, minced**
- **2 naan flatbreads**
- **½ cup part-skim ricotta cheese**
- **1 tsp. dried oregano**
- **½ cup roasted garlic tomato sauce**
- **½ cup loosely packed basil leaves**
- **1 cup shredded part-skim mozzarella cheese**
- **2 Tbsp. grated Parmesan cheese**
- **Sliced fresh basil, optional**

1. Preheat the oven to 400°. In a large skillet, heat 1 Tbsp. oil over medium-high heat; saute the eggplant and onion with salt and pepper until the eggplant begins to soften, 4-5 minutes. Stir in garlic; remove from heat.

2. Place flatbreads on a baking sheet. Spread with ricotta cheese; sprinkle with oregano. Spread with tomato sauce. Top with eggplant mixture and whole basil leaves. Sprinkle with mozzarella and Parmesan cheeses; drizzle with the remaining oil.

3. Bake until crust is golden brown and cheese is melted, 12-15 minutes. If desired, top with sliced basil.

½ pizza: 340 cal., 21g fat (7g sat. fat), 32mg chol., 996mg sod., 25g carb. (5g sugars, 3g fiber), 14g pro.

RAGIN' CAJUN EGGPLANT & SHRIMP SKILLET

We always have a large summer garden where lots of produce lingers into fall. That's when we harvest our onions, bell peppers, tomatoes and eggplant, some of the key ingredients of this dish. It gets Cajun flair from the Holy Trinity (onion, celery and bell pepper), shrimp and red pepper flakes.

—Barbara Hahn, Park Hills, MO

PREP: 30 MIN. • BAKE: 35 MIN. • MAKES: 4 SERVINGS

- **1 medium eggplant, peeled and cut into ½-in. cubes**
- **3 Tbsp. olive oil**
- **2 celery ribs, diced**
- **1 medium onion, diced**
- **1 small green pepper, seeded and diced**
- **3 plum tomatoes, diced**
- **1 tsp. crushed red pepper flakes**
- **½ tsp. pepper**
- **12 oz. uncooked shell-on shrimp (31-40 per lb.), peeled and deveined**
- **½ cup seasoned bread crumbs**
- **1½ cups shredded part-skim mozzarella cheese**

1. Place eggplant in a large saucepan; add water to cover. Bring to a boil. Reduce heat; simmer, covered, until tender, 3-4 minutes. Drain.

2. Preheat oven to 350°. In an ovenproof skillet, heat the oil over medium-high heat. Add celery, onion and green pepper; saute until tender, about 5 minutes. Reduce heat to medium; stir in tomatoes and eggplant. Saute 5 minutes. Stir in seasonings. Add shrimp and bread crumbs; saute 5 minutes longer, stirring well.

3. Bake 30 minutes. Remove skillet from oven; top with mozzarella cheese. Bake 5 minutes more.

1 serving: 399 cal., 21g fat (7g sat. fat), 131mg chol., 641mg sod., 26g carb. (9g sugars, 5g fiber), 28g pro.

GRILLED EGGPLANT PANINI WITH BASIL AIOLI

I love being able to use our homegrown fresh vegetables and herbs for meals. This sandwich is loaded with veggies and has a satisfying crunch.

—Joseph Sciascia, San Mateo, CA

PREP: 25 MIN. • GRILL: 20 MIN. • MAKES: 4 SERVINGS

- **¾ cup mayonnaise**
- **⅓ cup chopped fresh basil**
- **3 Tbsp. grated Parmesan cheese**
- **2 Tbsp. minced fresh chives**
- **1 Tbsp. lemon juice**
- **2 garlic cloves, minced**
- **½ tsp. salt**
- **½ tsp. pepper**
- **1 large eggplant, cut into 8 slices**
- **2 large sweet red peppers, cut into large pieces**
- **2 Tbsp. olive oil**
- **4 ciabatta rolls, split**
- **8 slices provolone cheese**

1. For aioli, place first 8 ingredients in a blender; cover and process until smooth.

2. Brush the vegetables with oil. Place in a broiling pan and broil 3-4 in. from heat, or grill, covered, over medium heat until tender, 4-5 minutes per side. Chop the peppers when cool enough to handle.

3. Spread cut sides of each roll with 2 Tbsp. aioli; top each with cheese. Layer bottoms with eggplant and peppers. Replace tops.

4. In a panini press, grill sandwiches until cheese is melted, 5-7 minutes. Serve remaining aioli with sandwiches or save for another use.

1 panini: 732 cal., 38g fat (11g sat. fat), 33mg chol., 1116mg sod., 83g carb. (12g sugars, 9g fiber), 23g pro.

RAGIN' CAJUN EGGPLANT & SHRIMP SKILLET

LEEK-STUFFED FLANK STEAK

LEEK-STUFFED FLANK STEAK

Colorful and tender, this special beef dish was a popular request for birthday dinners when I was growing up.

—Julie Etzel, Tualatin, OR

PREP: 30 MIN. • BAKE: 1¼ HOURS + STANDING • MAKES: 6 SERVINGS

- **1 beef flank steak (about 1½ lbs.)**
- **⅛ tsp. plus ½ tsp. salt, divided**
- **⅛ tsp. pepper**
- **4 bacon strips, diced**
- **3 leeks (white portion only), sliced**
- **1½ cups chopped sweet yellow pepper**
- **1½ cups chopped celery, divided**
- **½ lb. baby spinach, torn**
- **1 tsp. dried thyme**
- **1 tsp. dried basil**
- **2 garlic cloves, minced**
- **3 Tbsp. olive oil**
- **1 medium onion, cut into wedges**
- **1 cup water**
- **½ cup beef broth**
- **2 tsp. tomato paste**
- **1 bay leaf**

1. Cut flank steak horizontally from a long side to within ½ in. of the opposite side. Open the steak so it lies flat; cover with plastic wrap. Flatten it to ¼-in. thickness. Remove plastic; sprinkle the steak with ⅛ tsp. salt and pepper. Set aside. In a skillet, cook the bacon until crisp. Remove to paper towels. Discard the drippings, reserving 2 Tbsp. in pan.

2. In the bacon drippings, saute leeks, yellow peppers and 1 cup celery until tender. Stir in spinach, thyme, basil and bacon. Spoon over meat to within ½ in. of the edges. Roll up tightly jelly-roll style, starting with a long side. Tie with kitchen string.

3. Rub steak with garlic and remaining salt. In a large skillet, brown meat in oil on all sides. Place in a greased shallow roasting pan. Add onion and remaining celery. Combine all remaining ingredients; pour over steak. Cover loosely with foil.

4. Bake at 350° for 1 hour. Baste with drippings. Bake, uncovered, 15 minutes longer or until meat is tender. Let stand for 10-15 minutes. Remove string and slice. Discard bay leaf; thicken juices if desired.

1 slice: 366 cal., 23g fat (7g sat. fat), 66mg chol., 572mg sod., 13g carb. (5g sugars, 3g fiber), 27g pro.

BRIE-LEEK TARTLETS

I have a family of picky eaters, but everyone loves these mini tarts. I always make extra because they're gone as soon as I turn my back!

—Colleen MacDonald, Port Moody, BC

TAKES: 30 MIN. • MAKES: 15 SERVINGS

- **1 medium leek (white portion only), finely chopped**
- **3 Tbsp. butter**
- **1 garlic clove, minced**
- **½ cup heavy whipping cream**
- **Dash salt and white pepper**
- **Dash ground nutmeg**
- **1 pkg. (1.9 oz.) frozen miniature phyllo tart shells**
- **2 oz. Brie cheese, rind removed**
- **Minced fresh parsley, optional**

1. In a small skillet, saute leek in butter until tender. Add garlic; cook 1 minute longer. Stir in cream, salt, pepper and nutmeg; cook and stir until thickened, 1-2 minutes.

2. Place tart shells on a baking sheet. Slice cheese into 15 pieces; place 1 piece in each tart shell. Top each with 1½ tsp. leek mixture.

3. Bake at 350° until heated through, 6-8 minutes. If desired, sprinkle with parsley. Refrigerate leftovers.

1 tartlet: 86 cal., 7g fat (4g sat. fat), 21mg chol., 64mg sod., 4g carb. (0 sugars, 0 fiber), 2g pro.

LEEK POTATO PANCAKES

This comforting recipe came from my great-grandmother. She brought it over from England, where they always enjoyed leeks during the fall and winter.

—Suzanne Kesel, Cohocton, NY

PREP: 30 MIN. + CHILLING • COOK: 5 MIN./BATCH • MAKES: 6 SERVINGS

- **½ lb. russet potatoes, peeled and quartered (about 1 large)**
- **2 lbs. medium leeks (white portion only), thinly sliced**
- **4 large eggs, room temperature, lightly beaten**
- **½ cup dry bread crumbs**
- **⅓ cup grated Parmesan cheese**
- **1 tsp. salt**
- **¼ tsp. pepper**
- **¼ cup canola oil, divided**
- **6 Tbsp. sour cream**

1. Place the potato quarters in a large saucepan and cover with water. Bring to a boil. Reduce heat; cover and cook for 15-20 minutes or until tender, adding the leeks during last 3 minutes. Drain.

2. Transfer potato quarters to a large bowl; mash with eggs, bread crumbs, cheese, salt and pepper. Cover and refrigerate for 1 hour.

3. Heat 1 Tbsp. oil in a large cast-iron or other heavy skillet over medium heat. Drop batter by ¼ cupfuls into oil. Fry in batches until golden brown on both

sides, using remaining oil as needed. Drain on paper towels. Serve with sour cream.

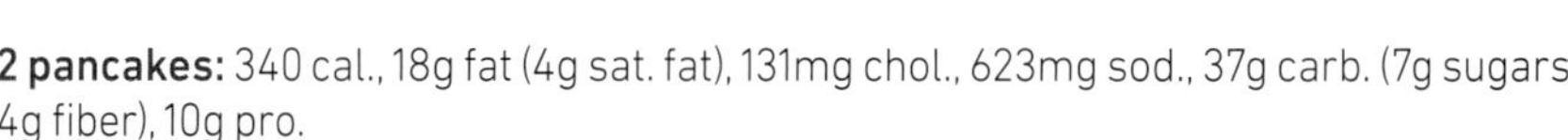
2 pancakes: 340 cal., 18g fat (4g sat. fat), 131mg chol., 623mg sod., 37g carb. (7g sugars, 4g fiber), 10g pro.

SICILIAN STEAMED LEEKS

I love the challenge of finding new ways to prepare leeks, a delicious but underused vegetable. This Italian-flavored side dish has become a family favorite.

—Roxanne Chan, Albany, CA

TAKES: 20 MIN. • MAKES: 6 SERVINGS

- **6 medium leeks (white portion only), halved lengthwise, cleaned**
- **1 large tomato, chopped**
- **1 small navel orange, peeled, sectioned and chopped**
- **2 Tbsp. minced fresh parsley**
- **2 Tbsp. sliced Greek olives**
- **1 tsp. capers, drained**
- **1 tsp. red wine vinegar**
- **1 tsp. olive oil**
- **½ tsp. grated orange zest**
- **½ tsp. pepper**
- **Crumbled feta cheese**

In a Dutch oven, place steamer basket over 1 in. of water. Place the leeks in basket. Bring water to a boil. Reduce heat to maintain a low boil; steam, covered, until tender, 8-10 minutes. Meanwhile, combine the next 9 ingredients. Transfer leeks to a serving platter. Spoon tomato mixture over top; sprinkle with cheese.

1 serving: 83 cal., 2g fat (0 sat. fat), 0 chol., 77mg sod., 16g carb. (6g sugars, 3g fiber), 2g pro. **Diabetic exchanges:** 1 starch, ½ fat.

SICILIAN STEAMED LEEKS

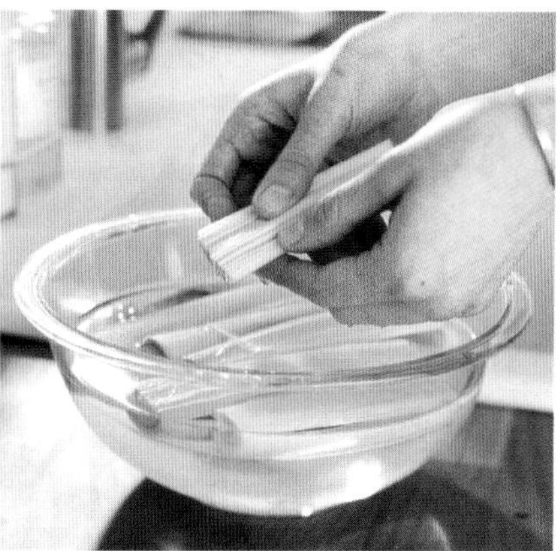

HOW-TO

Clean Leeks

- Cut off the root end and the tough green top.
- Halve the white part lengthwise.
- Soak the stalks in cold water for 10 minutes, then rinse to remove grit.

CHEDDAR POTATO CHOWDER

CHEDDAR POTATO CHOWDER

The original recipe for this chowder was quite high in fat. I found a way to use healthier ingredients while keeping the rich, home-style flavor we love.

—Ellie Rausch, Goodsoil, SK

PREP: 20 MIN. • **COOK:** 20 MIN. • **MAKES:** 7 SERVINGS

- **2 cups water**
- **2 cups diced unpeeled red potatoes**
- **1 cup diced carrot**
- **½ cup diced celery**
- **¼ cup chopped onion**
- **1 tsp. salt**
- **¼ tsp. pepper**
- **¼ cup all-purpose flour**
- **2 cups 2% milk**
- **2 cups shredded reduced-fat cheddar cheese**
- **1 cup cubed fully cooked ham**

1. In a Dutch oven, combine the first 7 ingredients. Bring to a boil. Reduce heat; cover and simmer for 10-12 minutes or until tender.

2. Meanwhile, place flour in a large saucepan; gradually whisk in milk. Bring to a boil over medium heat; cook and stir for 2 minutes or until thickened. Remove from the heat. Add cheese; stir until melted. Stir the ham and the cheese sauce into undrained vegetables; stir until combined.

1 cup: 212 cal., 9g fat (5g sat. fat), 29mg chol., 847mg sod., 18g carb. (0 sugars, 2g fiber), 16g pro.

SCALLOPED POTATOES WITH HAM

With a smooth sauce and chunks of ham, this dish is a sure family-pleaser. I changed my mother's version by adding parsley and thyme, and now my husband and children request these potatoes often.

—Wendy Rhoades, Yacolt, WA

PREP: 15 MIN. • **BAKE:** 1 HOUR 20 MIN. • **MAKES:** 4 SERVINGS

- **6 Tbsp. butter, divided**
- **¼ cup all-purpose flour**
- **1 tsp. dried parsley flakes**
- **1 tsp. salt**
- **½ tsp. dried thyme**
- **¼ tsp. pepper**
- **3 cups 2% milk**
- **6 cups thinly sliced peeled potatoes**
- **1½ cups chopped fully cooked ham**
- **1 small onion, grated**

1. Preheat oven to 375°. In a large saucepan, melt 4 Tbsp. butter over medium heat. Stir in flour, parsley, salt, thyme and pepper until smooth. Gradually add milk; bring to a boil. Cook and stir for 2 minutes.

2. Combine potatoes, ham and onion; place half in a greased 2½-qt. baking dish. Top with half of the sauce; repeat layers.

3. Cover and bake until potatoes are almost tender, 65-75 minutes. Dot with the remaining 2 Tbsp. butter. Bake, uncovered, until potatoes are tender, 15-20 minutes.

1 cup: 521 cal., 28g fat (16g sat. fat), 99mg chol., 2343mg sod., 47g carb. (10g sugars, 5g fiber), 19g pro.

Test Kitchen Tip: Before you peel potatoes, scrub them with a vegetable brush under cold water. Remove eyes or sprouts. If you have a lot of potatoes, place them in cold water after peeling to prevent discoloring.

5i LEMON OREGANO POTATOES

My husband made simply seasoned, roasted potatoes when we were first married. They've been a staple on our menus ever since.

—Kate Hilts, Grand Rapids, MI

PREP: 10 MIN. • BAKE: 35 MIN. • MAKES: 4 SERVINGS

- **3 large red or russet potatoes, peeled and cut into 1-in. cubes**
- **¼ cup olive oil**
- **3 Tbsp. lemon juice**
- **1 tsp. dried oregano**
- **½ tsp. salt**

Place potatoes in a saucepan and cover with water. Bring to a boil over medium heat. Reduce heat. Simmer, uncovered, for 5-8 minutes or until potatoes are crisp-tender; drain. Add the oil, lemon juice, oregano and salt and toss well to coat. Mixture should form a slight paste on the outside of the potatoes. Transfer to a greased rimmed baking sheet. Bake, uncovered, at 450° for 20-25 minutes or until potatoes just start to release from the baking sheet. Turn and continue roasting until tender and deep golden brown, 15-20 minutes longer.

1 cup: 214 cal., 14g fat (2g sat. fat), 0 chol., 303mg sod., 21g carb. (2g sugars, 2g fiber), 2g pro. **Diabetic exchanges:** 3 fat, 1½ starch.

❄ TEXAS GARLIC MASHED POTATOES

Flavored with garlic and caramelized onions, this creamy classic is likely to become the star of the meal.

—Richard Markle, Midlothian, TX

PREP: 20 MIN. • COOK: 30 MIN. • MAKES: 6 SERVINGS

- **1 whole garlic bulb**
- **1 tsp. plus 1 Tbsp. olive oil, divided**
- **1 medium white onion, chopped**
- **4 medium potatoes, peeled and quartered**
- **¼ cup butter, softened**
- **¼ cup sour cream**
- **¼ cup grated Parmesan cheese**
- **¼ cup 2% milk**
- **½ tsp. salt**
- **¼ tsp. pepper**

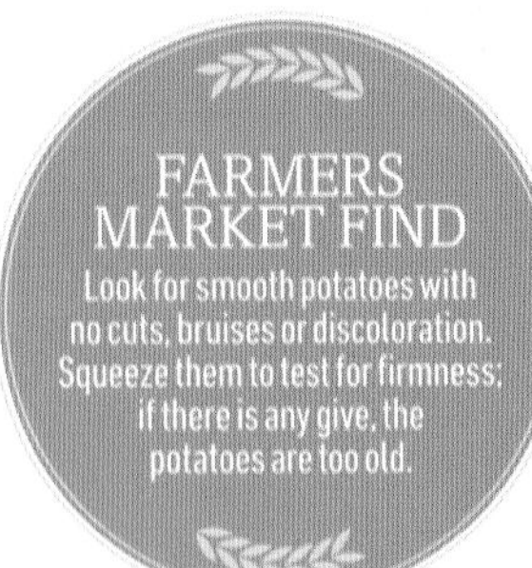

1. Preheat oven to 425°. Remove the papery outer skin from garlic bulb, but do not peel or separate cloves. Cut top off of the garlic bulb, exposing individual cloves. Brush cut cloves with 1 tsp. oil. Wrap in foil. Bake until cloves are soft, 30-35 minutes.

2. Meanwhile, place the remaining oil in a large skillet over low heat. Add the onion; cook 15-20 minutes or until golden brown, stirring occasionally. Transfer to a food processor. Process until blended; set aside.

3. Place potatoes in a large saucepan; add water to cover. Bring to a boil. Reduce heat; cook, uncovered, until tender, 15-20 minutes. Drain; return to pan. Squeeze softened garlic onto potatoes; add butter, sour cream, cheese, milk, salt, pepper and onion. Beat until mashed.

Freeze option: Place cooled mashed potato mixture in a freezer container and freeze. To use, partially thaw in refrigerator overnight. Microwave, covered, on high, stirring twice and adding a little milk if necessary, until heated through.

⅔ cup: 236 cal., 14g fat (7g sat. fat), 31mg chol., 313mg sod., 25g carb. (4g sugars, 2g fiber), 4g pro.

LEMON OREGANO POTATOES

HOW-TO

Roast Potatoes

- Place potatoes in a saucepan and cover with cold water. Bring to a boil over medium heat. Once it's bubbling, reduce the heat. Simmer, uncovered, until the potatoes are crisp-tender, 5-8 minutes. (You should be able to pierce them with a knife, but you don't need them to be like butter. A little resistance is desirable.) Drain.

- Set the potatoes into a large bowl. Pour in oil, salt and herbs or seasoning of your choice. Mix until potatoes are well coated.

- Pour the coated potatoes out onto a greased rimmed baking sheet. (Greasing helps prevent sticking.) Bake, uncovered, at 450° until the potatoes just start to release from the baking sheet, 20-25 minutes. Toss the potatoes. Continue roasting, tossing occasionally, until they're a deep golden brown, 15-20 minutes.

GRILLED THREE-POTATO SALAD

GRILLED THREE-POTATO SALAD

Everyone in our extended family loves to cook, so I put our favorite recipes in a book to be handed down from generation to generation. I couldn't leave out this twist on traditional potato salad.

—Suzette Jury, Keene, CA

PREP: 25 MIN. + COOLING • GRILL: 10 MIN. • MAKES: 6 SERVINGS

- **¾ lb. Yukon Gold potatoes**
- **¾ lb. red potatoes**
- **1 medium sweet potato, peeled**
- **½ cup thinly sliced green onions**
- **¼ cup canola oil**
- **2 to 3 Tbsp. white wine vinegar**
- **1 Tbsp. Dijon mustard**
- **1 tsp. salt**
- **½ tsp. celery seed**
- **¼ tsp. pepper**

1. Place potatoes and sweet potato in a Dutch oven; cover with water. Bring to a boil. Reduce heat; cover and simmer for 15-20 minutes or until tender. Drain and cool. Cut into 1-in. chunks.

2. Place potato mixture in a grill wok or basket. Grill, uncovered, over medium heat for 8-12 minutes or until browned, stirring frequently. Transfer to a large salad bowl; add onions.

3. Whisk the oil, vinegar, mustard, salt, celery seed and pepper. Drizzle over potato mixture and toss to coat. Serve warm or at room temperature.

¾ cup: 191 cal., 10g fat (1g sat. fat), 0 chol., 466mg sod., 24g carb. (3g sugars, 3g fiber), 3g pro. **Diabetic exchanges:** 2 fat, 1½ starch.

PESTO PASTA & POTATOES

Shhh—let the simplicity of this dish be your little secret! You'll need only five ingredients, including convenient prepared pesto. Plus, the beans and pasta cook in the same pot.

—Laura Flowers, Moscow, ID

TAKES: 30 MIN. • MAKES: 12 SERVINGS

- **1½ lbs. small red potatoes, halved**
- **12 oz. uncooked whole grain spiral pasta**
- **3 cups cut fresh or frozen green beans**
- **1 jar (6½ oz.) prepared pesto**
- **1 cup grated Parmigiano-Reggiano cheese**

1. Place potatoes in a large saucepan; add water to cover. Bring to a boil. Reduce heat; cook, uncovered, until tender, 8-10 minutes. Drain; transfer to a large bowl.

2. Meanwhile, cook pasta according to package directions, adding green beans during the last 5 minutes of cooking. Drain, reserving ¾ cup pasta water; add to potatoes. Toss with pesto, cheese and enough pasta water to moisten.

¾ cup: 261 cal., 10g fat (3g sat. fat), 11mg chol., 233mg sod., 34g carb. (2g sugars, 5g fiber), 11g pro. **Diabetic exchanges:** 2 starch, 2 fat.

SPICED SWEET POTATO SOUP

A bowlful of sweet potato soup from the slow cooker always warms us up body and soul.
—Lisa Speer, Palm Beach, FL

PREP: 20 MIN. • COOK: 6 HOURS • MAKES: 12 SERVINGS (2¼ QT.)

2 lbs. sweet potatoes (about 4 medium), peeled and chopped
1 large sweet onion, finely chopped
1 medium sweet red pepper, finely chopped
1½ tsp. curry powder
1 tsp. sea salt
½ tsp. ground cinnamon
¼ tsp. ground ginger
¼ tsp. ground allspice
¼ tsp. grated lemon zest
⅛ tsp. coarsely ground pepper
6 cups reduced-sodium chicken broth
Optional: Salted pumpkin seeds or pepitas

1. In a 5-qt. slow cooker, combine the first 11 ingredients. Cook, covered, on low 6-8 hours or until the vegetables are tender.

2. Puree the soup using an immersion blender. Or, cool soup slightly and puree in batches in a blender; return to slow cooker and heat through. If desired, top servings with pumpkin seeds.

¾ cup: 86 cal., 0 fat (0 sat. fat), 0 chol., 489mg sod., 19g carb. (5g sugars, 3g fiber), 3g pro.

GRILLED LIME-BALSAMIC SWEET POTATOES

For me, tailgating is about camaraderie and preparing food that's good to grill. These yummy wedges are a must!
—Raquel Perazzo, West New York, NJ

PREP: 15 MIN. • GRILL: 10 MIN./BATCH • MAKES: 8 SERVINGS

5 medium sweet potatoes (about 3 lbs.)
2 Tbsp. olive oil
1 tsp. salt
¼ tsp. pepper
¼ cup chopped fresh cilantro
¼ cup packed brown sugar
¼ cup lime juice
3 Tbsp. white or regular balsamic glaze

1. Peel and cut each sweet potato lengthwise into 8 wedges; place in a large bowl. Toss with oil, salt and pepper.

2. In batches, cook sweet potatoes on a greased grill rack, covered, over medium heat 8-10 minutes or until tender, turning occasionally.

3. In a large bowl, mix the remaining ingredients; add potatoes and toss to coat.

5 potato wedges: 197 cal., 4g fat (1g sat. fat), 0 chol., 309mg sod., 41g carb. (23g sugars, 4g fiber), 2g pro.

5i SWEET POTATO & ANDOUILLE HASH

When my husband trained for the Senior Olympics, I looked for healthier recipes like this spicy hash. Enjoy it with a fried egg on the side.

—Marla Clark, Albuquerque, NM

PREP: 15 MIN. • **COOK:** 25 MIN. • **MAKES:** 6 SERVINGS

- **2 Tbsp. olive oil**
- **½ lb. fully cooked andouille sausage or fully cooked Spanish chorizo, finely chopped**
- **4 cups finely chopped sweet potatoes (about 2 medium)**
- **4 celery ribs, finely chopped**
- **1 medium onion, finely chopped**
- **4 garlic cloves, minced**
- **½ tsp. salt**
- **¼ tsp. pepper**

1. In a Dutch oven, heat the oil over medium-high heat. Add sausage; cook and stir until browned.

2. Stir in remaining ingredients. Reduce heat to medium-low; cook, uncovered, 15-20 minutes or until the potatoes are tender, stirring occasionally.

¾ cup: 226 cal., 12g fat (3g sat. fat), 49mg chol., 602mg sod., 22g carb. (5g sugars, 4g fiber), 9g pro.

SWEET POTATO PANCAKES WITH CINNAMON CREAM

Featuring apples and a rich cinnamon topping, these cakes are a wonderful way to savor the flavors of fall.

—Tammy Rex, New Tripoli, PA

PREP: 25 MIN. • **COOK:** 5 MIN./BATCH • **MAKES:** 12 SERVINGS

- **1 pkg. (8 oz.) cream cheese, softened**
- **¼ cup packed brown sugar**
- **½ tsp. ground cinnamon**
- **½ cup sour cream**

PANCAKES

- **6 large eggs, room temperature**
- **¾ cup all-purpose flour**
- **½ tsp. ground nutmeg**
- **½ tsp. salt**
- **¼ tsp. pepper**
- **6 cups shredded peeled sweet potatoes (about 3 large)**
- **3 cups shredded peeled apples (about 3 large)**
- **⅓ cup grated onion**
- **½ cup canola oil**

1. In a small bowl, beat the cream cheese, brown sugar and cinnamon until blended; beat in sour cream. Set aside.

2. In a large bowl, whisk the eggs, flour, nutmeg, salt and pepper. Add the sweet potatoes, apples and onion; toss to coat.

3. In a large nonstick skillet, heat 2 Tbsp. oil over medium heat. Working in batches, drop sweet potato mixture by ⅓ cupfuls into the oil; press slightly to flatten. Fry for 2-3 minutes on each side until golden brown, using remaining oil as needed. Drain on paper towels. Serve with cinnamon topping.

2 pancakes with 2 Tbsp. topping: 325 cal., 21g fat (7g sat. fat), 114mg chol., 203mg sod., 30g carb. (15g sugars, 3g fiber), 6g pro.

CHAPTER 3

ROOT VEGETABLES

No longer reserved for spring menus, beets, carrots, fennel and other root vegetables are now year-round mealtime mainstays. You'll enjoy fresh earthy flavor every day with these incredible recipes.

BERRY-BEET SALAD

Here's a delightfully different salad that balances the hearty flavor of beets with the natural sweetness of berries. If you prefer, substitute crumbled feta for the goat cheese.

—Amy Lyons, Mounds View, MN

PREP: 20 MIN. • BAKE: 30 MIN. + COOLING • MAKES: 4 SERVINGS

- **1 each fresh red and golden beets**
- **¼ cup balsamic vinegar**
- **2 Tbsp. walnut oil**
- **1 tsp. honey**
- **Dash salt**
- **Dash pepper**
- **½ cup sliced fresh strawberries**
- **½ cup fresh raspberries**
- **½ cup fresh blackberries**
- **3 Tbsp. chopped walnuts, toasted**
- **1 shallot, thinly sliced**
- **4 cups torn mixed salad greens**
- **1 oz. fresh goat cheese, crumbled**
- **1 Tbsp. fresh basil, thinly sliced**

1. Place beets in an 8-in. square baking dish; add 1 in. of water. Cover and bake at 400° for 30-40 minutes or until tender.

2. Meanwhile, in a small bowl, whisk the vinegar, oil, honey, salt and pepper; set aside. Cool beets; peel and cut into thin slices.

3. In a large bowl, combine the beets, berries, walnuts and shallot. Pour dressing over beet mixture and toss gently to coat. Divide salad greens among 4 serving plates. Top with beet mixture; sprinkle with cheese and basil.

1 serving: 183 cal., 12g fat (2g sat. fat), 5mg chol., 124mg sod., 18g carb. (11g sugars, 5g fiber), 4g pro. **Diabetic exchanges:** 2 fat, 1 starch.

GOLDEN BEET & PEACH SOUP WITH TARRAGON

One summer we had a bumper crop of peaches from our two trees, so I had fun experimenting with different recipes. After seeing a beet soup recipe in a cookbook, I changed it a bit to include our homegrown golden beets and sweet peaches.

—Sue Gronholz, Beaver Dam, WI

PREP: 20 MIN. • BAKE: 40 MIN. + CHILLING • MAKES: 6 SERVINGS

- **2 lbs. fresh golden beets, peeled and cut into 1-in. cubes**
- **1 Tbsp. olive oil**
- **2 cups white grape-peach juice**
- **2 Tbsp. cider vinegar**
- **¼ cup plain Greek yogurt**
- **¼ tsp. finely chopped fresh tarragon**
- **2 medium fresh peaches, peeled and diced**
- **Fresh tarragon sprigs**

1. Preheat oven to 400°. Place beets in a 15x10x1-in. baking pan. Drizzle with oil; toss to coat. Roast until tender, 40-45 minutes. Cool slightly.

2. Transfer beets to a blender or food processor. Add juice and vinegar; process until smooth. Refrigerate at least 1 hour. In a small bowl, combine the Greek yogurt and chopped tarragon; refrigerate yogurt mixture.

3. To serve, divide beet mixture among individual bowls; place a spoonful of yogurt mixture in each bowl. Top with diced peaches and tarragon sprigs.

⅔ cup: 159 cal., 4g fat (1g sat. fat), 3mg chol., 129mg sod., 31g carb. (26g sugars, 4g fiber), 3g pro. **Diabetic exchanges:** 2 vegetable, 1 fruit, ½ fat.

BERRY-BEET
SALAD
FARMERS
MARKET FIND
Look for firm, smooth outer skin on the beet. If the greens are attached, make sure the stalk is bright green and crisp. Choose smaller beets of similar sizes to ensure even cooking.

HOW-TO

How To Peel Beets

After preparing, baking and cooling the beets, peel off what's left of the stems. Grab two clean paper towels and hold one in each hand. Pick up a beet with both hands. Hold the beet firmly and twist your hands in opposite directions. The skin should slide right off, and your hands will stay clean.

ROASTED BEETROOT & GARLIC HUMMUS

ROASTED BEETROOT & GARLIC HUMMUS

This beetroot hummus is so tasty, healthy and the prettiest pink snack I've ever seen. This is also a fantastic recipe to make in large batches and keep in the fridge for lunches and snacks throughout the week.
—Elizabeth Worndl, Toronto, ON

PREP: 25 MIN. • **BAKE:** 45 MIN. • **MAKES:** 4 CUPS

- **3 fresh medium beets (about 1 lb.)**
- **1 whole garlic bulb**
- **½ tsp. salt, divided**
- **½ tsp. coarsely ground pepper, divided**
- **1 tsp. plus ¼ cup olive oil, divided**
- **1 can (15 oz.) garbanzo beans or chickpeas, rinsed and drained**
- **3 to 4 Tbsp. lemon juice**
- **2 Tbsp. tahini**
- **½ tsp. ground cumin**
- **½ tsp. cayenne pepper**
- **¼ cup plain Greek yogurt, optional**
- **Minced fresh dill weed or parsley**
- **Assorted fresh vegetables**
- **Sliced or torn pita bread**

1. Preheat oven to 375°. Pierce beets with a fork; place in a microwave-safe bowl and cover loosely. Microwave the beets on high for 4 minutes, stirring halfway. Cool slightly. Wrap beets in individual foil packets.

2. Remove papery outer skin from garlic bulb, but do not peel or separate cloves. Cut in half crosswise. Sprinkle halves with ¼ tsp. salt and ¼ tsp. pepper; drizzle with 1 tsp. oil. Wrap in individual foil packets. Roast beets and garlic until cloves are soft, about 45 minutes.

3. Remove from oven; unwrap. Rinse beets with cold water; peel when cool enough to handle. Squeeze garlic from skins. Place beets and garlic in a food processor. Add garbanzo beans, lemon juice, tahini, cumin, cayenne pepper and remaining olive oil, salt and ground pepper. Process until smooth.

4. If desired, pulse 2 Tbsp. Greek yogurt with beet mixture, dolloping remaining yogurt over finished hummus. Sprinkle with dill or parsley. Serve with assorted vegetables and pita bread.

¼ cup: 87 cal., 5g fat (1g sat. fat), 0 chol., 131mg sod., 8g carb. (3g sugars, 2g fiber), 2g pro. **Diabetic exchanges:** 1 fat, ½ starch.

ORANGE-GLAZED BEETS

Beets were a popular vegetable in our house when I was growing up and this recipe is a real favorite of ours. It's very easy to make, and the orange gives it a delightful citrus flavor.
—Susan Punzal, Orchard Park, NY

TAKES: 25 MIN. • **MAKES:** 8 SERVINGS

- **¾ cup orange marmalade**
- **6 Tbsp. orange juice**
- **⅓ cup butter, cubed**
- **¼ tsp. salt**
- **¼ tsp. pepper**
- **3 cans (14½ oz. each) sliced beets, drained**

In a large skillet, combine the first 5 ingredients. Bring to a boil; cook and stir until thickened, 3-4 minutes. Add beets; cook and stir until most of the liquid is absorbed, 6-8 minutes longer.

½ cup: 194 cal., 8g fat (5g sat. fat), 20mg chol., 443mg sod., 32g carb. (27g sugars, 3g fiber), 2g pro.

CARROT SOUP WITH ORANGE & TARRAGON

A pretty orange color, a delicious hint of citrus and a garden-fresh flavor make this soup a requested dish at celebrations. Try sprinkling individual bowls with fresh tarragon before serving.

—Phyllis Schmalz, Kansas City, KS

PREP: 20 MIN. • **COOK:** 20 MIN. • **MAKES:** 8 SERVINGS (2 QT.)

- **2 lbs. fresh carrots, sliced**
- **2 medium onions, chopped**
- **2 Tbsp. butter**
- **6 cups reduced-sodium chicken broth**
- **1 cup orange juice**
- **2 Tbsp. brandy**
- **4 tsp. minced fresh tarragon or ½ tsp. dried tarragon**
- **1 tsp. salt**
- **1 tsp. pepper**
- **8 tarragon sprigs**

1. In a Dutch oven, saute carrots and onion in butter for 8-10 minutes or until the onion is tender. Add the broth; bring to a boil. Reduce heat; simmer, uncovered, for 10-12 minutes or until carrots are very tender. Cool slightly.

2. In a blender, process soup in batches until smooth. Return all to pan; stir in the orange juice, brandy and minced tarragon. Bring to a boil. Reduce heat; simmer, uncovered, for 5 minutes to allow flavors to blend. Season with salt and pepper. Garnish with tarragon sprigs before serving.

1 cup: 117 cal., 3g fat (2g sat. fat), 8mg chol., 823mg sod., 18g carb. (10g sugars, 4g fiber), 4g pro.

CAMPFIRE TROUT & CARROT DINNER

Your fresh catch will taste even better with this simple treatment that keeps the fish moist. Carrots are an excellent accompaniment, and they cook up perfectly in a separate foil packet.

—Wendy McGowan, Fontana, CA

PREP: 20 MIN. • **GRILL:** 20 MIN. • **MAKES:** 4 SERVINGS

- **4 bacon strips**
- **2 dressed trout (1 lb. each)**
- **4 lemon slices**
- **1 small onion, halved and sliced**
- **¼ tsp. salt**
- **⅛ tsp. pepper**

CARROTS

- **4 medium carrots, thinly sliced**
- **⅛ tsp. salt**
- **Dash pepper**
- **1 Tbsp. butter**
- **Lemon wedges**

1. Cook bacon until partially cooked but not crisp; drain. Place each trout on a double thickness of heavy-duty foil (about 20x18 in.). Place lemon and onion in the trout cavities; sprinkle with salt and pepper. Wrap trout with bacon. Fold foil around trout and seal tightly.

2. Place carrots on a double thickness of heavy-duty foil (about 20x18 in.); sprinkle with salt and pepper. Dot with butter. Fold foil around the carrots and seal tightly.

3. Grill carrots, covered, over medium heat for 10 minutes. Add trout packets to grill; cook 20-25 minutes longer or until fish flakes easily with a fork and carrots are tender. Serve with lemon wedges.

1 serving: 362 cal., 16g fat (6g sat. fat), 136mg chol., 530mg sod., 8g carb. (4g sugars, 2g fiber), 44g pro.

CARROT SOUP WITH ORANGE & TARRAGON

SWEET & TANGY CARROTS

With a brown sugar-mustard sauce, these simple simmered carrots bring bright flavor and color to the table.

—Paula Zsiray, Logan, UT

TAKES: 20 MIN. • MAKES: 8 SERVINGS

- **2 lbs. carrots, sliced**
- **¼ tsp. salt**
- **½ cup packed brown sugar**
- **3 Tbsp. butter**
- **2 Tbsp. Dijon mustard**
- **¼ tsp. white pepper**
- **2 Tbsp. minced fresh parsley**

1. Place 1 in. of water, carrots and salt in a large saucepan; bring to a boil. Reduce heat; cover and simmer until tender, 15-20 minutes. Drain.

2. Return carrots to pan; add the brown sugar, butter, mustard and pepper. Cook and stir over low heat until well coated. Sprinkle with minced parsley. Serve with a slotted spoon.

½ cup: 143 cal., 5g fat (3g sat. fat), 11mg chol., 257mg sod., 25g carb. (21g sugars, 3g fiber), 1g pro.

MARMALADE CANDIED CARROTS

My crisp-tender carrots have a citrus-sweet flavor that's perfect for special occasions. This is my favorite carrot recipe.

—Heather Clemmons, Supply, NC

TAKES: 30 MIN. • MAKES: 8 SERVINGS

- **2 lbs. fresh baby carrots**
- **⅔ cup orange marmalade**
- **3 Tbsp. brown sugar**
- **2 Tbsp. butter**
- **½ cup chopped pecans, toasted**
- **1 tsp. rum extract**

1. In a large saucepan, place steamer basket over 1 in. of water. Place carrots in basket. Bring water to a boil. Reduce the heat to maintain a low boil; steam, covered, 12-15 minutes or until carrots are crisp-tender.

2. Meanwhile, in a small saucepan, combine marmalade, brown sugar and butter; cook and stir over medium heat until mixture is thickened and reduced to about ½ cup. Stir in the pecans and rum extract.

3. Place the carrots in a large bowl. Add the marmalade mixture and toss gently to coat.

1 serving: 211 cal., 8g fat (2g sat. fat), 8mg chol., 115mg sod., 35g carb. (27g sugars, 4g fiber), 2g pro.

FARMERS MARKET FIND

When it comes to carrots, the darker the better, because darker carrots have more beta carotene. Look for carrots with a consistent color.

SWEET & TANGY CARROTS

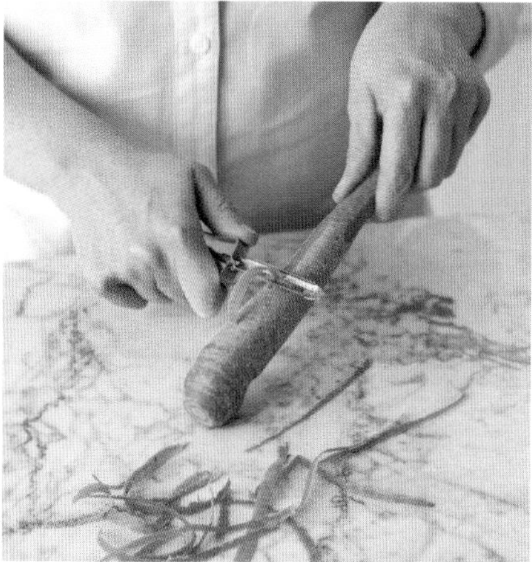

HOW-TO

Peel Carrots

- Hold the carrot at a 45° angle on a cutting board. Take the peeler in your other hand. Set the peeler at the middle of the carrot. Press downward toward the cutting board. Next, switch directions and peel back upward, stopping at the center of the carrot. Rotate the carrot a bit, and continue peeling in a down-and-up fashion until the bottom half of the carrot is peeled.
- Flip the carrot, holding onto the peeled end. The unpeeled end of the carrot should rest against the cutting board at a 45° angle.
- Repeat the exact steps as above. Cut down, then up and around the carrot until it's completely peeled.

SPICED CARROT CAKE

SPICED CARROT CAKE

My mom made this cake for my birthday one year because carrot cake is her favorite. Turns out, it's my favorite, too! Now when I make it, I add lots of spice. The pumpkin pie spice is a perfect shortcut but you could use a custom blend of cinnamon, ginger, nutmeg and cloves.

—Jaris Dykas, Knoxville, TN

PREP: 30 MIN. • **BAKE:** 20 MIN. + COOLING • **MAKES:** 16 SERVINGS

- 3 large eggs, room temperature
- 1 cup packed brown sugar
- ¾ cup fat-free plain yogurt
- ¼ cup canola oil
- 2 tsp. vanilla extract
- 2½ cups all-purpose flour
- 3 tsp. pumpkin pie spice
- 2 tsp. baking soda
- 1 tsp. salt
- 3 cups shredded carrots (about 6 medium)

FROSTING

- ½ cup heavy whipping cream
- 4 oz. reduced-fat cream cheese
- ½ cup confectioners' sugar

1. Preheat oven to 350°. Line bottoms of 2 greased 9-in. round baking pans with parchment; grease paper.

2. Beat first 5 ingredients until well blended. In another bowl, whisk together flour, pie spice, baking soda and salt; stir into egg mixture. Fold in carrots.

3. Transfer to prepared pans. Bake until a toothpick inserted in center comes out clean, 20-25 minutes. Cool cake in pans 10 minutes before removing to wire racks; remove paper. Cool completely.

4. For frosting, beat cream until soft peaks form. In another bowl, beat cream cheese and confectioners' sugar until smooth; gradually fold in whipped cream.

5. If cakes are domed, trim tops with a serrated knife. Spread frosting between layers and over top of cake. Refrigerate leftovers.

1 slice: 241 cal., 9g fat (3g sat. fat), 49mg chol., 375mg sod., 36g carb. (19g sugars, 1g fiber), 5g pro.

CURRY CARROT DIP

The flavors of sweet carrots, mustard and curry blend deliciously in this unique dip. Raw veggies are the perfect partners.

—Louise Weyer, Marietta, GA

TAKES: 30 MIN. • **MAKES:** 1 CUP

- 1 small onion, chopped
- 2 tsp. canola oil
- 4 medium carrots, sliced
- ⅓ cup water
- ¼ tsp. salt
- ¼ tsp. pepper
- ¼ tsp. curry powder
- 2 Tbsp. reduced-fat mayonnaise
- 2 tsp. prepared mustard
- Assorted raw vegetables

1. In a nonstick skillet, saute onion in oil. Add the carrots, water, salt, pepper and curry. Bring to a boil. Reduce heat; cover and simmer for 6 minutes or until the vegetables are tender. Uncover; cook for 8 minutes or until the liquid has evaporated. Cool.

2. Transfer to a food processor or a blender; cover and process until smooth. Add mayonnaise and mustard; mix well. Serve with vegetables.

2 Tbsp.: 40 cal., 3g fat (0 sat. fat), 1mg chol., 133mg sod., 4g carb. (2g sugars, 1g fiber), 0 pro.

FENNEL-JICAMA SALAD

FENNEL-JICAMA SALAD

This crunchy jicama salad contains no mayonnaise, making it a terrific dish to pass. Mint adds a refreshing flavor but can be omitted if you don't have it on hand.

—Stephanie Matthews, Tempe, AZ

TAKES: 20 MIN. • MAKES: 12 SERVINGS

- 1 medium jicama, cut into strips
- 1 fennel bulb, peeled and thinly sliced
- 1 large apple, thinly sliced
- 1 large pear, thinly sliced
- 1 small red onion, thinly sliced
- ½ cup canola oil
- ½ cup cider vinegar
- ⅓ cup sugar
- 1 Tbsp. lemon juice
- ½ tsp. salt
- ½ cup dried cherries
- 1 tsp. minced fresh mint

In a large bowl, combine the jicama, fennel, apple, pear and onion. In a small bowl, whisk the oil, vinegar, sugar, lemon juice and salt. Pour over salad and toss to coat. Sprinkle with cherries and mint. Refrigerate until serving.

¾ cup: 167 cal., 10g fat (1g sat. fat), 0 chol., 112mg sod., 21g carb. (15g sugars, 3g fiber), 1g pro. **Diabetic exchanges:** 2 fat, 1½ starch.

FARMERS MARKET FIND

Select fennel with creamy white bulbs, firm straight stalks and bright green fronds. Avoid withered bulbs or those with brown spots or yellowing. Smaller bulbs are more tender.

ROASTED CARROTS & FENNEL

This addictive combo is a fresh take on one of my mother's standard wintertime dishes. I usually add more carrots—as many as the pans will hold.

—Lily Julow, Lawrenceville, GA

PREP: 15 MIN. • BAKE: 40 MIN. • MAKES: 8 SERVINGS

- 2½ lbs. medium carrots, peeled and cut in half lengthwise
- 1 large fennel bulb, cut into ½-in. wedges
- 1 large red onion, cut into ½-in. wedges
- 1 medium lemon, thinly sliced
- ¼ cup olive oil
- 2 tsp. ground coriander
- 1 tsp. ground cumin
- ½ tsp. salt
- ¼ tsp. pepper
- Thinly sliced fresh basil leaves

1. Preheat oven to 375°. In a large bowl, combine the carrots, fennel, onion and lemon. Mix oil, coriander, cumin, salt and pepper; drizzle over carrot mixture and toss to coat. Transfer to 2 foil-lined 15x10x1-in. baking pans.

2. Roast 40-50 minutes or until vegetables are tender, stirring occasionally. Sprinkle with basil.

1 serving: 139 cal., 7g fat (1g sat. fat), 0 chol., 262mg sod., 18g carb. (9g sugars, 6g fiber), 2g pro. **Diabetic exchanges:** 2 vegetable, 1½ fat.

Test Kitchen Tip: To prepare fennel, trim off the fronds and stalks. Trim the base from the bulb. Remove and discard any yellowed or split outer layers. Cut in half and remove the core. Cut, slice or chop the bulb and stalks. Use the fronds as you would a minced herb or for a garnish.

KOHLRABI, CUCUMBER & TOMATO SALAD

This refreshing chilled salad is wonderful on hot days. It has a nice crunch and a delicious balance of sweet and spicy flavors.
—Kristina Segarra, Yonkers, NY

PREP: 30 MIN. + CHILLING • MAKES: 6 SERVINGS

- **2 Tbsp. olive oil**
- **1 medium red onion, finely chopped**
- **2 pickled hot cherry peppers, seeded and finely chopped**
- **2 garlic cloves, minced**
- **2 Tbsp. cider vinegar**
- **1 tsp. salt**
- **1 kohlrabi, peeled and cut into ½-in. pieces**
- **2 large yellow tomatoes, seeded and chopped**
- **2 mini cucumbers, cut into ½-in. pieces**
- **2 Tbsp. minced fresh cilantro**

1. In a small skillet, heat oil over medium-high heat. Add the onion; cook and stir 2-3 minutes or until crisp-tender. Add peppers and garlic; cook 2 minutes longer. Stir in vinegar and salt; remove from heat.

2. In a large bowl, combine the kohlrabi, tomatoes and cucumbers. Pour in onion mixture; gently toss to coat. Chill for 1 hour. Sprinkle with cilantro before serving.

¾ cup: 59 cal., 4g fat (1g sat. fat), 0 chol., 372mg sod., 6g carb. (2g sugars, 2g fiber), 2g pro. **Diabetic exchanges:** 1 vegetable, ½ fat.

CREAMED KOHLRABI

This might look like potato salad, but it's actually kohlrabi cubes covered in a velvety white sauce and accented with chives. Kohlrabi is a favorite vegetable of mine.
—Lorraine Foss, Puyallup, WA

TAKES: 30 MIN. • MAKES: 6 SERVINGS

- **4 cups cubed peeled kohlrabi (about 6 medium)**
- **2 Tbsp. butter**
- **2 Tbsp. all-purpose flour**
- **2 cups whole milk**
- **½ tsp. salt**
- **¼ tsp. pepper**
- **Dash paprika**
- **1 large egg yolk, lightly beaten**
- **Minced chives and additional paprika**

1. Place kohlrabi in a large saucepan; add 1 in. of water. Bring to a boil. Reduce heat; cover and simmer for 6-8 minutes or until crisp-tender.

2. Meanwhile, in a small saucepan, melt butter. Stir in flour until smooth; gradually add milk. Bring to a boil. Stir in the salt, pepper and paprika. Gradually stir a small amount of hot mixture into egg yolk; return all to the pan, stirring constantly. Bring to a gentle boil; cook and stir for 2 minutes.

3. Drain kohlrabi and place in a serving bowl; add sauce and stir to coat. Sprinkle with chives and additional paprika.

⅔ cup: 125 cal., 7g fat (4g sat. fat), 52mg chol., 276mg sod., 11g carb. (6g sugars, 3g fiber), 5g pro. **Diabetic exchanges:** 1½ fat, 1 vegetable, ½ starch.

KOHLRABI, CUCUMBER & TOMATO SALAD

HOW-TO

Seed Cucumbers

Here are two methods that will have your cucumbers seed-free in no time.

Method 1: Halves

Thoroughly rinse the cucumber in cool water. Lay the cucumber on a cutting board and cut the cucumber in half lengthwise with a sharp knife. Gently scoop out the seeds by gliding the tip of a spoon or a butter knife across the length of the flesh. Be careful to only remove the seeds and not too much of the flesh.

Method 2: Quarters

Just like in the method above, rinse the cucumber with cool water and cut it in half lengthwise with a sharp knife. Then, after the cucumber is cut in half, lay the halves flesh side down on the cutting board. Once more, cut the cucumber halves down the middle lengthwise, creating four quarters in total. Using the tip of a spoon or butter knife, carefully remove the seeds with a gliding motion.

Seed Tomatoes

To seed a tomato quickly, simply remove the stem and cut the tomato in half vertically. Hold half of the tomato over a bowl and gently squeeze seeds out. Use a small spoon to carefully scoop out remaining seeds. Slice, dice or chop the tomatoes as directed.

GRILLED ONION
& SKIRT STEAK TACOS

GRILLED ONION & SKIRT STEAK TACOS

I grew up watching my grandmother and mother in the kitchen. My grandparents came from Mexico, and this steak, marinated in beer and lime juice, honors their passion for cooking.

—Adan Franco, Milwaukee, WI

PREP: 15 MIN. + MARINATING • **GRILL:** 5 MIN. • **MAKES:** 8 SERVINGS

- **2 beef skirt or flank steaks (1 lb. each)**
- **1 bottle (12 oz.) beer**
- **¼ cup lime juice**
- **3 Tbsp. olive oil, divided**
- **8 spring onions or green onions**
- **1¼ tsp. salt, divided**
- **¾ tsp. pepper, divided**
- **Corn tortillas, minced fresh cilantro and lime wedges**

1. Pound beef with a meat mallet to tenderize. In a large bowl, mix beer, lime juice and 2 Tbsp. oil until blended. Add beef to marinade; turn to coat. Refrigerate, covered, at least 30 minutes.

2. Meanwhile, cut partially through onions, leaving tops intact. Drizzle with remaining oil; sprinkle with ¼ tsp. salt and ¼ tsp. pepper.

3. Drain beef, discarding marinade; sprinkle with the remaining salt and pepper. On a greased grill rack, grill steaks and onions, covered, over medium heat or broil 4 in. from heat until meat reaches desired doneness (for medium-rare, a thermometer should read 135°; medium, 140°; medium-well, 145°) and onions are crisp-tender, 2-4 minutes on each side. Cut steak diagonally across the grain into thin slices. Serve with tortillas, onions, cilantro and lime wedges.

1 serving: 288 cal., 14g fat (5g sat. fat), 67mg chol., 458mg sod., 7g carb. (3g sugars, 1g fiber), 31g pro.

5i ONION PIE

My grandmother and mother always make onion pie during the holidays, but it's good anytime. This is a savory side dish that you can serve with almost any meat or main course. It's especially tasty with roast beef.

—Mary West, Marstons Mills, MA

PREP: 15 MIN. • **BAKE:** 35 MIN. • **MAKES:** 8 SERVINGS

- **6 to 8 medium onions, thinly sliced**
- **2 Tbsp. canola oil**
- **6 large eggs**
- **1 cup soft bread crumbs**
- **½ cup grated Parmesan cheese**
- **½ cup minced fresh parsley**

1. In a large skillet, saute onions in oil until soft but not browned; drain well. In a large bowl, whisk eggs. Stir in the bread crumbs, cheese, parsley and onions.

2. Place in a greased 10-in. pie plate. Bake at 350° until a knife inserted in the center comes out clean, 35-40 minutes.

1 piece: 170 cal., 9g fat (3g sat. fat), 163mg chol., 176mg sod., 14g carb. (8g sugars, 3g fiber), 9g pro.

FOUR-ONION SOUP

This mellow, rich-tasting onion soup is such a mainstay for our family that I felt compelled to share the recipe. Topped with toasted French bread and melted cheese, it's very special.

—Margaret Adams, Pacific Grove, CA

PREP: 35 MIN. • **COOK:** 50 MIN. • **MAKES:** 6 SERVINGS

- **1 medium yellow onion**
- **1 medium red onion**
- **1 medium leek (white portion only)**
- **5 green onions with tops**
- **1 garlic clove, minced**
- **2 Tbsp. butter**
- **2 cans (14½ oz. each) beef broth**
- **1 can (10½ oz.) condensed beef consomme, undiluted**
- **1 tsp. Worcestershire sauce**
- **½ tsp. ground nutmeg**
- **1 cup shredded Swiss cheese**
- **6 slices French bread (¾ in. thick), toasted**
- **6 Tbsp. grated Parmesan cheese, optional**

1. Slice all onions and leek ¼ in. thick. In a large saucepan over medium-low heat, saute onions, leek and garlic in butter about 15 minutes or until tender and golden, stirring occasionally. Add broth, consomme, Worcestershire sauce and nutmeg; bring to a boil. Reduce heat; cover and simmer for 30 minutes.

2. Sprinkle 1 Tbsp. of Swiss cheese in the bottom of 6 ovenproof 8-oz. bowls. Ladle hot soup into bowls. Top each with a slice of bread. Sprinkle with the remaining Swiss cheese and, if desired, Parmesan cheese if desired.

3. Broil 6-8 in. from the heat until cheese melts. Serve immediately.

1 cup: 197 cal., 10g fat (6g sat. fat), 29mg chol., 783mg sod., 18g carb. (5g sugars, 2g fiber), 10g pro.

GOAT CHEESE & ONION PASTRIES

A flaky puff pastry crust holds sweet caramelized onions and creamy goat cheese for an easy yet upscale appetizer. The recipe is a must on all our entertaining menus.

—Heidi Ellis, Monument, CO

PREP: 30 MIN. • **BAKE:** 20 MIN. • **MAKES:** 1 DOZEN

- **6 bacon strips, chopped**
- **2 large onions, finely chopped**
- **3 shallots, thinly sliced**
- **½ tsp. sugar**
- **½ cup white wine**
- **2 tsp. minced fresh thyme or ½ tsp. dried thyme**
- **2 garlic cloves, minced**
- **¼ tsp. pepper**
- **1 sheet frozen puff pastry, thawed**
- **1 large egg white, beaten**
- **1 log (4 oz.) fresh goat cheese, cut into 12 slices**

1. Preheat oven to 400°. In a large skillet, cook bacon over medium heat until crisp, stirring occasionally. Remove with a slotted spoon; drain on paper towels. Discard drippings, reserving 2 tsp. in pan. Add onions, shallots and sugar to drippings; cook and stir over medium heat until vegetables are golden brown, 15-20 minutes.

2. Add wine, stirring to loosen browned bits from pan. Stir in thyme, garlic and pepper. Cook, uncovered, until liquid is evaporated, 2-3 minutes. Stir in bacon.

3. On a lightly floured surface, unfold puff pastry. Cut into three 9x3-in. rectangles. Transfer to a parchment-lined baking sheet. Brush dough with egg white; top with onion mixture and goat cheese. Bake until golden brown, 16-20 minutes. Cut each rectangle into 4 appetizers. Garnish with additional thyme if desired.

1 appetizer: 168 cal., 9g fat (3g sat. fat), 10mg chol., 186mg sod., 17g carb. (2g sugars, 2g fiber), 4g pro.

HOW-TO

Chop Onions

To quickly chop an onion, peel and cut it in half from the root to the top. Leaving the root attached, place the flat side down on work surface. Cut vertically through the onion, leaving the root end uncut. Cut across the onion, discarding root end. The closer the cuts, the more finely the onion will be chopped. This method can also be used for shallots.

GOAT CHEESE & ONION PASTRIES

PINEAPPLE-ONION PORK CHOPS

I prepared these tender pork chops for my teenage grandson's birthday meal. Brown sugar and pineapple provide sweetness for the onion-topped entree.

—Marjorie Bruner, Parchment, MI

PREP: 25 MIN. • BAKE: 25 MIN. • MAKES: 6 SERVINGS

- **¼ cup all-purpose flour**
- **½ tsp. salt**
- **¼ tsp. pepper**
- **6 boneless pork loin chops (¾ in. thick)**
- **3 Tbsp. butter**
- **½ cup water**
- **1 medium onion, sliced**
- **1½ cups pineapple juice**
- **2 Tbsp. brown sugar**
- **2 Tbsp. honey mustard**

1. In a large, shallow bowl, combine the flour, salt and pepper. Add pork chops and toss to coat. In a skillet, brown chops on both sides in butter. Transfer to a greased 13x9-in. baking dish. Add water to dish. Place onion over chops. Cover and bake at 350° for 20 minutes.

2. Meanwhile, in a saucepan, combine the pineapple juice, brown sugar and mustard. Bring to a boil. Reduce heat; simmer, uncovered, for 10 minutes. Pour over pork. Bake, uncovered, for 5-10 minutes or until meat juices run clear.

1 pork chop: 294 cal., 13g fat (6g sat. fat), 70mg chol., 332mg sod., 22g carb. (16g sugars, 1g fiber), 23g pro.

CARAMELIZED ONION & GARLIC PASTA

This full-flavored recipe is the result of my mom's love of pasta and our love of cooking together. With a bit of pepper heat and smoky bacon, the entree is excellent alone or paired with grilled chicken.

—Lacy Jo Matheson, Sault Ste. Marie, MI

PREP: 20 MIN. • COOK: 35 MIN. • MAKES: 6 SERVINGS

- **¼ cup butter, cubed**
- **2 large sweet onions, thinly sliced**
- **¼ tsp. crushed red pepper flakes**
- **⅛ tsp. salt**
- **8 garlic cloves, minced**
- **2 cups grape tomatoes, halved**
- **¼ cup balsamic vinegar**
- **¼ cup olive oil, divided**
- **1 pkg. (16 oz.) uncooked angel hair pasta**
- **9 bacon strips, cooked and crumbled**
- **⅔ cup shredded Parmesan cheese**
- **½ tsp. coarsely ground pepper**
- **Fresh basil leaves, optional**

1. In a large skillet over medium-high heat, melt the butter. Add the onions, pepper flakes and salt; saute until the onions are tender. Stir in garlic. Reduce the heat to medium-low; cook, stirring occasionally, for 30-40 minutes or until the onions are deep golden brown.

2. Add the tomatoes, vinegar and 2 Tbsp. oil to the skillet. Cook pasta according to package directions. Drain pasta; toss with onion mixture.

3. Drizzle with remaining olive oil. Sprinkle with bacon, cheese, and pepper; heat through. Garnish with basil if desired.

1½ cups: 574 cal., 24g fat (9g sat. fat), 37mg chol., 495mg sod., 71g carb. (10g sugars, 4g fiber), 18g pro.

CARAMELIZED ONION & GARLIC PASTA

FARMERS MARKET FIND

When shopping for onions, avoid those that have green shoots or sprouts growing out of them—these are too old for cooking and just want to grow.

HOW-TO

Buy Radishes

When shopping for radishes, look for vibrant colors. Bulbs should be bright red, smooth and firm, with no cracks. If greens are attached, make sure they're equally colorful and fresh-looking. Avoid those with wilted or discolored greens.

Store Radishes

You can trim radish greens and use them in salads; they have a peppery flavor and are loaded with vitamins and minerals. Store the bulbs in a plastic bag in the refrigerator for up to a week.

Prep Radishes

When preparing radishes, slice off the roots and wash thoroughly, patting them dry. Use radishes whole, sliced, diced or minced. If you find them too bitter overall, they can be cooked to tamp down the flavor.

RAVISHING RADISH SALAD

RAVISHING RADISH SALAD

Showcase radishes in all their glory with a fresh, crunchy salad. Herbs and fennel take it up another notch.

—Maggie Ruddy, Altoona, IA

PREP: 30 MIN. + CHILLING • MAKES: 6 SERVINGS

- **24 radishes, quartered**
- **1 tsp. salt**
- **1 tsp. pepper**
- **6 green onions, chopped**
- **½ cup thinly sliced fennel bulb**
- **6 fresh basil leaves, thinly sliced**
- **¼ cup snipped fresh dill**
- **¼ cup olive oil**
- **2 Tbsp. champagne vinegar**
- **2 Tbsp. honey**
- **2 garlic cloves, minced**
- **½ cup chopped walnuts, toasted**

1. Place radishes in a large bowl. Sprinkle with salt and pepper; toss to coat. Add the onions, fennel, basil and dill. In a small bowl, whisk the oil, vinegar, honey and garlic. Pour over salad and toss to coat.

2. Cover and refrigerate for at least 1 hour. Sprinkle with the walnuts immediately before serving.

⅔ cup: 177 cal., 15g fat (2g sat. fat), 0 chol., 408mg sod., 10g carb. (7g sugars, 2g fiber), 2g pro. **Diabetic exchanges:** 3 fat, 1 vegetable.

SAUTEED TARRAGON RADISHES

Who says radishes only belong in salads? Sauteed in wine and tarragon, these may just change the way you look at radishes forever. These can be served on their own, or added to your favorite au gratin recipe.

—Taste of Home *Test Kitchen*

TAKES: 25 MIN. • MAKES: 12 SERVINGS

- **½ cup unsalted butter, cubed**
- **6 lbs. radishes, quartered (about 9 cups)**
- **¼ cup white wine or water**
- **2 tsp. minced fresh tarragon or ½ tsp. dried tarragon**
- **½ tsp. salt**
- **¼ tsp. pepper**

In a 6-qt. stockpot, heat butter over medium heat. Add the radishes; cook and stir 2 minutes. Stir in wine; increase heat to medium-high. Cook, uncovered, until radishes are crisp-tender, 8-10 minutes. Stir in tarragon, salt and pepper.

¾ cup: 108 cal., 8g fat (5g sat. fat), 20mg chol., 188mg sod., 8g carb. (4g sugars, 4g fiber), 2g pro.

BOK CHOY & RADISHES

This is such a great-tasting, good-for-you recipe. With bok choy and radishes, the simple dish capitalizes on the flavors of spring.

—Ann Baker, Texarkana, TX

TAKES: 25 MIN. • MAKES: 8 SERVINGS

- **1 head bok choy**
- **2 Tbsp. butter**
- **1 Tbsp. olive oil**
- **12 radishes, thinly sliced**
- **1 shallot, sliced**
- **1 tsp. lemon-pepper seasoning**
- **¾ tsp. salt**

1. Cut off and discard root end of bok choy, leaving stalks with leaves. Cut the green leaves from stalks and cut the leaves into 1-in. slices; set aside. Cut white stalks into 1-in. pieces.

2. In a large cast-iron or other heavy skillet, cook bok choy stalks in butter and oil until crisp-tender, 3-5 minutes. Add the radishes, shallot, lemon pepper, salt and reserved leaves; cook and stir until heated through, about 3 minutes.

¾ cup: 59 cal., 5g fat (2g sat. fat), 8mg chol., 371mg sod., 3g carb. (2g sugars, 1g fiber), 2g pro. **Diabetic exchanges:** 1 vegetable, 1 fat.

RADISH, CARROT & CILANTRO SALAD

Bright carrots and radishes pop in this citrusy salad. My husband likes it with anything from the grill. I like to pile it on tacos.

—Christina Baldwin, Covington, LA

PREP: 20 MIN. + CHILLING • MAKES: 12 SERVINGS

- **1½ lbs. radishes, very thinly sliced**
- **1½ lbs. medium carrots, thinly sliced**
- **6 green onions, chopped**
- **¼ cup coarsely chopped fresh cilantro**

DRESSING

- **1 tsp. grated lemon zest**
- **1 tsp. grated orange zest**
- **3 Tbsp. lemon juice**
- **3 Tbsp. orange juice**
- **2 Tbsp. extra virgin olive oil**
- **½ tsp. salt**
- **¼ tsp. pepper**

In a large bowl, combine the radishes, carrots, onions and cilantro. In a small bowl, whisk dressing ingredients until blended. Pour over salad; toss to coat. Refrigerate, covered, at least 1 hour before serving.

⅔ cup: 51 cal., 2g fat (0 sat. fat), 0 chol., 145mg sod., 7g carb. (4g sugars, 2g fiber), 1g pro. **Diabetic exchanges:** 1 vegetable, ½ fat.

BOK CHOY & RADISHES

RUTABAGA CARROT CASSEROLE

FARMERS MARKET FIND

Select a firm, solid rutabaga that feels heavy for its size. Store unwashed rutabagas in the refrigerator crisper drawer for up to 2 weeks.

RUTABAGA CARROT CASSEROLE

This scoopable side with its sweet, crunchy topping makes a delightful alternative to the traditional sweet potato casserole.
—Joan Hallford, North Richland Hills, TX

PREP: 30 MIN. • BAKE: 30 MIN. • MAKES: 8 SERVINGS

- **1 large rutabaga, peeled and cubed**
- **3 large carrots, shredded**
- **1 large egg, beaten**
- **2 Tbsp. brown sugar**
- **1 Tbsp. butter**
- **½ tsp. salt**
- **¼ tsp. ground nutmeg**
- **Dash pepper**
- **1 cup cooked brown rice**
- **1 cup fat-free evaporated milk**

TOPPING

- **¼ cup all-purpose flour**
- **¼ cup packed brown sugar**
- **2 Tbsp. cold butter**
- **½ cup chopped pecans**

1. Place the rutabaga in a Dutch oven and cover with water. Bring to a boil. Cook, uncovered, until tender, 15-20 minutes, adding the carrots during the last 5 minutes of cooking; drain.

2. In a large bowl, mash the rutabaga mixture with egg, brown sugar, butter, salt, nutmeg and pepper. Stir in rice and milk. Transfer to an 11x7-in. baking dish coated with cooking spray.

3. For topping, in a small bowl, combine flour and brown sugar; cut in butter until crumbly. Stir in pecans. Sprinkle over top. Bake, uncovered, at 350° until bubbly, 30-35 minutes.

½ cup: 249 cal., 11g fat (3g sat. fat), 39mg chol., 267mg sod., 34g carb. (21g sugars, 4g fiber), 6g pro. **Diabetic exchanges:** 2 starch, 2 fat.

5i CABBAGE & RUTABAGA SLAW

This is a favorite crunchy slaw that's a perfect way to use cool-weather veggies. We love it as a side with any spicy main dish.
—Ann Sheehy, Lawrence, MA

PREP: 10 MIN. + CHILLING • MAKES: 4 SERVINGS

- **2 cups diced peeled rutabaga**
- **2 cups finely chopped cabbage**
- **½ cup finely chopped red onion**
- **¼ cup minced fresh Italian parsley**
- **½ cup reduced-fat apple cider vinaigrette**

Toss together all ingredients. Refrigerate, covered, to allow flavors to blend, about 3 hours.

1 cup: 126 cal., 6g fat (1g sat. fat), 0 chol., 144mg sod., 19g carb. (11g sugars, 3g fiber), 2g pro. **Diabetic exchanges:** 1 vegetable, 1 fat, ½ starch.

Test Kitchen Tip: To use rutabaga, trim off the top and bottom, then cut in half. Peel off wax before using. Rinse with cold water after peeling.

CHAPTER 4

HEARTY SQUASH

No matter what the season, there's always time for hearty, healthy, versatile squash. Turn here for ideas that use up bumper crops of summer zucchini as well as pumpkin side dishes that round out holiday menus.

51 ROASTED ACORN SQUASH & BRUSSELS SPROUTS

I love it when just a handful of ingredients and a few easy steps add up to a delicious dish, such as this squash with sprouts. Maple syrup lends a slight sweetness, and pecans toss in a toasty crunch.

—Angela Lemoine, Howell, NJ

PREP: 15 MIN. • BAKE: 30 MIN. • MAKES: 8 SERVINGS

- **1 medium acorn squash**
- **1 lb. fresh Brussels sprouts**
- **2 Tbsp. olive oil**
- **½ tsp. salt**
- **¼ tsp. pepper**
- **1¾ cups pecan halves**
- **¼ cup maple syrup**
- **3 Tbsp. butter**

1. Preheat oven to 375°. Cut squash lengthwise into quarters; remove and discard seeds. Cut each quarter crosswise into ½-in. slices; discard ends. Trim and halve Brussels sprouts.

2. Place squash and Brussels sprouts in a large bowl. Drizzle with oil; sprinkle with salt and pepper, and toss to coat. Transfer to 2 foil-lined 15x10x1-in. baking pans. Roast 30-35 minutes or until vegetables are tender, stirring occasionally.

3. Meanwhile, in a dry large skillet, toast pecans over medium-low heat 6-8 minutes or until lightly browned, stirring frequently. Add syrup and butter; cook and stir until butter is melted.

4. Sprinkle vegetables with pecan mixture; gently toss to combine.

¾ cup: 300 cal., 24g fat (5g sat. fat), 11mg chol., 198mg sod., 23g carb. (11g sugars, 5g fiber), 4g pro.

HOW-TO

Prepare Acorn Squash

- Cut off the top and bottom of the acorn squash. Cut the squash in half.
- Scoop out seeds with a spoon.
- Cut through each of the deep ridges to form wedges. Using a vegetable peeler, peel each wedge.
- Cut wedges into cubes of desired size.

FARMERS MARKET FIND

Acorn squash is aptly named, as it resembles an acorn. Its ridged shell can be dark green, golden orange or cream colored. The bright orange flesh is mild tasting, making it versatile to cook with.

ROASTED ACORN SQUASH & BRUSSELS SPROUTS

SPICED ACORN SQUASH

SPICED ACORN SQUASH

Working full time, I found I didn't always have time to cook my family's favorite foods. So I re-created many of them, including this sweet side dish, in the slow cooker.

—Carol Greco, Centereach, NY

PREP: 15 MIN. • COOK: 3½ HOURS • MAKES: 4 SERVINGS

- **¾ cup packed brown sugar**
- **1 tsp. ground cinnamon**
- **1 tsp. ground nutmeg**
- **2 small acorn squash, halved and seeded**
- **¾ cup raisins**
- **4 Tbsp. butter**
- **½ cup water**

1. In a small bowl, mix the brown sugar, cinnamon and nutmeg; spoon into squash halves. Sprinkle with raisins. Top each with 1 Tbsp. butter. Wrap each half individually in heavy-duty foil, sealing tightly.

2. Pour the water into a 5-qt. slow cooker. Place squash in slow cooker, cut side up (packets may be stacked). Cook, covered, on high 3½-4 hours or until squash is tender. Open foil carefully to allow steam to escape.

One squash half: 433 cal., 12g fat (7g sat. fat), 31mg chol., 142mg sod., 86g carb. (63g sugars, 5g fiber), 3g pro.

WAFFLE-IRON ACORN SQUASH

I love to get the kids involved in cooking. Cut with cookie cutters and baked in a waffle iron, these fun slices are tailor-made for children to help with.

—Donna Kelly, Draper, UT

PREP: 10 MIN. • BAKE: 5 MIN./BATCH • MAKES: 4 SERVINGS

- **3 Tbsp. maple syrup**
- **¾ tsp. ground chipotle pepper**
- **½ tsp. salt**
- **1 small acorn squash**

1. Preheat a greased waffle maker. Mix syrup, chipotle pepper and salt.

2. Cut squash crosswise into ½-in.-thick slices. Using round cookie cutters, cut out centers to remove squash strings and seeds. If necessary, halve slices to fit the waffle maker.

3. Bake slices in waffle maker just until tender and lightly browned, 3-4 minutes. Serve with syrup mixture.

1 serving: 98 cal., 0 fat (0 sat. fat), 0 chol., 463mg sod., 25g carb. (12g sugars, 2g fiber), 1g pro. **Diabetic exchanges:** 1½ starch.

Test Kitchen Tip: Cut slices just ½ in. thick. If slices are thicker, the waffle iron won't close all the way. A panini press also works to make this squash. The squash will be very tender after cooking this way. To keep the squash intact, drizzle the maple mixture over the slices instead of brushing it on.

SAUSAGE-STUFFED BUTTERNUT SQUASH

Fill butternut squash shells with a simple turkey sausage mixture for a quick, delicious meal. The bonus? It's surprisingly low in calories.

—Katia Slinger, West Jordan, UT

TAKES: 30 MIN. • MAKES: 4 SERVINGS

1 medium butternut squash (about 3 lbs.)
1 lb. Italian turkey sausage links, casings removed
1 medium onion, finely chopped
4 garlic cloves, minced
½ cup shredded Italian cheese blend
Crushed red pepper flakes, optional

1. Preheat broiler. Cut the squash lengthwise in half; discard seeds. Place squash in a large microwave-safe dish, cut side down; add ½ in. of water. Microwave, covered, on high until soft, 20-25 minutes. Cool slightly.

2. Meanwhile, in a large nonstick skillet, cook and crumble the sausage with onion over medium-high heat until no longer pink, 5-7 minutes. Add the garlic; cook and stir 1 minute.

3. Leaving ½-in.-thick shells, scoop flesh from squash and stir it into sausage mixture. Place squash shells on a baking sheet; fill with sausage mixture. Sprinkle with cheese.

4. Broil 4-5 in. from heat until cheese is melted, 1-2 minutes. If desired, sprinkle with pepper flakes. To serve, cut each half into 2 portions.

1 serving: 325 cal., 10g fat (4g sat. fat), 52mg chol., 587mg sod., 44g carb. (10g sugars, 12g fiber), 19g pro. **Diabetic exchanges:** 3 starch, 3 lean meat.

"MY HUSBAND AND I LOVED THIS! IT'S A KEEPER!"

—PENNSTATEMOM, TASTEOFHOME.COM

SAUSAGE-STUFFED
BUTTERNUT SQUASH

HOW-TO

Peel, Chop & Cut Butternut Squash

- Cut a half-inch off the top and bottom. Cut through the squash right at the spot where it starts to flare out to form the seed bulb.
- Using a vegetable peeler, remove the outer peel from both sections.
- Cut the bottom portion in half and remove the seeds with a spoon. Cut crosswise into slices and then into cubes of desired size.
- Cut the top portion into slices and then into cubes.

HONEY-THYME BUTTERNUT SQUASH

GINGER BUTTERNUT SQUASH BISQUE

The couple who introduced my husband and me served us this smooth vegetarian soup one freezing-cold evening. We've been warming up with bowlfuls on chilly days ever since.

—Cara McDonald, Winter Park, CO

PREP: 25 MIN. • **BAKE:** 40 MIN. + COOLING • **MAKES:** 6 SERVINGS

- **1 medium butternut squash (about 3 lbs.)**
- **1 Tbsp. olive oil**
- **2 medium carrots, finely chopped**
- **1 medium onion, chopped**
- **2 garlic cloves, minced**
- **2 tsp. minced fresh gingerroot**
- **2 tsp. curry powder**
- **1 can (14½ oz.) vegetable broth**
- **1 can (13.66 oz.) coconut milk**
- **1 tsp. salt**
- **½ tsp. pepper**
- **2 cups hot cooked brown rice**
- **¼ cup sweetened shredded coconut, toasted**
- **¼ cup salted peanuts, coarsely chopped**
- **¼ cup minced fresh cilantro**

1. Preheat oven to 400°. Cut squash lengthwise in half; remove and discard seeds. Place the squash in a greased shallow roasting pan, cut side down. Roast 40-45 minutes or until squash is tender. Cool slightly.

2. In a large saucepan, heat oil over medium heat. Add carrots and onion; cook and stir until tender. Add garlic, ginger and curry powder; cook and stir 1 minute longer. Add broth; bring to a boil. Reduce heat; simmer, uncovered, 10-12 minutes or until carrots are tender.

3. Scoop the flesh from squash; discard skins. Add squash, coconut milk, salt and pepper to carrot mixture; bring just to a boil, stirring occasionally. Remove from heat; cool slightly. Process in batches in a blender until smooth.

4. Return to pan; heat through. Top servings with rice, coconut, peanuts and cilantro.

1 cup: 386 cal., 21g fat (14g sat. fat), 0 chol., 749mg sod., 48g carb. (10g sugars, 10g fiber), 7g pro.

HONEY-THYME BUTTERNUT SQUASH

Love mashed potatoes? Replace the spuds with butternut squash and flavor it with honey, parsley and thyme. The result is special enough for a holiday but easy enough for any day of the week.

—Bianca Noiseux, Bristol, CT

TAKES: 30 MIN. • **MAKES:** 10 SERVINGS

- **1 large butternut squash (about 5 lbs.), peeled and cubed**
- **¼ cup butter, cubed**
- **3 Tbsp. half-and-half cream**
- **2 Tbsp. honey**
- **2 tsp. dried parsley flakes**
- **½ tsp. salt**
- **⅛ tsp. dried thyme**
- **⅛ tsp. coarsely ground pepper**

1. In a large saucepan, bring 1 in. of water to a boil. Add squash; cover and cook for 10-15 minutes or until tender.

2. Drain. Mash squash with the remaining ingredients.

¾ cup: 145 cal., 5g fat (3g sat. fat), 14mg chol., 161mg sod., 26g carb. (9g sugars, 7g fiber), 2g pro. **Diabetic exchanges:** 1½ starch, 1 fat.

PATTYPAN SAUTE

The summery tastes of fresh tomato and sweet red pepper complement the sauteed squash in this colorful side. It's a wonderful way to enjoy the bounty from your backyard garden.

—Taste of Home *Test Kitchen*

TAKES: 25 MIN. • MAKES: 4 SERVINGS

- **2 cups halved pattypan squash**
- **1 medium onion, halved and sliced**
- **2 tsp. canola oil**
- **2 garlic cloves, minced**
- **1 small sweet red pepper, cut into ½-in. pieces**
- **1 cup sliced fresh mushrooms**
- **1 medium tomato, chopped**
- **½ tsp. salt**
- **½ tsp. Italian seasoning**
- **⅛ tsp. pepper**
- **2 Tbsp. shredded Parmesan cheese**

1. In a large nonstick skillet, saute squash and onion in oil for 2 minutes. Add garlic; cook 1 minute longer. Add red pepper and mushrooms; saute until vegetables are crisp-tender, 5-7 minutes.

2. Stir in the tomato, salt, Italian seasoning and pepper; heat through. Sprinkle top with cheese.

¾ cup: 73 cal., 3g fat (1g sat. fat), 2mg chol., 343mg sod., 9g carb. (5g sugars, 2g fiber), 3g pro. **Diabetic exchanges:** 2 vegetable, ½ fat.

GRILLED PATTYPANS

Love Asian flavors? Grill pattypans until tender, then coat them with a tongue-tingling blend of hoisin sauce, apricot spreadable fruit, rice vinegar and ginger.

—Taste of Home *Test Kitchen*

TAKES: 15 MIN. • MAKES: 6 SERVINGS

- **6 cups pattypan squash (about 1½ lbs.)**
- **¼ cup apricot spreadable fruit**
- **2 tsp. hoisin sauce**
- **1 tsp. rice vinegar**
- **½ tsp. sesame oil**
- **¼ tsp. salt**
- **⅛ tsp. ground ginger**

1. Place squash in a grill wok or basket coated with cooking spray. Grill, covered, over medium heat until tender, 4 minutes on each side.

2. Meanwhile, in a small bowl, combine the remaining ingredients. Transfer squash to a serving bowl; add sauce and toss gently.

¾ cup: 54 cal., 0 fat (0 sat. fat), 0 chol., 127mg sod., 12g carb. (8g sugars, 1g fiber), 1g pro. **Diabetic exchanges:** 1 vegetable, ½ starch.

PATTYPAN SAUTE

HOW-TO

Roast Squash

- Roasting, as well as other dry-heat methods of cooking, make the flavor of squash rich and sweet. Simply start by cutting squash into uniform sizes for even cooking.
- Coat the squash with a bit of olive oil, adding the herbs and seasonings of your choice.
- Spread the squash in a single layer in a baking pan with a 1-in. side. Be sure not to overcrowd the pan.
- Roast the squash uncovered at 400° to 450° until squash is tender. Stir occasionally.

ROASTED PUMPKIN NACHOS

5i ROASTED PUMPKIN NACHOS

I'd always made these using corn off the cob during summer. Then one autumn day when I wanted something seasonal, I replaced the corn with roasted pumpkin—yum!

—Lesle Harwood, Douglassville, PA

PREP: 40 MIN. • BAKE: 10 MIN. • MAKES: 12 SERVINGS

- **4 cups cubed fresh pumpkin or butternut squash (about 1 lb.)**
- **2 Tbsp. olive oil**
- **¼ tsp. salt**
- **⅛ tsp. pepper**
- **1 pkg. (13 oz.) tortilla chips**
- **1 can (15 oz.) black beans, rinsed and drained**
- **1 jar (16 oz.) salsa**
- **3 cups shredded Mexican cheese blend**
- **Optional toppings: Minced fresh cilantro, sliced green onions and hot pepper sauce**

1. Preheat oven to 400°. Place pumpkin in a greased 15x10x1-in. baking pan. Drizzle with oil; sprinkle with salt and pepper. Toss to coat. Roast until tender, 25-30 minutes, stirring occasionally.

2. Reduce oven setting to 350°. On a greased 15x10x1-in. baking pan, layer half each of the chips, beans, pumpkin, salsa and cheese. Repeat layers. Bake until the cheese is melted, 8-10 minutes. Add toppings of your choice; serve immediately.

1 serving: 347 cal., 18g fat (6g sat. fat), 25mg chol., 559mg sod., 36g carb. (3g sugars, 4g fiber), 10g pro.

PUMPKIN & CHICKEN SAUSAGE HASH

It's hard to beat a breakfast of poached or fried eggs served on top of this hearty hash. It's wonderful as a side or main dish for lunch or dinner, too.

—Valerie Donn, Gaylord, MI

PREP: 15 MIN. • COOK: 25 MIN. • MAKES: 4 SERVINGS

- **2 Tbsp. olive oil**
- **2 cups cubed fresh pumpkin or butternut squash**
- **¼ tsp. salt**
- **¼ tsp. pepper**
- **½ cup chopped onion**
- **1 pkg. (12 oz.) fully cooked apple chicken sausage links or flavor of your choice, cut into ½-in. slices**
- **1 cup sliced fresh mushrooms**
- **½ cup chopped sweet red pepper**
- **½ cup chopped green pepper**
- **1 tsp. garlic powder**
- **¼ cup minced fresh parsley**

In a large skillet, heat the oil over medium heat. Add the pumpkin; sprinkle with salt and pepper. Cook and stir until crisp-tender, 8-10 minutes. Add onion; cook 3 minutes longer. Add sausage, mushrooms, red and green peppers and garlic powder. Cook and stir until the pumpkin is tender, 10-12 minutes. Top with parsley before serving.

1 serving: 260 cal., 14g fat (3g sat. fat), 60mg chol., 634mg sod., 19g carb. (13g sugars, 2g fiber), 16g pro. **Diabetic exchanges:** 2 lean meat, 1½ fat, 1 starch.

PUMPKIN SOUP WITH SOURDOUGH SAGE CROUTONS

This holiday-special recipe, which can also be prepared with butternut squash instead of pumpkin, includes just a few extra steps for making homemade croutons and a creamy topping. They're so worth it!

—Jenn Tidwell, Fair Oaks, CA

PREP: 35 MIN. • **COOK:** 30 MIN. • **MAKES:** 10 SERVINGS (2½ QT. SOUP, 2 CUPS CROUTONS, ½ CUP SWEET CREAM)

- 1 large onion, chopped
- 2 medium carrots, thinly sliced
- 3 Tbsp. olive oil
- 9 cups cubed fresh pumpkin
- 3 cans (14½ oz. each) chicken broth
- 2 Tbsp. minced fresh sage
- 1½ tsp. garlic powder
- ½ tsp. salt
- ½ tsp. pepper
- ⅛ tsp. ground nutmeg

SWEET CREAM

- 3 oz. cream cheese, softened
- ¼ cup 2% milk
- 2 Tbsp. confectioners' sugar

CROUTONS

- 3 slices sourdough bread, cubed
- 2 Tbsp. olive oil
- 2 Tbsp. butter, melted
- 2 Tbsp. minced fresh sage

1. In a Dutch oven, saute the onion and carrots in oil for 5 minutes. Add pumpkin; cook 5-6 minutes longer. Stir in the broth, sage, garlic powder, salt, pepper and nutmeg; bring to a boil. Reduce heat; cover and simmer until pumpkin is tender, 15-20 minutes.

2. Cool slightly. In a blender, process soup in batches until smooth. Return all to pan and heat through.

3. For sweet cream, combine ingredients until smooth. For croutons, place bread in a small bowl; drizzle with oil and butter. Sprinkle with sage and toss to coat. Transfer to a small skillet; cook and stir over medium heat until lightly toasted, 4-6 minutes.

4. Garnish servings with sweet cream and croutons.

1 cup soup with 3 Tbsp. croutons and 2 tsp. sweet cream: 199 cal., 13g fat (4g sat. fat), 18mg chol., 778mg sod., 19g carb. (7g sugars, 1g fiber), 4g pro.

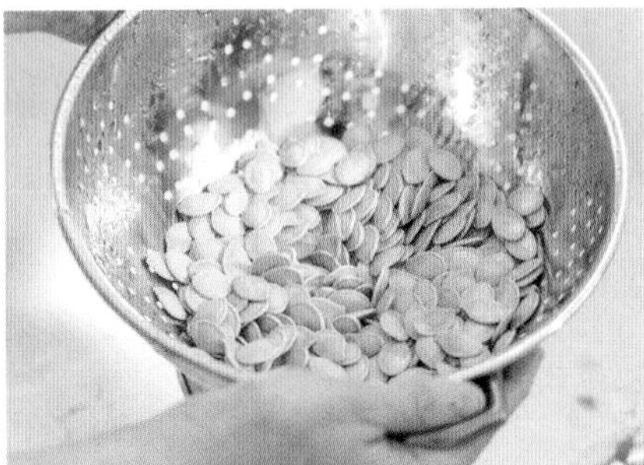

HOW-TO

Roast Pumpkin Seeds

- Preheat oven to 250°. Cut the top off a carving pumpkin. Scoop out the seeds and stringy pulp.
- Rinse seeds, discarding the pulp. Pat dry. Toss with melted butter, salt and Worcestershire sauce.
- Evenly spread the seeds in a greased, foil-lined 15x10x1-in. pan.
- Bake the seeds for 45 minutes, stirring occasionally. Increase oven temperature to 325°. Bake until lightly browned and dry, about 5 minutes. Serve the seeds warm or at room temperature. Cool completely before storing in an airtight container.

FARMERS MARKET FIND

Pumpkins are technically members of the gourd family but can be cooked like any winter squash. Varieties known as pie pumpkins are smaller than the jack-o'-lantern type and make for flavorful dishes.

PUMPKIN SOUP WITH SOURDOUGH SAGE CROUTONS

SALSA SPAGHETTI SQUASH

SALSA SPAGHETTI SQUASH

If you're craving pasta but are eating gluten-free or just want something lighter, try this delicious alternative.

—Clara Coulson Minney, Washington Court House, OH

TAKES: 30 MIN. • MAKES: 4 SERVINGS

- **1 medium spaghetti squash**
- **1 medium onion, chopped**
- **2 cups salsa**
- **1 can (15 oz.) black beans, rinsed and drained**
- **3 Tbsp. minced fresh cilantro**
- **1 medium ripe avocado, peeled and cubed**

1. Cut squash lengthwise in half; discard seeds. Place squash on a microwave-safe plate, cut side down. Microwave, uncovered, on high for 15-18 minutes or until tender.

2. Meanwhile, in a lightly oiled nonstick skillet, cook and stir onion over medium heat until tender. Stir in salsa, beans and cilantro; heat through. Gently stir in avocado; cook 1 minute longer.

3. When squash is cool enough to handle, use a fork to separate strands. Serve squash topped with salsa mixture.

1 cup: 308 cal., 9g fat (2g sat. fat), 0 chol., 822mg sod., 46g carb. (6g sugars, 16g fiber), 8g pro.

SPAGHETTI SQUASH PRIMAVERA

The bright yellow shell of a spaghetti squash becomes a fun bowl for this satisfying meatless entree.

—CoraLee Collis, Ankeny, IA

PREP: 25 MIN. • COOK: 20 MIN. • MAKES: 4 SERVINGS

- **1 large spaghetti squash (3½ lbs.)**
- **¼ cup sliced carrot**
- **¼ cup chopped red onion**
- **¼ cup chopped sweet red pepper**
- **¼ cup chopped green pepper**
- **2 tsp. canola oil**
- **1 cup thinly sliced yellow summer squash**
- **1 cup thinly sliced zucchini**
- **1 garlic clove, minced**
- **1 can (14½ oz.) Italian stewed tomatoes**
- **½ cup frozen corn, thawed**
- **½ tsp. salt**
- **½ tsp. dried oregano**
- **⅛ tsp. dried thyme**
- **4 tsp. grated Parmesan cheese**
- **2 Tbsp. minced fresh parsley**

1. Cut spaghetti squash in half; discard seeds. Place cut side up on a microwave-safe plate. Microwave, covered, on high for 9 minutes or until tender.

2. Meanwhile, in a large skillet, saute the carrot, onion and peppers in oil for 3 minutes. Add the yellow squash and zucchini; saute 2-3 minutes longer or until squash is tender. Add garlic; cook 1 minute longer. Reduce heat; add the tomatoes, corn, salt, oregano and thyme. Cook 5 minutes longer or until heated through, stirring occasionally.

3. Separate spaghetti squash strands with a fork. Spoon the vegetable mixture into squash; sprinkle with Parmesan cheese and parsley.

1 serving: 237 cal., 6g fat (1g sat. fat), 1mg chol., 633mg sod., 46g carb. (7g sugars, 9g fiber), 6g pro.

ITALIAN SPAGHETTI SQUASH

Here's the easiest way I know to prepare spaghetti squash. Just put it in the slow cooker for a delicious Italian side or light meal.

—Melissa Brooks, Sparta, WI

PREP: 15 MIN. • COOK: 6¼ HOURS • MAKES: 4 SERVINGS

- **1 medium spaghetti squash (3 lbs.)**
- **1 can (14½ oz.) diced tomatoes, undrained**
- **1 cup sliced fresh mushrooms**
- **½ tsp. salt**
- **½ tsp. dried oregano**
- **¼ tsp. pepper**
- **¾ cup shredded part-skim mozzarella cheese**

1. Halve squash lengthwise; discard seeds. Fill with tomatoes and mushrooms; sprinkle with seasonings. Place in an oval 7-qt. slow cooker, tilting 1 slightly to fit.

2. Cook, covered, on low until squash is tender, 6-8 hours. Sprinkle with cheese. Cook, covered, on low until cheese is melted, 10-15 minutes. To serve, cut each half into 2 portions.

¾ cup: 195 cal., 6g fat (3g sat. fat), 14mg chol., 661mg sod., 31g carb. (4g sugars, 7g fiber), 9g pro. **Diabetic exchanges:** 2 starch, 1 medium-fat meat.

CHEESY BACON SPAGHETTI SQUASH

This quick casserole is called cheesy for a reason! The recipe calls for Swiss, but feel free to stir in any kind you have on hand.

—Jean Williams, Stillwater, OK

TAKES: 30 MIN. • MAKES: 4 SERVINGS

- **1 large spaghetti squash (3½ lbs.)**
- **4 bacon strips, chopped**
- **3 Tbsp. butter**
- **1 Tbsp. brown sugar**
- **½ tsp. salt**
- **¼ tsp. pepper**
- **½ cup shredded Swiss cheese**

1. Halve squash lengthwise; discard seeds. Place squash on a microwave-safe plate, cut side down; microwave on high until tender, 15-20 minutes. Cool slightly. Separate strands with a fork.

2. In a large skillet, cook bacon over medium heat until crisp, stirring occasionally. With a slotted spoon, remove bacon to paper towels; reserve drippings.

3. In same pan, heat the drippings over medium heat; stir in butter, brown sugar, salt and pepper until blended. Add squash; toss and heat through. Remove from heat; stir in cheese. Top with bacon.

1 cup: 381 cal., 26g fat (12g sat. fat), 54mg chol., 627mg sod., 32g carb. (4g sugars, 6g fiber), 10g pro.

ITALIAN SPAGHETTI SQUASH

HOW-TO

Prep & Cook Spaghetti Squash

- Halve the squash horizontally and discard the seeds.
- Place the squash cut side down in a greased baking dish; bake it at 350° for 45-60 minutes or until the shell can be pierced easily with a fork. Cool enough to handle.
- Turn the squash over and use a fork to separate the squash into strands resembling spaghetti.

SLOW-COOKED
SUMMER SQUASH

SLOW-COOKED SUMMER SQUASH

We love squash, but I needed ideas that went beyond just adding cheese. This was a huge hit with our family.

—Joan Hallford, North Richland Hills, TX

PREP: 15 MIN. • COOK: 2½ HOURS • MAKES: 8 SERVINGS

- **1 lb. medium yellow summer squash**
- **1 lb. medium zucchini**
- **2 medium tomatoes, chopped**
- **¼ cup thinly sliced green onions**
- **½ tsp. salt**
- **¼ tsp. pepper**
- **1 cup vegetable broth**
- **1½ cups Caesar salad croutons, coarsely crushed**
- **½ cup shredded cheddar cheese**
- **4 bacon strips, cooked and crumbled**

1. Cut squash into ¼-in.-thick slices. In a 3- or 4-qt. slow cooker, combine squash, tomatoes and green onions. Add salt, pepper and broth. Cook, covered, on low until tender, 2½-3½ hours. Remove squash with a slotted spoon.

2. To serve, top with croutons, cheese and bacon.

¾ cup: 111 cal., 6g fat (2g sat. fat), 12mg chol., 442mg sod., 10g carb. (4g sugars, 2g fiber), 6g pro. **Diabetic exchanges:** 1 vegetable, 1 fat.

Test Kitchen Tip: If you prefer, substitute 1½ cups crushed buttery crackers for the Caesar salad croutons.

SUMMER SQUASH & PEPPER SAUTE

This colorful side is so pretty on the table, and the taste keeps you coming back for more. I always have the recipe handy because it complements just about any main dish.

—Shirley Warren, Thiensville, WI

TAKES: 20 MIN. • MAKES: 4 SERVINGS

- **2 yellow summer squash, halved lengthwise and cut into ¼-in. slices**
- **1 medium sweet orange pepper, cut into thin strips**
- **2 Tbsp. butter**
- **3 green onions, chopped**
- **2 tsp. brown sugar**
- **2 tsp. lemon juice**
- **½ tsp. dried basil**
- **½ tsp. salt**
- **¼ tsp. pepper**

Saute squash and orange pepper in butter in a large skillet until crisp-tender. Add remaining ingredients; cook 4-5 minutes longer or until sugar is dissolved and vegetables are tender.

¾ cup: 90 cal., 6g fat (4g sat. fat), 15mg chol., 352mg sod., 8g carb. (6g sugars, 2g fiber), 2g pro. **Diabetic exchanges:** 1½ fat, 1 vegetable.

5i BAKED PARMESAN-BREADED SQUASH

Yellow summer squash crisps beautifully when baked. You don't have to turn the pieces—just keep an eye on them.

—Debi Mitchell, Flower Mound, TX

PREP: 20 MIN. • BAKE: 20 MIN. • MAKES: 6 SERVINGS

- **4 cups thinly sliced yellow summer squash (3 medium)**
- **3 Tbsp. olive oil**
- **½ tsp. salt**
- **½ tsp. pepper**
- **⅛ tsp. cayenne pepper**
- **¾ cup panko bread crumbs**
- **¾ cup grated Parmesan cheese**

1. Preheat oven to 450°. Place squash in a large bowl. Add oil and seasonings; toss to coat.

2. In a shallow bowl, mix the panko bread crumbs and cheese. Dip squash in crumb mixture to coat both sides, patting to help coating adhere. Place on parchment-lined baking sheets. Bake 20-25 minutes or until golden brown, rotating pans halfway through baking.

⅔ cup: 137 cal., 10g fat (2g sat. fat), 7mg chol., 346mg sod., 8g carb. (0 sugars, 2g fiber), 5g pro. **Diabetic exchanges:** 2 fat, 1 vegetable.

SHRIMP & SQUASH STIR-FRY

When my garden is bursting with tomatoes, garlic and corn, I toss them into this quick stir-fry and cook some rice. Dinner's done!

—Lindsay Honn, Huntingdon, PA

TAKES: 20 MIN. • MAKES: 4 SERVINGS

- **2 Tbsp. olive oil**
- **2 small yellow summer squash, sliced**
- **1 small onion, chopped**
- **1 lb. uncooked shrimp (26-30 per lb.), peeled and deveined**
- **1½ cups fresh or frozen corn, thawed**
- **1 cup chopped tomatoes**
- **4 garlic cloves, minced**
- **½ tsp. salt**
- **¼ tsp. pepper**
- **¼ tsp. crushed red pepper flakes, optional**
- **¼ cup chopped fresh basil**
- **Hot cooked brown rice, optional**

1. In a large skillet, heat oil over medium-high heat. Add squash and onion; stir-fry until squash is crisp-tender, 2-3 minutes.

2. Add next 6 ingredients and, if desired, pepper flakes; stir-fry until shrimp turn pink, 3-4 minutes longer. Top with basil. Serve with rice if desired.

1 serving: 239 cal., 9g fat (1g sat. fat), 138mg chol., 443mg sod., 19g carb. (8g sugars, 3g fiber), 22g pro. **Diabetic exchanges:** 3 lean meat, 1½ fat, 1 starch, 1 vegetable.

SHRIMP & SQUASH STIR-FRY

YELLOW SUMMER SQUASH RELISH

My friends can barely wait for the growing season to arrive so I can make this incredible squash relish. The color really dresses up a hot dog.

—Ruth Hawkins, Jackson, MS

PREP: 1 HOUR + MARINATING • PROCESS: 15 MIN. • MAKES: 6 PINTS

- **10 cups shredded yellow summer squash (about 4 lbs.)**
- **2 large onions, chopped**
- **1 large green pepper, chopped**
- **6 Tbsp. canning salt**
- **4 cups sugar**
- **3 cups cider vinegar**
- **1 Tbsp. each celery seed, ground mustard and ground turmeric**
- **½ tsp. ground nutmeg**
- **½ tsp. pepper**

1. In a large container, combine squash, onions, green pepper and salt. Cover and refrigerate overnight. Drain; rinse and drain again.

2. In a Dutch oven, combine sugar, vinegar and seasonings; bring to a boil. Add the squash mixture; return to a boil. Reduce the heat; simmer 15 minutes. Remove from heat.

3. Carefully ladle hot mixture into 6 hot 1-pint jars, leaving ½-in. headspace. Remove air bubbles and adjust headspace, if necessary, by adding hot mixture. Wipe rims. Center lids on jars; screw on bands until fingertip tight.

4. Place jars into canner with simmering water, ensuring that they are completely covered with water. Bring to a boil; process for 15 minutes. Remove jars and cool. Refrigerate remaining relish for up to 1 week.

2 Tbsp.: 39 cal., 0 fat (0 sat. fat), 0 chol., 5mg sod., 9g carb. (9g sugars, 0 fiber), 0 pro.

CHEESY SUMMER SQUASH FLATBREADS

When you want a meatless meal with Mediterranean style, these flatbreads smothered with squash, hummus and mozzarella deliver the goods.

—Matthew Hass, Ellison Bay, WI

TAKES: 30 MIN. • MAKES: 4 SERVINGS

- **3 small yellow summer squash, sliced ¼ in. thick**
- **1 Tbsp. olive oil**
- **½ tsp. salt**
- **2 cups fresh baby spinach, coarsely chopped**
- **2 naan flatbreads**
- **⅓ cup roasted red pepper hummus**
- **1 carton (8 oz.) fresh mozzarella cheese pearls**
- **Pepper**

1. Preheat oven to 425°. Toss squash with oil and salt; spread evenly in a 15x10x1-in. baking pan. Roast until tender, 8-10 minutes. Transfer to a bowl; stir in spinach.

2. Place naan on a baking sheet; spread with hummus. Top with squash mixture and cheese. Bake on a lower oven rack just until cheese is melted, 4-6 minutes. Sprinkle with pepper.

½ topped flatbread: 332 cal., 20g fat (9g sat. fat), 47mg chol., 737mg sod., 24g carb. (7g sugars, 3g fiber), 15g pro.

YELLOW SUMMER SQUASH RELISH

ZUCCHINI-VEGETABLE STRATA

❄ ZUCCHINI-VEGETABLE STRATA

With the abundance of zucchini my family has in the fall, this is the perfect dish to use some of what we have. Cheesy and rich, the classic warm breakfast dish is sure to please!

—Colleen Doucette, Truro, NS

PREP: 55 MIN. + CHILLING • **BAKE:** 40 MIN. • **MAKES:** 8 SERVINGS

- **3 large zucchini, halved lengthwise and cut into ¾-in. slices**
- **1 each medium red, yellow and orange peppers, cut into 1-in. pieces**
- **2 Tbsp. olive oil**
- **1 tsp. dried oregano**
- **½ tsp. salt**
- **½ tsp. pepper**
- **½ tsp. dried basil**
- **1 medium tomato, chopped**
- **1 loaf (1 lb.) unsliced crusty Italian bread**
- **½ cup shredded sharp cheddar cheese**
- **½ cup shredded Asiago cheese**
- **6 large eggs**
- **2 cups fat-free milk**

1. Preheat oven to 400°. Toss zucchini and peppers with oil and seasonings; transfer to a 15x10x1-in. pan. Roast until tender, 25-30 minutes, stirring once. Stir in tomato; cool slightly.

2. Trim ends from bread; cut bread into 1-in. slices. In a greased 13x9-in. baking dish, layer half of each of the following: bread, roasted vegetables and cheeses. Repeat layers. Whisk together eggs and milk; pour evenly over top. Refrigerate, covered, 6 hours or overnight.

3. Preheat oven to 375°. Remove casserole from refrigerator while the oven heats. Bake, uncovered, until golden brown, 40-50 minutes. Let stand for 5-10 minutes before cutting.

Freeze option: Cover and freeze unbaked casserole. To use, partially thaw casserole in refrigerator overnight. Remove from refrigerator 30 minutes before baking. Preheat oven to 375°. Bake casserole as directed, increasing time as necessary to heat through and for a thermometer inserted in center to read 165°.

1 piece: 349 cal., 14g fat (5g sat. fat), 154mg chol., 642mg sod., 40g carb. (9g sugars, 4g fiber), 17g pro. **Diabetic exchanges:** 2 starch, 1 vegetable, 1 medium-fat meat, 1 fat.

HOW-TO

Buy Zucchini

In this case, bigger isn't better. For the best flavor, look for zucchini that are about 6 inches long and 2 inches in diameter. The skin should be glossy and a bit prickly. Give the fruit a light squeeze. It should be firm; it should not give under slight pressure. Make sure it's free of cuts, gouges and blemishes. An inch of stem should be attached.

Store Zucchini

You can keep unwashed zucchini in a perforated plastic bag in the fridge for up to 5 days. Or, freeze it: Slice the fruit into rounds and place them in a freezer bag. They will keep in the freezer for up to 1 year.

Prep Zucchini

Wash the zucchini with cool water before preparing. The skin does not need to be peeled prior to eating.

BLACKENED TILAPIA WITH ZUCCHINI NOODLES

I love quick and bright meals like this one-skillet wonder. Homemade pico de gallo is easy to make the night before.

—Tammy Brownlow, Dallas, TX

TAKES: 30 MIN. • MAKES: 4 SERVINGS

- **2 large zucchini (about 1½ lbs.)**
- **1½ tsp. ground cumin**
- **¾ tsp. salt, divided**
- **½ tsp. smoked paprika**
- **½ tsp. pepper**
- **¼ tsp garlic powder**
- **4 tilapia fillets (6 oz. each)**
- **2 tsp. olive oil**
- **2 garlic cloves, minced**
- **1 cup pico de gallo**

1. Trim ends of zucchini. Using a spiralizer, cut zucchini into thin strands.

2. Mix cumin, ½ tsp. salt, smoked paprika, pepper and garlic powder; sprinkle generously onto both sides of tilapia. In a large nonstick skillet, heat oil over medium-high heat. In batches, cook tilapia until the fish just begins to flake easily with a fork, 2-3 minutes per side. Remove from pan; keep warm.

3. In the same pan, cook zucchini with garlic over medium-high heat until slightly softened, 1-2 minutes, tossing constantly with tongs (do not overcook). Sprinkle with remaining salt. Serve with tilapia and pico de gallo.

1 serving: 203 cal., 4g fat (1g sat. fat), 83mg chol., 522mg sod., 8g carb. (5g sugars, 2g fiber), 34g pro. **Diabetic exchanges:** 5 lean meat, 1 vegetable, ½ fat.

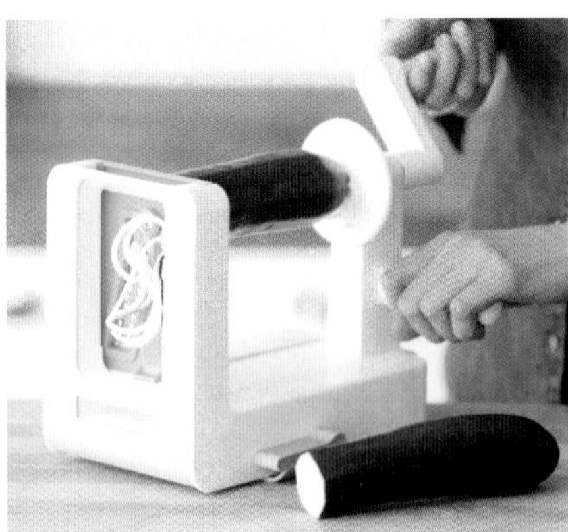

HOW-TO

How to Make Zucchini Noodles

- Begin by trimming off the ends of the zucchini. Peel the skin from the zucchini if desired. Align zucchini within spiralizer device so one end meets the blade, then poke the claw insert into the opposite end so it's held in place.
- Crank the spiralizer handle, applying light pressure to feed the zucchini into the grating blades. Keep turning until the zucchini has been completely spiralized into strands or noodles.
- Add oil to a large nonstick skillet over medium-high heat. Toss in the zucchini noodles with herbs or seasonings. Cook noodles 1-2 minutes. Make sure the zucchini cooks only slightly, to preserve its fresh, crunchy texture. As the noodles cook, toss them constantly with a pair of tongs so they don't overcook.

BLACKENED TILAPIA WITH ZUCCHINI NOODLES

ITALIAN SAUSAGE & ZUCCHINI SOUP

Everyone in my family likes this soup. Sometimes I use mini farfalle in this soup because my grandchildren say it looks like tiny butterflies. The recipe also works in a slow cooker.

—Nancy Murphy, Mount Dora, FL

TAKES: 30 MIN. • MAKES: 6 SERVINGS (2 QT.)

- **½ lb. bulk Italian sausage**
- **1 medium onion, chopped**
- **1 medium green pepper, chopped**
- **3 cups beef broth**
- **1 can (14½ oz.) diced tomatoes, undrained**
- **1 Tbsp. minced fresh basil or 1 tsp. dried basil**
- **1 Tbsp. minced fresh parsley or 1 tsp. dried parsley flakes**
- **1 medium zucchini, cut into ½-in. pieces**
- **½ cup uncooked orzo pasta**

1. In a large saucepan, cook sausage, onion and pepper over medium heat until sausage is no longer pink and vegetables are tender, breaking up sausage into crumbles, 4-6 minutes; drain.

2. Add the broth, tomatoes, basil and parsley; bring to a boil. Stir in zucchini and orzo; return to a boil. Cook, covered, 10-12 minutes or until zucchini and orzo are tender.

1¼ cups: 191 cal., 9g fat (3g sat. fat), 20mg chol., 789mg sod., 20g carb. (5g sugars, 2g fiber), 9g pro.

THYMED ZUCCHINI SAUTE

This simple and flavorful dish is a tasty and healthy way to use up zucchini.

—Bobby Taylor, Ulster Park, NY

TAKES: 15 MIN. • MAKES: 4 SERVINGS

- **1 Tbsp. olive oil**
- **1 lb. medium zucchini, quartered lengthwise and halved**
- **¼ cup finely chopped onion**
- **½ vegetable bouillon cube, crushed**
- **2 Tbsp. minced fresh parsley**
- **1 tsp. minced fresh thyme or ¼ tsp. dried thyme**

In a large skillet, heat oil over medium-high heat. Add zucchini, onion and bouillon; cook and stir 4-5 minutes or until zucchini is crisp-tender. Sprinkle with herbs.

Note: This recipe was prepared with Knorr vegetable bouillon.

¾ cup: 53 cal., 4g fat (1g sat. fat), 0 chol., 135mg sod., 5g carb. (2g sugars, 2g fiber), 2g pro. **Diabetic exchanges:** 1 vegetable

SAUTEED SQUASH WITH TOMATOES & ONIONS

My favorite meals show a love of family and food. This zucchini dish with tomatoes is like a scaled-down ratatouille.

—Adan Franco, Milwaukee, WI

TAKES: 20 MIN. • MAKES: 8 SERVINGS

- **2 Tbsp. olive oil**
- **1 medium onion, finely chopped**
- **4 medium zucchini, chopped**
- **2 large tomatoes, finely chopped**
- **1 tsp. salt**
- **¼ tsp. pepper**

1. In a large skillet, heat oil over medium-high heat. Add onion; cook and stir until tender, 2-4 minutes. Add zucchini; cook and stir 3 minutes.

2. Stir in the tomatoes, salt and pepper; cook and stir 4-6 minutes longer or until the squash is tender. Serve with a slotted spoon.

¾ cup: 60 cal., 4g fat (1g sat. fat), 0 chol., 306mg sod., 6g carb. (4g sugars, 2g fiber), 2g pro. **Diabetic exchanges:** 1 vegetable, ½ fat.

BEEF & BULGUR-STUFFED ZUCCHINI BOATS

My mom frequently cooked the giant zucchini that she grew in her garden. I adapted this recipe from one of her favorite weeknight meals. Though I love the taste of fresh-picked zucchini, ones from the grocery store cook up fine, too.

—Susan Peterson, Blaine, MN

PREP: 35 MIN. • BAKE: 30 MIN. • MAKES: 4 SERVINGS

- **4 medium zucchini**
- **1 lb. lean ground beef (90% lean)**
- **1 large onion, finely chopped**
- **1 small sweet red pepper, chopped**
- **1½ cups tomato sauce**
- **½ cup bulgur**
- **¼ tsp. pepper**
- **½ cup salsa**
- **½ cup shredded reduced-fat cheddar cheese**

1. Preheat oven to 350°. Cut each zucchini in half lengthwise. Scoop out flesh, leaving a ¼-in. shell; chop flesh.

2. In a large skillet, cook beef, onion and red pepper over medium heat until meat is no longer pink, 6-8 minutes, breaking it into crumbles; drain. Stir in the tomato sauce, bulgur, pepper and zucchini flesh. Bring to a boil. Reduce heat; simmer, uncovered, 12-15 minutes or until bulgur is tender. Stir in the salsa. Spoon into zucchini shells.

3. Place in a 13x9-in. baking dish coated with cooking spray. Bake, covered, for 20 minutes. Sprinkle with cheese. Bake, uncovered, 10-15 minutes longer or until zucchini is tender and filling is heated through.

2 stuffed zucchini halves: 361 cal., 13g fat (6g sat. fat), 81mg chol., 714mg sod., 31g carb. (9g sugars, 7g fiber), 32g pro.

ZUCCHINI PANZANELLA SALAD

I learned how to make panzanella from a dear friend's grandmother. This is a version I crave during the summer. It's a tasty way to use day-old bread and your garden's bounty of zucchini.

—Felicity Wolf, Kansas City, MO

PREP: 20 MIN. + COOLING • BAKE: 40 MIN. • MAKES: 14 CUPS

- **3 medium zucchini, cut into ¼-in. slices**
- **¼ cup olive oil, divided**
- **1 French bread baguette (10½ oz.), cubed**
- **1½ cups heirloom mini or cherry tomatoes, halved**
- **1 medium green pepper, coarsely chopped**
- **½ medium red onion, thinly sliced**
- **¼ cup balsamic vinegar**
- **1 tsp. jarred roasted minced garlic**
- **1 tsp. Italian seasoning**
- **½ tsp. crushed red pepper flakes**
- **1 tsp. kosher salt**
- **½ tsp. coarsely ground pepper**
- **1½ cups fresh mozzarella cheese pearls**

1. Place zucchini in a 15x10x1-in. baking pan. Toss with 1 Tbsp. olive oil. Bake, uncovered, at 400° until tender and lightly browned, 25-30 minutes, stirring halfway. Remove from the oven and cool.

2. Meanwhile, in a large bowl, toss bread cubes with 1 Tbsp. olive oil. Transfer to a baking sheet. Bake at 400° until lightly browned, 12-14 minutes, stirring occasionally.

3. Place the cooled zucchini, toasted bread, tomatoes, green pepper and red onion in a large bowl. In a small bowl, whisk together the vinegar, garlic, seasonings and remaining oil. Drizzle over salad; toss gently to combine. Add the mozzarella and stir to combine. Serve immediately.

1 cup: 152 cal., 8g fat (3g sat. fat), 13mg chol., 301mg sod., 16g carb. (4g sugars, 1g fiber), 5g pro. **Diabetic exchanges:** 1½ fat, 1 starch.

Test Kitchen Tips: If the raw onion is too pungent for you, roast it with the zucchini. Use ⅓ cup prepared balsamic vinaigrette if you're short on time.

ZUCCHINI & CHEESE ROULADES

My husband enjoys this recipe so much that he even helps me roll up the roulades! You can change the filling any way you'd like—I have used feta instead of Parmesan or sun-dried tomatoes in the place of the olives.

—April McKinney, Murfreesboro, TN

TAKES: 25 MIN. • MAKES: 2 DOZEN

- **1 cup part-skim ricotta cheese**
- **¼ cup grated Parmesan cheese**
- **2 Tbsp. minced fresh basil or 2 tsp. dried basil**
- **1 Tbsp. capers, drained**
- **1 Tbsp. chopped Greek olives**
- **1 tsp. grated lemon zest**
- **1 Tbsp. lemon juice**
- **⅛ tsp. salt**
- **⅛ tsp. pepper**
- **4 medium zucchini**

1. In a small bowl, mix the first 9 ingredients.

2. Slice the zucchini lengthwise into twenty-four ⅛-in.-thick slices. On a greased grill rack, cook the zucchini in batches, covered, over medium heat. Grill zucchini until tender, 2-3 minutes on each side.

3. Place 1 Tbsp. ricotta mixture on the end of each zucchini slice. Roll up and secure each with a toothpick.

1 appetizer: 24 cal., 1g fat (1g sat. fat), 4mg chol., 58mg sod., 2g carb. (1g sugars, 0 fiber), 2g pro.

ZUCCHINI
PANZANELLA SALAD

CHAPTER 5

LEAFY GREENS

When it comes to healthy eating, garden-fresh greens rise to the top of the ingredient list. From classic salads and change-of-pace sides to healthy entrees and warm-you-up soups, the versatility of these staples simply can't be beat.

ARUGULA & BROWN RICE SALAD

I double the recipe for this tasty arugula entree salad when I need to bring a dish to a potluck or party. I love that I'm always asked for the recipe.

—Mindy Oswalt, Winnetka, CA

TAKES: 25 MIN. • **MAKES:** 4 SERVINGS

- **1 pkg. (8.8 oz.) ready-to-serve brown rice**
- **7 cups fresh arugula or baby spinach (about 5 oz.)**
- **1 can (15 oz.) garbanzo beans or chickpeas, rinsed and drained**
- **1 cup crumbled feta cheese**
- **¾ cup loosely packed basil leaves, torn**
- **½ cup dried cherries or cranberries**

DRESSING

- **¼ cup olive oil**
- **¼ tsp. grated lemon zest**
- **2 Tbsp. lemon juice**
- **¼ tsp. salt**
- **⅛ tsp. pepper**

1. Heat rice according to package directions. Transfer to a large bowl; cool slightly.

2. Stir arugula, beans, cheese, basil and cherries into rice. In a small bowl, whisk dressing ingredients. Drizzle over salad; toss to coat. Serve immediately.

2 cups: 473 cal., 22g fat (5g sat. fat), 15mg chol., 574mg sod., 53g carb. (17g sugars, 7g fiber), 13g pro.

ARUGULA PIZZA

This pizza is fantastic served as an appetizer when family or friends get together. My girlfriends and I love it because it has that sophisticated gourmet touch, and it's healthy, too! This also serves four for a main course.

—Annette Riva, Naperville, IL

TAKES: 20 MIN. • **MAKES:** 16 PIECES

- **½ cup pizza sauce**
- **1 prebaked 12-in. pizza crust (14 oz.)**
- **1 cup shaved Parmesan cheese**
- **3 oz. thinly sliced prosciutto**
- **2 cups fresh arugula**
- **Additional fresh arugula, optional**

Preheat oven to 425°. Spread sauce over pizza crust. Layer with ½ cup Parmesan cheese, prosciutto and arugula; top with remaining cheese. Bake directly on oven rack until the edges are lightly browned, 10-12 minutes. Cut into small squares. If desired, top with more arugula.

2 pieces : 204 cal., 7g fat (3g sat. fat), 17mg chol., 689mg sod., 23g carb. (2g sugars, 1g fiber), 12g pro.

FARMERS MARKET FIND

Arugula is also known as garden rocket. It is a tender, bitter green with a distinct peppery, mustard flavor.

ARUGULA & BROWN RICE SALAD

STRAWBERRY ARUGULA SALAD WITH FETA

STRAWBERRY ARUGULA SALAD WITH FETA

The combination of peppery arugula, sweet strawberries and robust feta cheese may sound unusual, but one bite wins over taste buds.

—Carla Horne, Meridian, MS

TAKES: 15 MIN. • MAKES: 12 SERVINGS

- **6 cups fresh arugula or baby spinach**
- **1½ cups sliced fresh strawberries**
- **½ cup slivered almonds or pine nuts**
- **½ cup crumbled garlic and herb feta cheese**
- **4 green onions, chopped**

VINAIGRETTE

- **⅓ cup olive oil**
- **1 Tbsp. Dijon mustard**
- **1 Tbsp. red wine vinegar**
- **2 tsp. lemon juice**
- **1½ tsp. balsamic vinegar**
- **1 tsp. minced fresh rosemary or ¼ tsp. dried rosemary, crushed**
- **1 tsp. fresh sage or ¼ tsp. dried sage leaves**
- **½ tsp. celery seed**
- **⅛ tsp. pepper**

In a salad bowl, combine the first 5 ingredients. In a small bowl, whisk the vinaigrette ingredients. Drizzle over salad; toss to coat.

¾ cup: 106 cal., 9g fat (2g sat. fat), 3mg chol., 88mg sod., 4g carb. (2g sugars, 1g fiber), 2g pro.

Test Kitchen Tip: Take this salad to the family reunion, block party or church picnic by making the vinaigrette a day early, and packing up the salad ingredients individually. Toss it all together at the event for a fast, fresh and fabulous contribution.

ARUGULA SALAD WITH SHAVED PARMESAN

Fresh arugula, golden raisins, crunchy almonds and shaved Parmesan combine in this perfect dinner salad. I first put it together for my mom, and the whole family ended up loving it!

—Nicole Rash, Yucca Valley, CA

TAKES: 15 MIN. • MAKES: 4 SERVINGS

- **6 cups fresh arugula**
- **¼ cup golden raisins**
- **¼ cup sliced almonds, toasted**
- **3 Tbsp. olive oil**
- **1 Tbsp. lemon juice**
- **¼ tsp. salt**
- **¼ tsp. freshly ground pepper**
- **⅓ cup shaved or shredded Parmesan cheese**

In a large bowl, combine the arugula, raisins and almonds. Drizzle with oil and lemon juice. Sprinkle with salt and pepper; toss to coat. Divide salad among 4 plates; top with cheese.

1 cup: 181 cal., 15g fat (3g sat. fat), 4mg chol., 242mg sod., 10g carb. (7g sugars, 2g fiber), 4g pro. **Diabetic exchanges:** 3 fat, ½ starch.

GRILLED CABBAGE

I don't really like cabbage, but I fixed this recipe and couldn't believe how good it was! We threw some burgers on the grill and our dinner was complete. I never thought I'd skip dessert because I was full from eating too much cabbage!

—Elizabeth Wheeler, Thornville, OH

TAKES: 30 MIN. • MAKES: 8 SERVINGS

- **1 medium head cabbage (about 1½ lbs.)**
- **⅓ cup butter, softened**
- **¼ cup chopped onion**
- **½ tsp. garlic salt**
- **¼ tsp. pepper**

1. Cut cabbage into 8 wedges; place on a double thickness of heavy-duty foil (about 24x12 in.). Spread cut sides with butter. Sprinkle with onion, garlic salt and pepper.

2. Fold foil around cabbage and seal tightly. Grill, covered, over medium heat until tender, about 20 minutes. Open foil carefully to allow steam to escape.

1 wedge: 98 cal., 8g fat (5g sat. fat), 20mg chol., 188mg sod., 7g carb. (4g sugars, 3g fiber), 2g pro. **Diabetic exchanges:** 1½ fat, 1 vegetable.

NEW WORLD STUFFED CABBAGE

European immigrants brought their favorite stuffed cabbage recipes to the New World in the late 19th century. Here's my take on that tradition.

—Katherine Stefanovich, Desert Hot Springs, CA

PREP: 45 MIN. • BAKE: 2 HOURS • MAKES: 6 SERVINGS

- **1 medium head cabbage**
- **1 can (16 oz.) sauerkraut, divided**
- **3 bacon strips, diced**
- **1 cup finely chopped onion**
- **2 garlic cloves, minced**
- **¼ cup all-purpose flour**
- **1 Tbsp. Hungarian paprika**
- **¼ tsp. cayenne pepper**
- **1 can (16 oz.) crushed tomatoes**
- **2 cups beef broth**
- **½ cup long grain rice, cooked**
- **1 lb. ground turkey**
- **2 Tbsp. chopped fresh parsley**
- **1 tsp. salt**
- **½ tsp. pepper**
- **1 large egg, beaten**

1. Remove core from head of cabbage. Place in a large saucepan and cover with water. Bring to a boil; boil until outer leaves loosen from head. Lift out the cabbage; remove softened leaves. Return to boiling water to soften more leaves. Repeat until all leaves are removed. Remove tough center stalk from each leaf. Set aside 12 large leaves for rolls; reserve the balance to use as the recipe directs. Spoon half of the sauerkraut into a Dutch oven; set aside.

2. In a heavy saucepan, fry bacon until crisp. Remove to paper towels. In drippings, saute onion and garlic until tender. Remove half to a bowl to cool. To remaining onion mixture, add flour, paprika and cayenne pepper. Cook and stir for 1 to 2 minutes. Stir in tomatoes and broth; bring to a boil. Remove from the heat and set aside. To cooled onion mixture, add rice, turkey, parsley, salt, pepper, egg and bacon; mix well.

3. Place 3-4 Tbsp. mixture on each cabbage leaf. Roll up, tucking in sides. Place the rolls, seam side down, on sauerkraut in Dutch oven. Cover with remaining sauerkraut. Chop remaining cabbage leaves; place over sauerkraut. Pour tomato mixture over all, adding water to cover if necessary. Cover and bake at 325° for about 2 hours.

2 cabbage rolls: 352 cal., 13g fat (4g sat. fat), 90mg chol., 1508mg sod., 38g carb. (11g sugars, 9g fiber), 24g pro.

GRILLED CABBAGE

HOW-TO

Core & Chop Cabbage

- After splitting the cabbage in half, cut a "V" to remove the core. Cut the cabbage halves into wedges.
- Chop or shred as finely as you wish. Chopped cabbage holds more water and stays crunchier over time. Shredded gets softer as it sits. The choice is up to you!

HOW-TO

Ferment Cabbage

- Cut quartered cabbage into ⅛-in.-thick slices; combine with canning salt.
- Squeeze cabbage until it becomes wilted and releases liquid.
- Place the crock weight over the cabbage, submerging it in the brine.
- If using a crock, attach air lock as directed. If using a glass container, cover with a towel or a lid that isn't screwed on. It must be loose.

HOMEMADE SAUERKRAUT

51 HOMEMADE SAUERKRAUT

Put down that jar! You only need a few ingredients (and a little patience) to make fresh, flavorful sauerkraut at home. Get those brats ready!

—Josh Rink, Milwaukee, WI

PREP: 45 MIN. + STANDING • MAKES: 40 SERVINGS (ABOUT 10 CUPS)

- **6 lbs. cabbage (about 2 heads)**
- **3 Tbsp. canning salt**
- **Optional: 2 peeled and thinly sliced Granny Smith apples, 2 thinly sliced sweet onions, 2 tsp. caraway seeds and 1 tsp. ground coriander**

1. Quarter cabbages and remove cores; slice ⅛ in. thick. In an extra-large bowl, combine salt and cabbage. With clean hands, squeeze cabbage until it wilts and releases liquid, about 10 minutes. If desired, add optional ingredients.

2. Firmly pack cabbage mixture into 4-qt. fermenting crock or large glass container, removing as many air bubbles as possible. If the cabbage mixture is not covered by 1-2 in. of liquid, make enough brine to cover by 1-2 in. To make brine, combine 4½ tsp. canning salt per 1 qt. of water in a saucepan; bring to a boil until salt is dissolved. Cool brine before adding to crock.

3. Place crock weight over cabbage; the weight should be submerged in the brine. Or, place an inverted dinner plate or glass pie plate over cabbage. The plate should be slightly smaller than the container opening, but large enough to cover most of the shredded cabbage mixture. Weigh down the plate with 2 or 3 sealed quart jars filled with water. If using a glass container with a lid, cover the opening loosely so any gas produced by the fermenting cabbage can escape. Alternately, you can cover the opening with a clean, heavy towel. If using a crock, seal it according manufacturer's instructions.

4. Store crock, undisturbed, between 70° and 75° for 3-4 weeks (bubbles will form and aroma will change). Cabbage must be kept submerged below the surface of the fermenting liquid throughout fermentation. Check crock 2-3 times each week; skim and remove any scum that may form on top of liquid. Fermentation is complete when bubbling stops. Transfer to individual containers. Cover and store in the refrigerator for up to 3 months.

¼ cup: 11 cal., 0 fat (0 sat. fat), 0 chol., 344mg sod., 3g carb. (1g sugars, 1g fiber), 1g pro.

Test Kitchen Tip: A fermenting vessel is worth the investment if you plan to make sauerkraut frequently, particularly because of the included weight and the water seal features. The water seal allows gases to escape but prevents other contaminants from entering. We recommend placing the vessel in a Tupperware-style bin during the fermentation process, as the liquid can sometimes bubble over as gas is released.

KALE & BACON SALAD WITH HONEY-HORSERADISH VINAIGRETTE

This salad incorporates kale into a meal without sacrificing flavor. It is also wonderful made with collard or mustard greens.

—Elizabeth Warren, Oklahoma City, OK

PREP: 35 MIN. • MAKES: 8 SERVINGS

- **10 kale leaves, stems removed, thinly sliced**
- **¼ cup loosely packed basil leaves, thinly sliced**
- **½ cup alfalfa sprouts**
- **4 bacon strips, cooked and crumbled**
- **½ cup crumbled feta cheese**
- **½ medium ripe avocado, peeled and thinly sliced**
- **1 hard-boiled large egg, chopped**
- **1 cup grape tomatoes, chopped**

VINAIGRETTE

- **⅓ cup olive oil**
- **3 Tbsp. lemon juice**
- **2 Tbsp. prepared horseradish**
- **2 Tbsp. honey**
- **1½ tsp. garlic powder**
- **1½ tsp. spicy brown mustard**
- **¼ tsp. crushed red pepper flakes**
- **⅛ tsp. pepper**
- **Dash salt**

1. On a serving platter or individual plates, combine kale and basil. Top with sprouts, bacon, feta cheese, avocado, egg and grape tomatoes.

2. In a small bowl, whisk the vinaigrette ingredients. Drizzle over salads; serve immediately.

1 serving: 236 cal., 15g fat (3g sat. fat), 34mg chol., 248mg sod., 21g carb. (6g sugars, 4g fiber), 8g pro.

BUCATINI WITH SAUSAGE & KALE

I was short on time, but wanted to make an elegant dinner. This hearty pasta dish was the tasty outcome.

—Angela Lemoine, Howell, NJ

TAKES: 30 MIN. • MAKES: 6 SERVINGS

- **1 pkg. (12 oz.) bucatini pasta or fettuccine**
- **2 tsp. plus 3 Tbsp. olive oil, divided**
- **1 lb. regular or spicy bulk Italian sausage**
- **5 garlic cloves, thinly sliced**
- **8 cups chopped fresh kale (about 5 oz.)**
- **¾ tsp. salt**
- **¼ tsp. pepper**
- **Shredded Romano cheese**

1. Cook pasta according to package directions, decreasing time by 3 minutes. Drain, reserving 2 cups pasta water. Toss pasta with 2 tsp. oil.

2. In a 6-qt. stockpot, cook the sausage over medium heat until no longer pink, 5-7 minutes, breaking sausage into large crumbles. Add garlic and remaining oil; cook and stir 2 minutes. Stir in kale, salt and pepper; cook, covered, over medium-low heat until kale is tender, about 10 minutes, stirring occasionally.

3. Add pasta and reserved pasta water; bring to a boil. Reduce heat; simmer, uncovered, until pasta is al dente and liquid is absorbed, about 3 minutes, tossing to combine. Sprinkle with cheese.

1⅓ cups: 512 cal., 30g fat (8g sat. fat), 51mg chol., 898mg sod., 43g carb. (2g sugars, 3g fiber), 19g pro.

BUCATINI WITH SAUSAGE & KALE

HOW-TO

Trim Kale

If your kale is thin and tender, just snip off the bottom of the stems with kitchen shears. If the stems are thicker, you'll need to remove them from the leaves completely. Place each leaf on a cutting board, fold the leaf in half lengthwise and use a knife to carefully slice away the stem.

KALE CAESAR SALAD

I love Caesar salads, so I created this blend of kale and romaine lettuces with a creamy Caesar salad dressing. It's perfect paired with chicken or steak for a light weeknight meal.
—Rashanda Cobbins, Milwaukee, WI

TAKES: 15 MIN. • MAKES: 8 SERVINGS

- **4 cups chopped fresh kale**
- **4 cups torn romaine**
- **1 cup Caesar salad croutons**
- **½ cup shredded Parmesan cheese**
- **½ cup mayonnaise**
- **2 Tbsp. lemon juice**
- **1 Tbsp. Worcestershire sauce**
- **2 tsp. Dijon mustard**
- **2 tsp. anchovy paste**
- **1 garlic clove, minced**
- **¼ tsp. salt**
- **¼ tsp. pepper**

In a large salad bowl, toss kale, romaine, croutons and cheese. For the dressing, combine the remaining ingredients in a small bowl; pour over the salad and toss to coat. Serve immediately.

1 cup: 148 cal., 13g fat (3g sat. fat), 10mg chol., 417mg sod., 6g carb. (1g sugars, 1g fiber), 3g pro. **Diabetic exchanges:** 2½ fat, 1 vegetable.

SPICY SWEET POTATO KALE CANNELLINI SOUP

While I prefer heartier soups in the winter, sometimes I want a meatless alternative to the classic beef stew. This recipe is a healthy option packed with earthy sweet potatoes, apples, beans and kale. It really keeps me warm on cold days.
—Marybeth Mank, Mesquite, TX

PREP: 25 MIN. • COOK: 40 MIN. • MAKES: 12 SERVINGS (3 QT.)

- **2 Tbsp. olive oil**
- **1 medium onion, finely chopped**
- **3 garlic cloves, minced**
- **3 lbs. sweet potatoes (about 5 medium), cubed**
- **2 medium Granny Smith apples, peeled and chopped**
- **1 tsp. honey**
- **1 tsp. rubbed sage**
- **¾ to 1 tsp. crushed red pepper flakes**
- **½ tsp. salt**
- **¼ tsp. pepper**
- **3 cans (14½ oz. each) vegetable broth**
- **2 cans (15 oz. each) cannellini beans, rinsed and drained**
- **3 cups chopped fresh kale**
- **½ cup heavy whipping cream**
- **Optional toppings: Olive oil, giardiniera and shredded Parmesan cheese**

1. In a 6-qt. stockpot, heat oil over medium-high heat. Add onion; cook and stir until tender, 6-8 minutes. Add garlic; cook 1 minute longer. Stir in sweet potatoes, apples, honey, seasonings and broth. Bring to a boil. Reduce heat; simmer, covered, until potatoes are tender, 25-30 minutes.

2. Puree soup using an immersion blender, or cool soup slightly and puree in batches in a blender; return to pan. Add beans and kale; cook, uncovered, over medium heat until kale is tender, 10-15 minutes, stirring occasionally. Stir in the cream. Serve with toppings as desired.

1 cup: 250 cal., 6g fat (3g sat. fat), 14mg chol., 615mg sod., 44g carb. (16g sugars, 7g fiber), 5g pro. **Diabetic exchanges:** 3 starch, 1 lean meat, ½ fat.

SPICY SWEET POTATO
KALE CANNELLINI SOUP

FLAMBOYANT FLAMENCO
SUMMER SALAD

TOMATO-MELON CHICKEN SALAD

Nothing says summer like picking watermelon, tomatoes and raspberries, then tossing them together with fresh salad greens. The addition of grilled chicken makes it a satisfying yet still summery meal.
—Betsy Hite, Wilton, CA

TAKES: 15 MIN. • MAKES: 6 SERVINGS

- **4 medium tomatoes, cut into wedges**
- **2 cups cubed seedless watermelon**
- **1 cup fresh raspberries**
- **¼ cup minced fresh basil**
- **¼ cup olive oil**
- **2 Tbsp. balsamic vinegar**
- **¼ tsp. salt**
- **¼ tsp. pepper**
- **9 cups torn mixed salad greens**
- **4 grilled chicken breasts (4 oz. each), sliced**

In a large bowl, combine the tomatoes, watermelon and raspberries. In a small bowl, whisk the basil, oil, vinegar, salt and pepper. Drizzle over tomato mixture; toss to coat. Divide salad greens among 6 serving plates; top with tomato mixture and chicken.

1 serving: 266 cal., 13g fat (2g sat. fat), 64mg chol., 215mg sod., 15g carb. (9g sugars, 4g fiber), 26g pro. **Diabetic exchanges:** 3 lean meat, 2 vegetable, 2 fat.

FLAMBOYANT FLAMENCO SUMMER SALAD

I came up with this salad simply by choosing the best-looking vegetables at a local farmers market—the colors were so beautiful! Turn it into a full vegetarian meal by adding roasted garbanzo beans or cooked white beans.
—Crystal Schlueter, Northglenn, CO

TAKES: 25 MIN. • MAKES: 8 SERVINGS

- **3 medium rainbow carrots**
- **4 medium blood oranges, peeled and segmented**
- **½ small red onion, thinly sliced**
- **½ medium fresh beet, thinly sliced**
- **½ medium watermelon radish, thinly sliced**
- **2 radishes, thinly sliced**
- **2 Tbsp. chopped pistachios, toasted**
- **2 Tbsp. chopped oil-packed sun-dried tomatoes**
- **1 Tbsp. capers, drained**
- **¼ tsp. salt**
- **¼ tsp. pepper**
- **¼ cup white balsamic vinaigrette**
- **4 cups torn leaf lettuce**
- **¼ cup shaved Manchego or Parmesan cheese**

Using a vegetable peeler, shave carrots lengthwise into very thin slices; place in a large bowl. Add oranges, red onion, beet, radishes, pistachios, tomatoes, capers, salt and pepper. Drizzle with vinaigrette; lightly toss to coat. Arrange lettuce on a platter; top with vegetable mixture. Top with cheese.

1 cup: 103 cal., 6g fat (1g sat. fat), 4mg chol., 203mg sod., 12g carb. (8g sugars, 3g fiber), 2g pro. **Diabetic exchanges:** 1 vegetable, 1 fat, ½ fruit.

GREEN SALAD WITH TANGY BASIL VINAIGRETTE

I think a tart-tangy dressing turns basic salads into something special. This idea works for weeknight dining, but it's impressive enough for company and it pairs perfectly with just about anything.
—Kristin Rimkus, Snohomish, WA

TAKES: 15 MIN. • MAKES: 4 SERVINGS

- **3 Tbsp. white wine vinegar**
- **4½ tsp. minced fresh basil**
- **4½ tsp. olive oil**
- **1½ tsp. honey**
- **¼ tsp. salt**
- **⅛ tsp. pepper**
- **6 cups torn mixed salad greens**
- **1 cup cherry tomatoes, halved**
- **2 Tbsp. shredded Parmesan cheese**

In a small bowl, whisk the first 6 ingredients until blended. In a large bowl, combine salad greens and tomatoes. Drizzle with vinaigrette; toss to coat. Sprinkle with the cheese.

1 cup: 89 cal., 6g fat (1g sat. fat), 2mg chol., 214mg sod., 7g carb. (4g sugars, 2g fiber), 3g pro. **Diabetic exchanges:** 1 vegetable, 1 fat.

GRILLED PIZZA WITH GREENS & TOMATOES

This smoky grilled pizza scores big because it encourages my husband and son to eat greens and it showcases fresh produce.
—Sarah Gray, Erie, CO

PREP: 15 MIN. + RISING • GRILL: 10 MIN. • MAKES: 2 PIZZAS (4 SLICES EACH)

- **1½ cups all-purpose flour**
- **1½ cups whole wheat flour**
- **2 tsp. kosher salt**
- **1 tsp. active dry yeast**
- **3 Tbsp. olive oil, divided**
- **1¼ to 1½ cups warm water (120° to 130°)**

TOPPING

- **2 Tbsp. olive oil**
- **10 cups beet greens, coarsely chopped**
- **4 garlic cloves, minced**
- **2 Tbsp. balsamic vinegar**
- **¾ cup prepared pesto**
- **¾ cup shredded Italian cheese blend**
- **½ cup crumbled feta cheese**
- **2 medium heirloom tomatoes, thinly sliced**
- **¼ cup fresh basil leaves, chopped**

1. Place the flours, salt and yeast in a food processor; pulse until blended. While processing, add 2 Tbsp. oil and enough water in a steady stream until dough forms a ball. Turn dough onto a floured surface; knead until smooth and elastic, 6-8 minutes.

2. Place in a greased bowl, turning once to grease the top. Cover and let rise in a warm place until almost doubled, about 1½ hours.

3. Punch down dough. On a lightly floured surface, divide dough into 2 portions. Press or roll each portion into a 10-in. circle; place each on a piece of greased foil (about 12 in. square). Brush tops with remaining oil; cover and let rest 10 minutes.

4. For topping, in a 6-qt. stockpot, heat oil over medium-high heat. Add beet greens; cook and stir 3-5 minutes or until tender. Add garlic; cook 30 seconds longer. Remove from heat; stir in vinegar.

5. Carefully invert pizza crusts onto lightly oiled grill rack; remove foil. Grill, covered, over medium heat 3-5 minutes or until bottoms are lightly browned. Turn; grill for 1-2 minutes or until second side begins to brown.

6. Remove from grill. Spread with pesto; top with beet greens, cheeses and tomatoes. Return pizzas to grill. Cook, covered, over medium heat 2-4 minutes or until cheese is melted. Sprinkle with basil.

1 slice: 398 cal., 21g fat (5g sat. fat), 11mg chol., 1007mg sod., 42g carb. (3g sugars, 6g fiber), 12g pro.

GRILLED PIZZA
WITH GREENS & TOMATOES

VEGGIE
NICOISE SALAD

VEGGIE NICOISE SALAD

When my co-workers and I throw a potluck, we tend to focus on fresh produce. This salad combines some of our favorite ingredients in one dish—and with the hard-boiled eggs and kidney beans, it delivers enough protein to satisfy those eating healthy.

—Elizabeth Kelley, Chicago, IL

PREP: 40 MIN. • COOK: 25 MIN. • MAKES: 8 SERVINGS

- **⅓ cup olive oil**
- **¼ cup lemon juice**
- **2 tsp. minced fresh oregano**
- **2 tsp. minced fresh thyme**
- **1 tsp. Dijon mustard**
- **1 garlic clove, minced**
- **¼ tsp. coarsely ground pepper**
- **⅛ tsp. salt**
- **1 can (16 oz.) kidney beans, rinsed and drained**
- **1 small red onion, halved and thinly sliced**
- **1 lb. small red potatoes (about 9), halved**
- **1 lb. fresh asparagus, trimmed**
- **½ lb. fresh green beans, trimmed**
- **12 cups torn romaine (about 2 small bunches)**
- **6 hard-boiled large eggs, quartered**
- **1 jar (6½ oz.) marinated quartered artichoke hearts, drained**
- **½ cup Nicoise or kalamata olives**

1. For vinaigrette, whisk together the first 8 ingredients. In another bowl, toss kidney beans and onion with 1 Tbsp. vinaigrette. Set aside bean mixture and remaining vinaigrette.

2. Place potatoes in a saucepan and cover with water. Bring to a boil. Reduce heat; simmer, covered, until tender, 10-15 minutes. Drain. While potatoes are warm, toss with 1 Tbsp. vinaigrette; set aside.

3. In a pot of boiling water, cook asparagus just until crisp-tender, 2-4 minutes. Remove with tongs and immediately drop into ice water. Drain and pat dry. In same pot of boiling water, cook green beans until crisp-tender, 3-4 minutes. Remove the beans; place in ice water. Drain and pat dry.

4. To serve, toss asparagus with 1 Tbsp. vinaigrette; toss green beans with 2 tsp. vinaigrette. Toss romaine with remaining vinaigrette; place on a platter. Arrange vegetables, kidney bean mixture, eggs, artichoke hearts and olives over top.

1 serving: 329 cal., 19g fat (4g sat. fat), 140mg chol., 422mg sod., 28g carb. (6g sugars, 7g fiber), 12g pro. **Diabetic exchanges:** 3 fat, 2 vegetable, 2 medium-fat meat, 1½ starch.

"VERY VERSATILE SALAD! DEPENDING ON WHAT'S IN SEASON, YOU CAN OMIT OR ADD THE VEGGIES OF YOUR CHOICE. LOOKS LOVELY, TOO!"

—CHOC52, TASTEOFHOME.COM

COLORFUL CORNBREAD SALAD

I live in the South, and we think bacon and cornbread make everything better, even salad!

—Rebecca Clark, Warrior, AL

PREP: 45 MIN. + CHILLING • MAKES: 14 SERVINGS

- **1 pkg. (8½ oz.) cornbread/muffin mix**
- **1 cup mayonnaise**
- **½ cup sour cream**
- **1 envelope ranch salad dressing mix**
- **1 to 2 Tbsp. adobo sauce from canned chipotle peppers**
- **4 to 6 cups torn romaine**
- **4 medium tomatoes, chopped**
- **1 medium green pepper, chopped**
- **1 medium onion, chopped**
- **1 lb. bacon strips, cooked and crumbled**
- **4 cups shredded cheddar cheese**
- **Optional: Additional tomato and crumbled bacon**

1. Preheat oven to 400°. Prepare the cornbread batter according to package directions. Pour into a greased 8-in. square baking pan. Bake until a toothpick inserted in the center comes out clean, 15-20 minutes. Cool completely in pan on a wire rack.

2. Coarsely crumble cornbread into a large bowl. In a small bowl, mix mayonnaise, sour cream, salad dressing mix and adobo sauce.

3. In a 3-qt. trifle bowl or glass bowl, layer a third of the cornbread and half of each of the following: romaine, tomatoes, pepper, onion, bacon, cheese and mayonnaise mixture. Repeat layers. Top with remaining cornbread and, if desired, additional chopped tomato and bacon. Refrigerate, covered, 2-4 hours before serving.

¾ cup: 407 cal., 31g fat (11g sat. fat), 61mg chol., 821mg sod., 18g carb. (6g sugars, 2g fiber), 14g pro.

BACON AVOCADO SALAD

Everyone in my family loves this romaine salad with bacon and avocados—even the younger kids!

—Noreen McCormick Danek, Cromwell, CT

TAKES: 25 MIN. • MAKES: 10 SERVINGS

- **¾ cup extra virgin olive oil**
- **¼ cup red wine vinegar**
- **4 tsp. sugar**
- **2 garlic cloves, minced**
- **1 tsp. salt**
- **1 tsp. Dijon mustard**

SALAD

- **1 bunch romaine, chopped (about 12 cups)**
- **¾ lb. bacon strips, cooked and crumbled**
- **3 medium tomatoes, chopped**
- **1 medium red onion, halved and thinly sliced**
- **3 medium ripe avocados, peeled and cubed**
- **2 Tbsp. lemon juice**
- **1 cup crumbled Gorgonzola or feta cheese**

1. Place first 6 ingredients in a jar with a tight-fitting lid; shake well until blended. Refrigerate until serving.

2. In a large bowl, combine romaine, bacon, tomatoes and onion. Toss the avocados with lemon juice and add to salad. Sprinkle with cheese. Serve with dressing, shaking the jar to blend again if needed.

1⅓ cups: 339 cal., 31g fat (7g sat. fat), 22mg chol., 626mg sod., 10g carb. (4g sugars, 5g fiber), 9g pro.

SPINACH & BACON PIZZA

Our go-to pizza is a snap to make using packaged pizza crust and ready-to-serve bacon. The kids don't even mind the spinach on top!

—Annette Riva, Naperville, IL

TAKES: 20 MIN. • MAKES: 6 SLICES

- **1 prebaked 12-in. pizza crust**
- **⅓ cup pizza sauce**
- **1 cup shaved Parmesan cheese**
- **2 cups fresh baby spinach, thinly sliced**
- **8 ready-to-serve fully cooked bacon strips, cut into 1-in. pieces**

Preheat oven to 450°. Place crust on an ungreased baking sheet. Spread with sauce; top with ½ cup cheese, spinach and bacon. Sprinkle with the remaining cheese. Bake until the cheese is melted, 8-10 minutes.

1 slice: 269 cal., 10g fat (4g sat. fat), 10mg chol., 726mg sod., 31g carb. (2g sugars, 2g fiber), 15g pro. **Diabetic exchanges:** 2 starch, 2 medium-fat meat.

Test Kitchen Tip: Thinly sliced tomatoes, fresh mushrooms and red onion make tasty additions to this colorful pizza.

SPINACH SALAD WITH RHUBARB DRESSING

Spinach gets a makeover with this tangy topping, which really perks it up. A friend shared a similar salad dressing recipe with me and I modified it a bit. The rhubarb adds rosy color and mouthwatering flavor.

—Twila Mitchell, Lindsborg, KS

PREP: 20 MIN. + CHILLING • MAKES: 6 SERVINGS

- **2 cups chopped fresh or frozen rhubarb**
- **½ cup sugar**
- **¼ cup white vinegar**
- **¾ cup vegetable oil**
- **3 Tbsp. grated onion**
- **1½ tsp. Worcestershire sauce**
- **½ tsp. salt**

SALAD

- **6 cups torn fresh spinach**
- **6 bacon strips, cooked and crumbled**
- **½ cup bean sprouts**
- **½ cup shredded cheddar cheese**
- **1 to 2 hard-boiled large eggs, chopped**

1. In a saucepan, combine rhubarb, sugar and vinegar; cook over medium heat until the rhubarb is tender, about 6 minutes. Drain, reserving about 6 Tbsp. juice; discard pulp.

2. Pour juice into a jar with tight-fitting lid; add oil, onion, Worcestershire sauce and salt. Shake well. Refrigerate for at least 1 hour.

3. Just before serving, combine salad ingredients in a large bowl. Add the dressing and toss to coat.

1 cup: 423 cal., 35g fat (7g sat. fat), 49mg chol., 454mg sod., 21g carb. (18g sugars, 2g fiber), 8g pro.

FARMERS MARKET FIND

Like most greens, spinach doesn't keep well in the fridge if the leaves are wet or damp. Pat the greens dry with a clean towel or paper towel before storing.

SPINACH ORANGE SALAD

People always enjoy the bold flavors in this delightful salad. I think it's both delicious and beautiful.

—Zita Wilensky, North Miami Beach, FL

TAKES: 15 MIN. • MAKES: 8 SERVINGS

- **⅓ cup olive oil**
- **¼ cup orange juice**
- **3 Tbsp. vinegar**
- **1 garlic clove, minced**
- **1 tsp. minced fresh parsley**
- **¼ tsp. salt**
- **Dash pepper**
- **8 cups torn spinach or mixed greens**
- **3 medium oranges, peeled and sliced**
- **1 cup sliced red onion**
- **½ cup crumbled blue cheese**
- **¼ cup slivered almonds, toasted**

In a small bowl, whisk the first 7 ingredients. On a serving platter or individual plates, arrange greens, oranges and onion. Drizzle with dressing. Sprinkle with cheese and almonds.

1 serving: 162 cal., 13g fat (3g sat. fat), 6mg chol., 216mg sod., 8g carb. (6g sugars, 2g fiber), 4g pro.

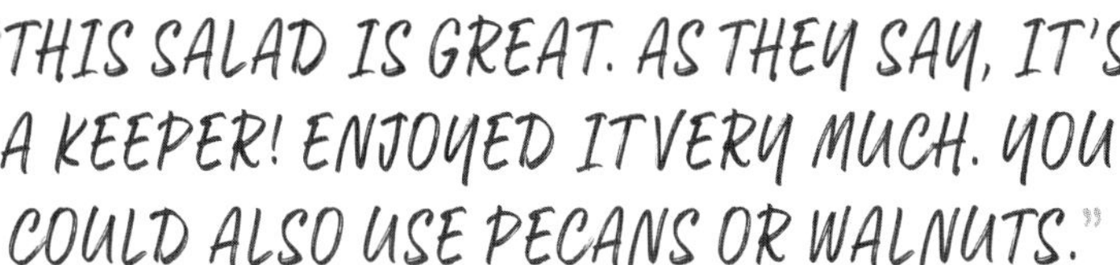

—SUSANH54, TASTEOFHOME.COM

HOW-TO

Buy Spinach

Select fresh, crisp greens with bright color. Avoid those with withered, yellow or blemished leaves or stems.

Store Spinach

Wrap greens in moist paper towels in a bag and keep in the refrigerator's crisper drawer for up to 3 days.

Prep Spinach

Wash in cool water to remove any dirt or grit that has become trapped in the leaves. Spin in a salad spinner to remove water or drain in a colander.

CHAPTER 6

BEST BERRIES

Looking to add color, flavor and bit of nutrition to your family favorites? Turn to berries! From breads and desserts to beverages and entrees, these tasty gems make everything a bit more special.

BLACKBERRY SANGRIA

My light, tasty beverage is so refreshing. I like to serve it with spoons so everyone can enjoy the fresh berries once the sangria is gone.

—Linda Cifuentes, Mahomet, IL

PREP: 10 MIN. + CHILLING • MAKES: 10 SERVINGS

1 bottle (750 ml) sparkling white wine
2½ cups white cranberry juice
⅔ cup light or coconut rum
⅓ cup each fresh blackberries, blueberries and raspberries
⅓ cup chopped fresh strawberries
Ice cubes

In a large pitcher, mix wine, juice and rum; add fruit. Refrigerate at least 2 hours; serve over ice.

¾ cup: 134 cal., 0 fat (0 sat. fat), 0 chol., 5mg sod., 12g carb. (10g sugars, 1g fiber), 0 pro.

CEDAR PLANK SALMON WITH BLACKBERRY SAUCE

Here's my favorite entree for a warm-weather cookout. The salmon has a rich grilled taste that's enhanced by the savory blackberry sauce. It's a nice balance of sweet, smoky and spicy.

—Stephanie Matthews, Tempe, AZ

PREP: 20 MIN. + SOAKING • GRILL: 15 MIN. • MAKES: 6 SERVINGS (¾ CUP SAUCE)

2 cedar grilling planks
2 cups fresh blackberries
2 Tbsp. white wine
1 Tbsp. brown sugar
1½ tsp. honey
1½ tsp. chipotle hot pepper sauce
¼ tsp. salt, divided
¼ tsp. pepper, divided
¼ cup finely chopped shallots
1 garlic clove, minced
6 salmon fillets (5 oz. each)

1. Soak grilling planks in water for at least 1 hour.

2. In a food processor, combine the blackberries, wine, brown sugar, honey, hot pepper sauce, ⅛ tsp. salt and ⅛ tsp. pepper; cover and process until blended. Strain and discard seeds. Stir shallots and garlic into the sauce; set aside.

3. Place planks on grill over medium-high heat. Cover and heat until planks create a light to medium smoke and begin to crackle, about 3 minutes (this indicates planks are ready). Turn the planks over.

4. Sprinkle salmon with remaining salt and pepper. Place on planks. Grill, covered, over medium heat for 12-15 minutes or until fish flakes easily with a fork. Serve with the sauce.

1 fillet with 2 Tbsp. sauce: 304 cal., 16g fat (3g sat. fat), 84mg chol., 186mg sod., 10g carb. (6g sugars, 3g fiber), 29g pro. **Diabetic exchanges:** 4 lean meat, ½ starch.

FARMERS MARKET FIND

Buy enough blackberries to double the sauce. You'll love it over grilled chicken and pork as well.

BLACKBERRY SANGRIA

GRANDMA'S BLACKBERRY CAKE

GRANDMA'S BLACKBERRY CAKE

A lightly seasoned spice cake lets the wonderful flavor of blackberries shine through.

—Diana Martin, Moundsville, WV

PREP: 15 MIN. • BAKE: 45 MIN. • MAKES: 9 SERVINGS

- **1 cup fresh blackberries**
- **2 cups all-purpose flour, divided**
- **½ cup butter, softened**
- **1 cup sugar**
- **2 large eggs, room temperature**
- **1 tsp. baking soda**
- **1 tsp. ground cinnamon**
- **1 tsp. ground nutmeg**
- **½ tsp. salt**
- **¼ tsp. ground cloves**
- **¼ tsp. ground allspice**
- **¾ cup buttermilk**
- **Optional: Whipped cream and confectioners' sugar**

1. Preheat oven to 350°. Toss blackberries with ¼ cup flour; set aside. In a large bowl, cream butter and sugar until light and fluffy, 5-7 minutes. Beat in eggs. Combine baking soda, cinnamon, nutmeg, salt, cloves, allspice and remaining 1¾ cups flour; add to creamed mixture alternately with buttermilk, beating well after each addition. Fold in blackberries.

2. Pour into a greased and floured 9-in. square baking pan. Bake until a toothpick inserted in center comes out clean, 45-50 minutes. Cool on a wire rack. If desired, serve with whipped cream and top with confectioners' sugar and additional fresh blackberries.

1 piece: 312 cal., 12g fat (7g sat. fat), 75mg chol., 410mg sod., 47g carb. (24g sugars, 2g fiber), 5g pro.

—NAMZIM, TASTEOFHOME.COM

HOW-TO

Freeze Fresh Berries

To freeze fresh berries and grapes, place them in a single layer on a baking sheet, and put them in the freezer until frozen (about 1½ hours). Then transfer to freezer bags. The fruit won't stick together, so you can pour out any portion you desire.

HUMBLE BUMBLE BLACKBERRY BARS

While developing a treat for my bingo group, I asked my husband for ideas. He suggested a fruity bar. This berry bar is lightly sweet and so easy.
—Nancy Phillips, Portland, ME

PREP: 30 MIN. • BAKE: 45 MIN. + COOLING • MAKES: 15 SERVINGS

- ½ cup butter, softened
- ¾ cup sugar
- 1 large egg, room temperature
- 2½ cups all-purpose flour
- ½ tsp. baking powder
- ¼ tsp. salt
- ¼ cup packed brown sugar
- 1 tsp. ground cinnamon

FILLING

- 2 cups chunky applesauce
- ½ tsp. ground cinnamon
- ⅛ tsp. ground nutmeg
- 2 cups fresh blackberries
- 2 cups fresh raspberries

1. Preheat oven to 350°. In a large bowl, cream the butter and sugar until light and fluffy, 5-7 minutes. Beat in egg. In another bowl, whisk flour, baking powder and salt; gradually beat into creamed mixture. Reserve ½ cup crumb mixture for the topping. Press remaining mixture onto bottom of a greased 13x9-in. baking pan. Bake until lightly browned, 12-15 minutes. Cool on a wire rack.

2. Stir brown sugar and cinnamon into reserved topping; set aside. In a large bowl, combine applesauce, cinnamon and nutmeg until blended. Spread over crust; top with berries and reserved topping. Bake until golden brown, 30-35 minutes. Cool in pan on a wire rack. Cut into bars.

1 piece: 228 cal., 7g fat (4g sat. fat), 29mg chol., 109mg sod., 39g carb. (20g sugars, 3g fiber), 3g pro.

MAPLE BLACKBERRY MOJITO

This refreshing cocktail takes advantage of prime berry season during the summer months. I've also used other types of fruit, including raspberries, kiwi and strawberries.
—Donna Noel, Gray, ME

TAKES: 10 MIN. • MAKES: 1 SERVING

- 4 fresh or frozen blackberries, thawed
- 5 fresh mint leaves
- 1 Tbsp. maple syrup
- 1 lime wedge
- ¼ cup club soda, chilled
- 1½ oz. light rum
- ½ to ¾ cup ice cubes

In a glass, muddle the blackberries and mint with maple syrup. Squeeze lime wedge into the glass. Stir in club soda and rum. Strain into a chilled glass; serve with ice.

½ cup: 160 cal., 0 fat (0 sat. fat), 0 chol., 18mg sod., 16g carb. (13g sugars, 1g fiber), 0 pro.

Test Kitchen Tip: To muddle, place the ingredients in the glass per the recipe. With a muddler, gently crush and bruise the ingredients until their aromas are released. An ice cream scoop is a good stand-in if you don't have a muddler.

HUMBLE BUMBLE
BLACKBERRY BARS

HOW-TO

Buy Blackberries

Select berries that are plump; avoid those that are bruised, mushy or moldy. Avoid packages with juice-stained bottoms.

Store Blackberries

Blackberries are highly perishable and fragile. Store unwashed berries in their container for 1-2 days or freeze washed and drained blackberries in a freezer container up to 1 year.

Prep Blackberries

Gently wash berries before using. Eat them on their own or follow a recipe's directions for slicing, chopping or even pureeing.

GRILLED HALIBUT WITH BLUEBERRY SALSA

GRILLED HALIBUT WITH BLUEBERRY SALSA

Give halibut a new, summery spin with blueberries. The salsa may seem sophisticated, but it's really a cinch to prepare.
—Donna Goutermont, Sequim, WA

TAKES: 30 MIN. • MAKES: 6 SERVINGS

- **2 cups fresh blueberries, divided**
- **1 small red onion, chopped**
- **¼ cup minced fresh cilantro**
- **1 jalapeno pepper, seeded and chopped**
- **2 Tbsp. orange juice**
- **1 Tbsp. balsamic vinegar**
- **1 tsp. plus 2 Tbsp. olive oil, divided**
- **⅛ tsp. plus 1 tsp. salt, divided**
- **⅛ tsp. pepper**
- **6 halibut fillets (5 oz. each)**

1. In a small bowl, coarsely mash 1 cup blueberries. Stir in the onion, cilantro, jalapeno, orange juice, vinegar, 1 tsp. oil, ⅛ tsp. salt, pepper and remaining blueberries. Cover and chill until serving.

2. Meanwhile, drizzle fillets with remaining oil; sprinkle with remaining salt. Grill halibut, covered, over medium heat for 4-5 minutes on each side or until fish flakes easily with a fork. Serve with salsa.

1 fillet with ⅓ cup salsa: 239 cal., 9g fat (1g sat. fat), 45mg chol., 521mg sod., 9g carb. (6g sugars, 1g fiber), 30g pro. **Diabetic exchanges:** 4 lean meat, 1 fat, ½ starch.

SKILLET BLUEBERRY SLUMP

My mother-in-law made a slump of wild blueberries with dumplings and served it warm with a pitcher of farm cream. We've been eating slump this way for nearly 60 years!
—Eleanore Ebeling, Brewster, MN

PREP: 25 MIN. • BAKE: 20 MIN. • MAKES: 6 SERVINGS

- **4 cups fresh or frozen blueberries**
- **½ cup sugar**
- **½ cup water**
- **1 tsp. grated lemon zest**
- **1 Tbsp. lemon juice**
- **1 cup all-purpose flour**
- **2 Tbsp. sugar**
- **2 tsp. baking powder**
- **½ tsp. salt**
- **1 Tbsp. butter**
- **½ cup 2% milk**
- **Vanilla ice cream**

1. Preheat oven to 400°. In a 10-in. ovenproof skillet, combine the first 5 ingredients; bring to a boil. Reduce heat; simmer, uncovered, 9-11 minutes or until slightly thickened, stirring occasionally.

2. Meanwhile, in a small bowl, whisk flour, sugar, baking powder and salt. Cut in butter until mixture resembles coarse crumbs. Slowly add the milk; stir just until moistened.

3. Drop batter in 6 portions on top of the simmering blueberry mixture. Transfer to oven. Bake, uncovered, 17-20 minutes or until dumplings are golden brown. Serve warm with ice cream.

1 serving: 239 cal., 3g fat (2g sat. fat), 7mg chol., 355mg sod., 52g carb. (32g sugars, 3g fiber), 4g pro.

BUTTERMILK BLUEBERRY PANCAKES

Here's the classic blueberry pancake—light as a feather, bursting with flavor and ready in no time!

—Ann Moran, Islesford, ME

TAKES: 30 MIN. • MAKES: 12 PANCAKES

- **2 cups all-purpose flour**
- **1 Tbsp. sugar**
- **½ tsp. baking soda**
- **¼ tsp. salt**
- **⅛ tsp. baking powder**
- **2 cups buttermilk**
- **2 large eggs, room temperature, lightly beaten**
- **1 Tbsp. canola oil**
- **1 cup fresh or frozen blueberries**
- **Optional: Butter and maple syrup**

1. In a large bowl, whisk flour, sugar, baking soda, salt and baking powder. In another bowl, whisk buttermilk, eggs and oil. Stir into the dry ingredients just until moistened.

2. Pour batter by ¼ cupfuls onto a greased hot griddle. Sprinkle 1 Tbsp. blueberries on each pancake. Turn when bubbles form on top. Cook until the second side is golden brown. If desired, serve with butter and syrup and top with additional blueberries.

2 pancakes: 250 cal., 5g fat (1g sat. fat), 74mg chol., 322mg sod., 41g carb. (9g sugars, 2g fiber), 9g pro.

BLUEBERRY, BASIL & GOAT CHEESE PIE

To send off a friend who was moving, I made a galette of blueberries, creamy goat cheese and fresh basil. Bake one, share it and make a precious memory of your own.

—Ashley Lecker, Green Bay, WI

PREP: 15 MIN. • BAKE: 40 MIN. • MAKES: 6 SERVINGS

- **Pastry for single-crust pie**
- **2 cups fresh blueberries**
- **2 Tbsp. plus 2 tsp. sugar, divided**
- **1 Tbsp. cornstarch**
- **1 Tbsp. minced fresh basil**
- **1 large egg**
- **1 tsp. water**
- **¼ cup crumbled goat cheese**
- **Fresh basil leaves, torn**

1. Preheat oven to 375°. On a floured sheet of parchment, roll dough into a 10-in. circle. Transfer to a baking sheet.

2. Mix blueberries, 2 Tbsp. sugar, cornstarch and basil. Spoon blueberry mixture over pastry to within 2 in. of edge. Fold pastry edge over filling, pleating as you go and leaving the center uncovered.

3. Whisk egg and water; brush over pastry. Sprinkle with the remaining sugar. Bake 30 minutes. Sprinkle with the goat cheese; bake until crust is golden and filling is bubbly, about 10 minutes longer. Transfer to a wire rack to cool. Top with torn basil leaves before serving.

1 piece: 308 cal., 18g fat (11g sat. fat), 77mg chol., 241mg sod., 34g carb. (11g sugars, 2g fiber), 5g pro.

Pastry for single-crust pie (9 in.): Combine 1¼ cups all-purpose flour and ¼ tsp. salt; cut in ½ cup cold butter until crumbly. Gradually add 3-5 Tbsp. ice water, tossing with a fork until dough holds together when pressed. Wrap and refrigerate 1 hour.

BUTTERMILK BLUEBERRY PANCAKES

BLUEBERRY ZUCCHINI SQUARES

I saw a bar recipe using apple and lemon zest on a muffin mix box. I tried it from scratch with fresh blueberries and shredded zucchini instead. It's a nifty combo.
—Shelly Bevington, Hermiston, OR

PREP: 30 MIN. • BAKE: 30 MIN. + COOLING • MAKES: 2 DOZEN

- **2 cups shredded zucchini (do not pack)**
- **½ cup buttermilk**
- **1 Tbsp. grated lemon zest**
- **3 Tbsp. lemon juice**
- **1 cup butter, softened**
- **2½ cups sugar**
- **2 large eggs, room temperature**
- **3¼ cups plus 2 Tbsp. all-purpose flour, divided**
- **1 tsp. baking soda**
- **½ tsp. salt**
- **2 cups fresh or frozen blueberries**

GLAZE

- **2 cups confectioners' sugar**
- **¼ cup buttermilk**
- **1 Tbsp. grated lemon zest**
- **2 tsp. lemon juice**
- **⅛ tsp. salt**

1. Preheat oven to 350°. Grease a 15x10x1-in. baking pan.

2. In a small bowl, combine zucchini, buttermilk, lemon zest and lemon juice; toss to combine. In a large bowl, cream the butter and sugar until light and fluffy, 5-7 minutes. Beat in eggs, 1 at a time. In another bowl, whisk 3¼ cups flour, baking soda and salt; gradually add to creamed mixture alternately with zucchini mixture, mixing well after each addition. Toss blueberries with remaining flour; fold into batter.

3. Transfer batter to prepared pan, spreading evenly (pan will be full). Bake 30-35 minutes or until light golden brown and a toothpick inserted in center comes out clean. Cool completely in pan on a wire rack.

4. In a small bowl, mix glaze ingredients until smooth; spread over top. Let stand until set.

1 piece: 270 cal., 8g fat (5g sat. fat), 36mg chol., 197mg sod., 47g carb. (33g sugars, 1g fiber), 3g pro.

GRILLED CHICKEN SALAD WITH BLUEBERRY VINAIGRETTE

We love adding grilled chicken to our salads in the summer, but the real star here is the vinaigrette made with blueberry preserves and maple syrup. This salad is perfect with a fresh baguette and a frosty glass of minted lemonade.

—Susan Gauthier, Falmouth, ME

PREP: 20 MIN. + MARINATING • GRILL: 10 MIN. • MAKES: 4 SERVINGS

- **2 boneless skinless chicken breast halves (6 oz. each)**
- **1 Tbsp. olive oil**
- **1 garlic clove, minced**
- **¼ tsp. salt**
- **¼ tsp. pepper**

VINAIGRETTE

- **¼ cup olive oil**
- **¼ cup blueberry preserves**
- **2 Tbsp. balsamic vinegar**
- **2 Tbsp. maple syrup**
- **¼ tsp. ground mustard**
- **⅛ tsp. salt**
- **Dash pepper**

SALADS

- **1 pkg. (10 oz.) ready-to-serve salad greens**
- **1 cup fresh blueberries**
- **½ cup canned mandarin oranges**
- **1 cup crumbled goat cheese**

1. Toss the chicken with oil, garlic, salt and pepper; refrigerate, covered, 30 minutes. In a small bowl, whisk together vinaigrette ingredients; refrigerate, covered, until serving.

2. Grill chicken, covered, over medium heat until a thermometer reads 165°, 5-7 minutes per side. Let stand 5 minutes before slicing.

3. Place greens on a serving plate; top with chicken, blueberries and mandarin oranges. Whisk vinaigrette again; drizzle over salad. Top with cheese.

1 serving: 455 cal., 26g fat (7g sat. fat), 82mg chol., 460mg sod., 36g carb. (27g sugars, 4g fiber), 24g pro.

HOW-TO

Buy Blueberries

Look for plump berries with a deep blue hue. Avoid blueberries that are discolored.

Store Blueberries

Once you get a carton home, sift through to ensure there aren't any spoiled or moldy blueberries. If there are, remove them from the carton so they don't spoil the intact berries. Store unwashed in the carton in the fridge for up to 10 days.

Prep Blueberries

Remove any stems from blueberries, and wash berries under cool running water before eating or using as directed in recipe.

WHITE BALSAMIC BLUEBERRY, CORN & FETA SALAD

I'm not typically a huge fan of summer corn, but when it comes to this sweet, salty, refreshing salad, I can't put my fork down. I find that grilling the corn inside of the husk makes it easier to remove all the corn silk from each cob.
—Colleen Delawder, Herndon, VA

PREP: 30 MIN. + SOAKING • GRILL: 20 MIN. • MAKES: 10 SERVINGS

- **8 medium ears sweet corn**
- **3 Tbsp. olive oil**
- **3 Tbsp. white balsamic vinegar**
- **1 Tbsp. minced fresh chives, plus more for garnish**
- **¾ tsp. kosher salt**
- **¼ tsp. pepper**
- **1 cup fresh blueberries**
- **½ cup crumbled feta cheese**

1. Carefully peel back corn husks to within 1 in. of bottoms; remove silk. Rewrap corn in husks; secure with kitchen string. Place in a stockpot; cover with cold water. Soak 20 minutes; drain.

2. Grill corn, covered, over medium heat about 20 minutes or until tender, turning often. Cut string and peel back husks. Cool slightly. Cut corn from cobs; transfer to a large bowl.

3. In a small bowl, whisk the oil, vinegar, chives, salt and pepper. Pour over corn; toss to coat. Gently fold in the blueberries and feta. Garnish with additional chives as desired.

¾ cup: 133 cal., 6g fat (1g sat. fat), 3mg chol., 210mg sod., 19g carb. (8g sugars, 2g fiber), 4g pro. **Diabetic exchanges:** 1 starch, 1 fat.

Test Kitchen Tip: If you don't have white balsamic vinegar, you can use traditional balsamic vinegar instead, but the corn and feta will take on a darker color.

MAPLE BLUEBERRY CRISP

With sweet blueberries and a tender crumb topping, this yummy crisp makes a wonderful treat following a brunch or evening meal. Sometimes I top servings with a scoop of vanilla ice cream.
—Mona Wright, Villa Rica, GA

PREP: 15 MIN. • BAKE: 35 MIN. • MAKES: 9 SERVINGS

- **4 cups fresh or frozen blueberries**
- **½ cup maple syrup**
- **2 Tbsp. cornstarch**
- **1 tsp. ground cinnamon**
- **1¼ cups all-purpose flour**
- **¾ cup packed brown sugar**
- **½ cup cold butter**
- **1 tsp. almond extract**
- **Vanilla ice cream, optional**

1. Preheat oven to 375°. In a large bowl, combine blueberries, syrup, cornstarch and cinnamon. Transfer to a greased 8-in square baking dish. In a small bowl, combine flour and brown sugar. Cut in butter until mixture resembles coarse crumbs; stir in extract. Sprinkle over top.

2. Bake until filling is bubbly and topping is golden brown, 35-40 minutes. If desired, serve with ice cream.

1 serving: 315 cal., 11g fat (6g sat. fat), 27mg chol., 82mg sod., 54g carb. (35g sugars, 2g fiber), 2g pro.

WHITE BALSAMIC BLUEBERRY,
CORN & FETA SALAD

"THIS COMBINATION OF SWEET, SALTY, CRUNCHY AND TENDER WORKS BEAUTIFULLY."

—ALLISONO, TASTEOFHOME.COM

CRANBERRY PUMPKIN BREAD

CRANBERRY PUMPKIN BREAD

Use up leftover cranberries and pumpkin deliciously in this moist quick bread. It's very good with the turkey casserole I make the day after Thanksgiving.

—Dixie Terry, Goreville, IL

PREP: 20 MIN. • BAKE: 70 MIN. + COOLING • MAKES: 2 LOAVES (16 SLICES EACH)

- **3¾ cups all-purpose flour**
- **3 cups sugar**
- **4 tsp. pumpkin pie spice**
- **2 tsp. baking soda**
- **1 tsp. salt**
- **4 large eggs, room temperature**
- **1 can (15 oz.) solid-pack pumpkin**
- **½ cup canola oil**
- **2 cups fresh or frozen cranberries, thawed**
- **1 cup chopped walnuts**

1. In a large bowl, combine the flour, sugar, pumpkin pie spice, baking soda and salt. In another bowl, whisk the eggs, pumpkin and oil; stir into dry ingredients just until moistened. Fold in cranberries and walnuts.

2. Spoon into 2 greased 9x5-in. loaf pans. Bake at 350° for 70-80 minutes or until a toothpick inserted in the center comes out clean. Cool 10 minutes before removing from pans to wire racks to cool completely.

1 slice: 197 cal., 6g fat (1g sat. fat), 27mg chol., 162mg sod., 32g carb. (19g sugars, 1g fiber), 4g pro.

CRANBERRY BOG BARS

Sweet and chewy, these fun bars combine the flavors of oats, cranberries, brown sugar and pecans. I like to sprinkle the squares with confectioners' sugar before serving.

—Sally Wakefield, Gans, PA

PREP: 25 MIN. • BAKE: 25 MIN. • MAKES: 2 DOZEN

- **1¼ cups butter, softened, divided**
- **1½ cups packed brown sugar, divided**
- **3½ cups old-fashioned oats, divided**
- **1 cup all-purpose flour**
- **1 can (14 oz.) whole-berry cranberry sauce**
- **½ cup finely chopped pecans**

1. In a large bowl, cream 1 cup butter and 1 cup brown sugar until light and fluffy, 5-7 minutes. Combine 2½ cups oats and flour. Gradually add to the creamed mixture until crumbly. Press into a greased 13x9-in. baking pan. Spread with cranberry sauce.

2. In a microwave-safe bowl, melt the remaining butter; stir in pecans and the remaining brown sugar and oats. Sprinkle over cranberry sauce. Bake at 375° until lightly browned, 25-30 minutes. Cool on a wire rack. Cut into bars.

1 bar: 239 cal., 12g fat (6g sat. fat), 25mg chol., 88mg sod., 32g carb. (18g sugars, 2g fiber), 2g pro.

BAKED CRANBERRY PUDDING

This old-fashioned pudding is a cranberry lover's delight. Serve warm topped with whipped cream for an elegant look, or in bowls with rich cream poured over for a homey touch.

—Lucy Meyring, Walden, Colorado

TAKES: 20 MIN. + STANDING • BAKE: 55 MIN. + COOLING MAKES: 10 SERVINGS.

- 2 large eggs, separated
- 1 cup packed brown sugar
- ½ cup heavy whipping cream
- ¼ cup butter, melted
- 2 teaspoons vanilla extract
- 1-½ cups all-purpose flour
- 3 tablespoons grated orange zest
- 1 teaspoon baking powder
- 1 teaspoon ground cinnamon
- ½ teaspoon ground nutmeg
- ½ teaspoon cream of tartar, divided
- ⅛ teaspoon salt
- 3 cups coarsely chopped cranberries

TOPPING:

- 1-½ cups sugar
- ½ cup orange juice
- 2-½ cups whole cranberries
- Optional: Orange zest strips and whipped cream

1. Place egg whites in a large bowl; let stand at room temperature for 30 minutes. Preheat oven to 350°.

2. In a large bowl, beat brown sugar, cream, melted butter, vanilla and egg yolks until well blended. In another bowl, whisk flour, orange zest, baking powder, cinnamon, nutmeg, ¼ tsp. cream of tartar and salt. Add chopped cranberries; toss to coat. Gradually add to sugar mixture, mixing well. (Batter will be stiff.)

3. Add remaining cream of tartar to egg whites; with clean beaters, beat on medium speed until soft peaks form. Fold into batter. Transfer to a greased 9-in. springform pan. Bake until a toothpick inserted in center comes out clean, 45-50 minutes.

4. Meanwhile, for topping, combine sugar and orange juice in a small saucepan. Bring to a boil, stirring frequently; cook until sugar is dissolved, 2-3 minutes. Add cranberries; return to a boil. Reduce heat; simmer, uncovered, until berries pop, stirring occasionally, 6-8 minutes. Remove from heat; cover and keep warm.

5. When pudding tests done, place springform pan in a 15x10x1-in. baking pan. Spoon cranberry mixture over top. Bake 10 minutes longer.

6. Cool pudding on a wire rack 10 minutes. Loosen sides from pan with a knife; remove rim from pan. Cool at least 1 hour before serving.

7. If made ahead, pudding can be warmed in a 350° oven for 10 minutes. If desired, top with orange zest and serve with whipped cream.

1 slice: 402 calories, 10g fat (6g saturated fat), 71mg cholesterol, 143mg sodium, 75g carbohydrate (57g sugars, 3g fiber), 4g protein.

APRICOT-APPLE CRANBERRY SAUCE

APRICOT-APPLE CRANBERRY SAUCE

Though I prefer this as a side dish, my sister swears it makes the best topping in the world for a slice of Thanksgiving turkey.

—Aysha Schurman, Ammon, Idaho

PREP: 15 MIN. • **COOK:** 15 MIN. + CHILLING • **MAKES:** 20 SERVINGS

- **4 cups fresh or frozen cranberries**
- **1⅔ cups sugar**
- **1⅔ cups water**
- **¾ cup orange juice**
- **¼ cup chopped dried apricots**
- **¼ cup chopped dried apples**
- **¼ cup dried cranberries**
- **1 tsp. grated lemon zest**
- **1 tsp. grated orange zest**

In a large saucepan, combine the first 7 ingredients. Cook over medium heat until berries pop, about 15 minutes. Remove from the heat; stir in lemon and orange zests. Transfer to a bowl; refrigerate until chilled.

¼ cup: 91 cal., 0 fat (0 sat.fat), 0 chol., 3mg sod., 24g carb., (21g sugars, 1g fiber), 0 pro.

❄ TANGY CRANBERRY CHICKEN

My husband loves chicken when it's nice and moist, as in this recipe. I serve it over hot rice with a salad and warm rolls. The ruby red sauce has a wonderful sweet-tart flavor.

—Dorothy Bateman, Carver, MA

PREP: 20 MIN. • **COOK:** 20 MIN. **MAKES:** 6 SERVINGS

- **½ cup all-purpose flour**
- **½ tsp. salt**
- **¼ tsp. pepper**
- **6 boneless skinless chicken breast halves (4 oz. each)**
- **3 Tbsp. butter**
- **1 cup water**
- **1 cup fresh or frozen cranberries**
- **½ cup packed brown sugar**
- **Dash ground nutmeg**
- **1 Tbsp. red wine vinegar, optional**
- **Hot cooked rice**

1. In a shallow dish, combine flour, salt and pepper; dredge chicken in the flour mixture. In a skillet, melt butter over medium heat. Brown the chicken on both sides. Remove and keep warm.

2. Add water, cranberries, brown sugar, nutmeg and, if desired, vinegar to the pan; cook and stir until the berries burst, about 5 minutes. Return the chicken to skillet. Cover and simmer 20-30 minutes or until the chicken is tender, basting occasionally with the sauce. Serve with hot cooked rice.

Freeze option: Place the chicken in freezer containers; top with sauce. If desired, place rice in separate freezer containers. Cool and freeze. To use, partially thaw in refrigerator overnight. Microwave, covered, on high in a microwave-safe dish until heated through, gently stirring; add water to chicken if necessary.

1 serving: 284 cal., 9g fat (1g sat. fat), 73mg chol., 122mg sod., 22g carb. (0 sugars, 0 fiber), 28g pro.

RHUBARB ELDERBERRY CRISP

Rhubarb and elderberries are quite abundant around these parts, so I combined the two in this wonderful crisp. It's been well received by friends.

—Carolyn Scouten, Wyalusing, PA

PREP: 20 MIN. • **BAKE:** 50 MIN. • **MAKES:** 10 SERVINGS

- **1 cup all-purpose flour**
- **¾ cup quick-cooking oats**
- **1½ cups sugar, divided**
- **1 tsp. ground cinnamon**
- **½ cup cold butter**
- **3 cups diced fresh rhubarb or frozen rhubarb**
- **2 cups elderberries or blackberries**
- **2 Tbsp. cornstarch**
- **1 cup water**
- **1 tsp. vanilla extract**

1. In a large bowl, combine the flour, oats, ½ cup sugar and cinnamon; cut in butter until mixture resembles coarse crumbs. Set aside half for topping.

2. Press remaining crumb mixture into an ungreased 11x7-in. baking dish. Top with rhubarb and berries.

3. In a small saucepan, combine cornstarch and remaining sugar. Gradually stir in water; bring to a boil. Reduce the heat; cook and stir until thickened, 1-2 minutes. Remove from the heat; stir in vanilla.

4. Pour over the fruit. Sprinkle with the reserved crumb mixture. Bake at 350° for 50-55 minutes or until golden brown. Serve warm or cold.

¾ cup: 302 cal., 10g fat (6g sat. fat), 25mg chol., 97mg sod., 52g carb. (34g sugars, 4g fiber), 3g pro.

ELDERBERRY PIE WITH CRUMB TOPPING

This pie has a wide appeal since it uses different types of berries.

—Jan Meinke, Parma, OH

PREP: 15 MIN. + STANDING • **BAKE:** 45 MIN. • **MAKES:** 8 SERVINGS

- **1½ cups fresh or frozen blueberries**
- **1½ cups fresh or frozen blackberries**
- **1½ cups fresh or frozen elderberries or raspberries**
- **1 Tbsp. lemon juice**
- **1 cup sugar**
- **4 Tbsp. quick-cooking tapioca**
- **1 unbaked pastry shell (9 in.)**

TOPPING

- **¾ cup all-purpose flour**
- **½ cup sugar**
- **⅓ cup butter**

1. In a large bowl, sprinkle berries with lemon juice. Combine sugar and tapioca. Add to berries; toss gently to coat. Let stand for 15 minutes. Spoon into pastry shell.

2. For topping, combine flour and sugar in a small bowl. Cut in butter until crumbly. Sprinkle over filling. Bake at 400° for 45 minutes or until filling is bubbly and topping is browned. Cool on a wire rack.

1 piece: 445 cal., 15g fat (8g sat. fat), 25mg chol., 180mg sod., 77g carb. (45g sugars, 4g fiber), 3g pro.

RASPBERRY-WALNUT PORK SALAD

Raspberry, rosemary, Gorgonzola and walnuts combine to make a pork dish that's bursting with flavor. Use homemade preserves for extra flair.

—Virginia Anthony, Jacksonville, FL

PREP: 30 MIN. • COOK: 20 MIN. • MAKES: 6 SERVINGS

- **1½ lbs. pork tenderloins, cut into 1-in. slices**
- **⅓ cup ground walnuts**
- **2 Tbsp. all-purpose flour**
- **½ tsp. salt, divided**
- **½ tsp. coarsely ground pepper, divided**
- **4½ tsp. walnut oil**
- **⅓ cup chopped shallot**
- **1 medium pear, chopped**
- **¾ cup reduced-sodium chicken broth**
- **¾ cup seedless raspberry preserves**
- **½ cup raspberry vinegar**
- **2 tsp. minced fresh rosemary or ½ tsp. dried rosemary, crushed**
- **2 tsp. minced fresh sage**
- **2 pkg. (6 oz. each) fresh baby spinach**
- **½ cup crumbled Gorgonzola cheese**
- **½ cup chopped walnuts, toasted**

1. Flatten pork slices to ½-in. thickness. In a shallow dish, combine the ground walnuts, flour, ¼ tsp. salt and ¼ tsp. pepper. Add pork, a few pieces at a time, and turn to coat.

2. In a large skillet over medium heat, cook pork in oil in batches for 2-3 minutes on each side or until meat is no longer pink. Remove and keep warm.

3. In the same skillet, saute shallot until tender. Add pear; cook 1 minute longer. Add the broth, preserves and vinegar. Bring to a boil; cook for 6-8 minutes or until slightly thickened. Stir in the rosemary, sage and remaining salt and pepper. Remove from the heat.

4. Place spinach in a large bowl. Add pear mixture; toss to coat. Divide among 6 plates; top each with pork. Sprinkle with cheese and chopped walnuts.

1 serving: 398 cal., 17g fat (4g sat. fat), 71mg chol., 415mg sod., 34g carb. (25g sugars, 2g fiber), 30g pro.

HOW-TO

Buy Raspberries

Since raspberries stop ripening once they are picked, you should plan to buy them a few days before eating or using them. Choose raspberries that are plump with even coloring.

Store Raspberries

Keep raspberries in a container that provides air circulation, and place them in the front of the refrigerator, where it isn't its coldest. Don't put them in the crisper bin—the moisture they create will speed up spoilage. Do not wash raspberries until ready to use them.

Prep Raspberries

Gently but thoroughly wash raspberries under cold running water.

RASPBERRY BLINTZES

RASPBERRY BLINTZES

My mother is a wonderful cook who always likes to prepare (and improve on!) dishes she's sampled at restaurants. That's what I did with these blintzes, and my family loves my fruity version even more than the original.

—Patricia Larsen, Thayne, WY

PREP: 25 MIN. • COOK: 15 MIN. • MAKES: 8 SERVINGS

BLINTZES

- **9 large eggs, room temperature**
- **1 cup all-purpose flour**
- **¼ cup cornstarch**
- **⅛ tsp. salt**
- **3 cups 2% milk**

FILLING

- **2 pkg. (8 oz. each) cream cheese, softened**
- **½ cup confectioners' sugar**
- **Pureed raspberries or strawberries**
- **Optional: Whipped cream and fresh raspberries or strawberries**

1. In a large bowl, beat the eggs. Add the flour, cornstarch and salt; stir until smooth. Stir in milk.

2. Heat a lightly greased 8-in. nonstick skillet; pour ⅓ cup batter into the center of skillet. Lift and tilt pan to evenly coat bottom. Cook until top appears dry; turn and cook 15-20 seconds longer. Keep in a warm oven, covered with foil. Repeat with remaining batter.

3. For filling, in a small bowl, beat cream cheese and confectioners' sugar until smooth. Place about 2 Tbsp. in the center of each blintz; overlap sides and ends on top of filling. Place folded side down. Serve with pureed berries; garnish with whipped cream and fresh berries if desired.

2 blintzes: 340 cal., 19g fat (10g sat. fat), 283mg chol., 237mg sod., 29g carb. (13g sugars, 0 fiber), 14g pro.

5i SWEET RASPBERRY TEA

You only need a handful of ingredients to stir together this bright and refreshing sipper as the weather heats up.

—Taste of Home *Test Kitchen*

PREP: 10 MIN. • COOK: 15 MIN. + CHILLING • MAKES: 15 SERVINGS (3¾ QT.)

- **4 qt. water, divided**
- **10 tea bags**
- **1 pkg. (12 oz.) frozen unsweetened raspberries, thawed and undrained**
- **1 cup sugar**
- **3 Tbsp. lime juice**

1. In a saucepan, bring 2 qt. water to a boil; remove from heat. Add tea bags; steep, covered, 5-8 minutes according to taste. Discard tea bags.

2. Place raspberries, sugar and remaining water in a large saucepan; bring to a boil, stirring to dissolve sugar. Reduce heat; simmer, uncovered, 3 minutes. Press mixture through a fine-mesh strainer into a bowl; discard pulp and seeds.

3. In a large pitcher, combine tea, raspberry syrup and lime juice. Refrigerate, covered, until cold.

1 cup: 63 cal., 0 fat (0 sat. fat), 0 chol., 0 sod., 16g carb. (15g sugars, 1g fiber), 0 pro.

RUBY RASPBERRY SLAW

Give ordinary coleslaw a "berry" tangy twist with this dish that's sure to get raves at your next picnic or potluck.

—Deborah Biggs, Omaha, NE

PREP: 15 MIN. + CHILLING • MAKES: 6 SERVINGS

- **2 cups shredded red cabbage**
- **2 cups shredded cabbage**
- **1 cup shredded carrots**
- **¼ cup prepared raspberry vinaigrette**
- **3 Tbsp. mayonnaise**
- **¼ tsp. pepper**
- **½ cup fresh raspberries**

In a large bowl, combine the cabbage and carrots. In a small bowl, whisk the vinaigrette, mayonnaise and pepper until blended. Add to cabbage mixture; toss to coat. Refrigerate, covered, 10 minutes. Top with raspberries.

¾ cup: 122 cal., 11g fat (1g sat. fat), 3mg chol., 144mg sod., 6g carb. (2g sugars, 2g fiber), 1g pro. **Diabetic exchanges:** 2 fat, 1 vegetable.

LEMON WHIRLIGIGS WITH RASPBERRIES

Golden homemade whirligigs with a tart lemon flavor float on a ruby raspberry sauce in this delectable dessert. I love serving it to guests. My children also like it made with blackberries.

—Vicki Ayres, Wappingers Falls, NY

PREP: 35 MIN. • BAKE: 25 MIN. • MAKES: 10 SERVINGS

- **⅔ cup sugar**
- **2 Tbsp. cornstarch**
- **¼ tsp. ground cinnamon**
- **⅛ tsp. ground nutmeg**
- **⅛ tsp. salt**
- **1 cup water**
- **3 cups fresh raspberries**

WHIRLIGIGS

- **1 cup all-purpose flour**
- **2 tsp. baking powder**
- **½ tsp. salt**
- **3 Tbsp. shortening**
- **1 large egg, room temperature, lightly beaten**
- **2 Tbsp. half-and-half cream**
- **¼ cup sugar**
- **2 Tbsp. butter, melted**
- **1 tsp. grated lemon zest**
- **Optional: Heavy whipping cream and additional raspberries**

1. In a small saucepan, combine the sugar, cornstarch, cinnamon, nutmeg and salt. Stir in the water until smooth. Bring to a boil; cook and stir for 2 minutes or until thickened.

2. Place raspberries in an ungreased 1½-qt. shallow baking dish; pour hot sauce over top. Bake, uncovered, at 400° for 10 minutes. Remove from the oven; set aside.

3. For whirligigs, combine the flour, baking powder and salt in a small bowl. Cut in shortening until crumbly. Combine egg and half-and-half; stir into crumb mixture to form a stiff dough.

4. Shape into a ball. On a lightly floured surface. roll out into a 12x6-in. rectangle. In a small bowl, combine the sugar, butter and lemon zest; spread over dough to within ½ in. of edges. Roll up, jelly roll style, starting with a long side. Cut into 10 slices; pat each slice slightly to flatten. Place on berry mixture.

5. Bake, uncovered, at 400° for 15 minutes or until whirligigs are golden. Garnish servings with cream and raspberries if desired.

1 serving: 206 cal., 7g fat (3g sat. fat), 29mg chol., 259mg sod., 34g carb. (20g sugars, 3g fiber), 2g pro.

RASPBERRY
FRUIT SALAD

RASPBERRY FRUIT SALAD

Though fresh fruit steals the show in this morning medley, the subtle honey sauce makes it an especially sweet treat. It takes just 10 minutes to assemble the easy, brunch-perfect salad.

—Dorothy Dinnean, Harrison, AR

TAKES: 10 MIN. • **MAKES:** 8 SERVINGS

- **2 medium firm bananas, chopped**
- **2 cups fresh blueberries**
- **2 cups fresh raspberries**
- **2 cups sliced fresh strawberries**
- **5 Tbsp. honey**
- **1 tsp. lemon juice**
- **¾ tsp. poppy seeds**

In a large bowl, combine the bananas and berries. In a small bowl, combine the honey, lemon juice and poppy seeds. Pour over fruit and toss to coat.

¾ cup: 117 cal., 1g fat (0 sat. fat), 0 chol., 2mg sod., 30g carb. (23g sugars, 5g fiber), 1g pro.

Test Kitchen Tip: Don't have those fruits on hand? Try blackberries, mangoes or peaches instead.

FARMERS MARKET FIND

Try melting white chocolate and spreading it over the cooled pie crust. It will add a rich layer and keep the crust crispy.

BEST EVER FRESH STRAWBERRY PIE

BEST EVER FRESH STRAWBERRY PIE

Next time you get a pint or two of perfectly ripe strawberries, make my favorite pie. It combines fresh berries and a lemony cream cheese layer. If you're in a hurry, use a premade pie shell.

—Janet Leach, Granger, WA

PREP: 1 HOUR + CHILLING • **COOK:** 10 MIN. + CHILLING • **MAKES:** 8 SERVINGS

- **2 cups all-purpose flour**
- **2 tsp. sugar**
- **½ tsp. salt**
- **⅔ cup shortening**
- **1 Tbsp. white vinegar**
- **4 to 5 Tbsp. 2% milk**

FILLING

- **1 pkg. (8 oz.) cream cheese, softened**
- **¾ cup confectioners' sugar**
- **2 tsp. grated lemon zest**
- **½ tsp. lemon extract**

TOPPING

- **6 cups fresh strawberries, hulled (about 2 lbs.)**
- **¾ cup sugar**
- **1 Tbsp. cornstarch**
- **¼ tsp. salt**
- **1 cup water**
- **1 pkg. (3 oz.) strawberry gelatin**
- **1 tsp. butter**

1. In a large bowl, mix the flour, sugar and salt; cut in shortening until crumbly. Gradually add vinegar and milk, tossing with a fork until dough holds together when pressed. Shape into a disk; wrap and refrigerate 1 hour or overnight.

2. On a lightly floured surface, roll dough to a ⅛-in.-thick circle; transfer to a 9-in. deep-dish pie plate. Trim crust to ½ in. beyond rim of plate; flute edge. Refrigerate 30 minutes. Preheat oven to 425°.

3. Line crust with a double thickness of foil. Fill with pie weights, dried beans or uncooked rice. Bake on a lower oven rack 20-25 minutes or until edges are golden brown. Remove foil and weights; bake 3-6 minutes longer or until bottom is golden brown. Cool completely on a wire rack.

4. In a bowl, beat cream cheese, confectioners' sugar, lemon zest and extract until blended. Spread carefully onto bottom of crust. Refrigerate while preparing topping.

5. Place strawberries in a large bowl. In a small saucepan, mix sugar, cornstarch, salt and water until blended; bring to a boil over medium heat, stirring constantly. Cook and stir 1-2 minutes longer or until thickened and clear. Remove from heat; stir in gelatin until dissolved. Stir in butter. Pour over strawberries, tossing gently to coat. Arrange over filling. Refrigerate 4 hours or until set.

1 piece: 564 cal., 27g fat (10g sat. fat), 33mg chol., 359mg sod., 75g carb. (47g sugars, 3g fiber), 7g pro.

HOW-TO

Buy Strawberries

Look for strawberries that are a uniform bright red; if the berry has any white areas, that means it isn't ripe enough and will have a flat flavor. The stems and leaf caps should be bright green.

Store Strawberries

You can store strawberries in the fridge for 1 to 2 days. No need to place them in any special container.

Prep Strawberries

Wash strawberries by placing them in a bowl and adding cold water. Swish them to remove any sandy soil. Avoid soaking them for prolonged periods. Once they're clean, cut off the stem and leaves.

CHOCOLATE-COVERED STRAWBERRY COBBLER

This cobbler came about because I love chocolate-covered strawberries. Top it with whipped cream, either plain or with a little chocolate syrup stirred in.

—Andrea Bolden, Unionville, TN

PREP: 15 MIN. • **BAKE:** 35 MIN. + STANDING • **MAKES:** 12 SERVINGS

- **1 cup butter, cubed**
- **1½ cups self-rising flour**
- **2¼ cups sugar, divided**
- **¾ cup 2% milk**
- **1 tsp. vanilla extract**
- **⅓ cup baking cocoa**
- **4 cups fresh strawberries, quartered**
- **2 cups boiling water**
- **Whipped cream and additional strawberries**

1. Preheat oven to 350°. Place butter in a 13x9-in. baking pan; heat pan in oven about 3-5 minutes or until butter is melted. Meanwhile, in a large bowl, combine flour, 1¼ cups sugar, milk and vanilla until well blended. In a small bowl, mix cocoa and remaining sugar.

2. Remove baking pan from oven; add batter. Sprinkle with strawberries and cocoa mixture; pour boiling water evenly over top (do not stir). Bake 35-40 minutes or until a toothpick inserted into cake portion comes out clean. Let stand 10 minutes. Serve warm with whipped cream and additional strawberries.

1 serving: 368 cal., 16g fat (10g sat. fat), 42mg chol., 316mg sod., 55g carb. (41g sugars, 2g fiber), 3g pro.

STRAWBERRY MIMOSAS

Here's a tasty twist on the classic mimosa. To make this refreshing drink friendly for kids, simply substitute lemon-lime soda or ginger ale for the champagne.

—Kelly Maxwell, Plainfield, IL

TAKES: 15 MIN. • **MAKES:** 12 SERVINGS

- **7 cups sliced fresh strawberries (about 2 qt.)**
- **3 cups orange juice**
- **4 cups champagne, chilled**

GARNISHES

Optional: Fresh strawberries and orange slices

1. Place half of the strawberries and orange juice in a blender; cover and process until smooth. Press through a fine mesh strainer. Repeat with remaining strawberries and orange juice.

2. Pour a scant ⅔ cup strawberry mixture into a glass. Top with about ⅓ cup champagne. If desired, serve with a strawberry and an orange slice.

1 cup: 112 cal., 0 fat (0 sat. fat), 0 chol., 1mg sod., 15g carb. (10g sugars, 2g fiber), 1g pro.

CHOCOLATE-COVERED
STRAWBERRY COBBLER

SEARED SALMON WITH
STRAWBERRY BASIL RELISH

SEARED SALMON WITH STRAWBERRY BASIL RELISH

Take a sweet new approach to salmon by topping it off with a relish of strawberries, basil, honey and pepper.
—Stacy Mullens, Gresham, OR

TAKES: 20 MIN. • MAKES: 6 SERVINGS

- **6 salmon fillets (4 oz. each)**
- **1 Tbsp. butter, melted**
- **¼ tsp. salt**
- **⅛ tsp. freshly ground pepper**

RELISH

- **1¼ cups finely chopped fresh strawberries**
- **1 Tbsp. minced fresh basil**
- **1 Tbsp. honey**
- **Dash freshly ground pepper**

1. Brush fillets with melted butter; sprinkle with salt and pepper. Heat a large skillet over medium-high heat. Add the fillets, skin side up, in batches if necessary; cook 2-3 minutes on each side or until fish just begins to flake easily with a fork.

2. In a small bowl, toss strawberries with basil, honey and pepper. Serve salmon with relish.

1 salmon fillet with 3 Tbsp. relish: 215 cal., 12g fat (3g sat. fat), 62mg chol., 169mg sod., 6g carb. (5g sugars, 1g fiber), 19g pro. **Diabetic exchanges:** 3 lean meat, ½ starch, ½ fat.

ROASTED STRAWBERRY SHEET CAKE

My grandma loved summer berry cakes. Almost any time I'd call her during the warmer months, she'd invite me over to taste her latest masterpiece. This cake is an ode to her.
—Kristin Bowers, Rancho Palos Verdes, CA

PREP: 1 HOUR • BAKE: 30 MIN. + COOLING • MAKES: 24 SERVINGS

- **4 lbs. halved fresh strawberries**
- **½ cup sugar**

CAKE

- **1 cup butter, softened**
- **1½ cups sugar**
- **2 large eggs, room temperature**
- **2 tsp. almond extract**
- **3 cups all-purpose flour**
- **3 tsp. baking powder**
- **2 tsp. salt**
- **1 cup 2% milk**
- **¼ cup turbinado (washed raw) sugar**

1. Preheat oven to 350°. Place strawberries on a parchment-lined rimmed baking sheet. Sprinkle with sugar and toss to coat. Bake until just tender, 35-40 minutes. Cool slightly.

2. Meanwhile, grease a 15x10x1-in. baking pan. In a large bowl, cream butter and sugar until light and fluffy, 5-7 minutes. Add eggs, 1 at a time, beating well after each addition. Beat in extract. In another bowl, whisk flour, baking powder and salt; add to creamed mixture alternately with milk, beating well after each addition (batter may appear curdled).

3. Transfer to prepared pan. Top with 3 cups roasted strawberries; sprinkle with turbinado sugar. Reserve remaining strawberries for serving. Bake until a toothpick inserted in center comes out clean, 30-35 minutes. Cool completely in pan on a wire rack. Serve with reserved roasted strawberries.

1 piece: 235 cal., 9g fat (5g sat. fat), 37mg chol., 329mg sod., 37g carb. (23g sugars, 2g fiber), 3g pro.

Test Kitchen Tip: It's important to just halve the strawberries, not quarter them. If they're too small, they will sink too far into the cake.

STRAWBERRY GELATO

You'll love this smooth and creamy gelato with bright strawberry flavor and just a hint of sea salt and honey.

—Shelly Bevington, Hermiston, OR

PREP: 10 MIN. + CHILLING • PROCESS: 25 MIN. • MAKES: 12 SERVINGS (1½ QT.)

- **2 cups whole milk**
- **2 Tbsp. light corn syrup**
- **1 Tbsp. honey**
- **¾ cup sugar**
- **½ tsp. sea salt**
- **2½ cups fresh strawberries (about 12 oz.), halved**
- **½ cup heavy whipping cream**
- **1 tsp. lemon juice**

FARMERS MARKET FIND

Feel free to give this gelato a try with fresh raspberries or blackberries. If your berries are tart, you may want to add a touch more sugar or honey to the recipe.

1. Place first 6 ingredients in a blender; cover and process until blended. While processing, gradually add the cream, processing just until combined. Remove to a bowl; stir in lemon juice. Refrigerate, covered, until cold, about 4 hours.

2. Fill the cylinder of ice cream maker no more than two-thirds full; freeze according to manufacturer's directions. (Refrigerate any remaining mixture until ready to freeze.)

3. Transfer ice cream to freezer containers, allowing headspace for expansion. Freeze until firm, 3-4 hours.

½ cup: 160 cal., 6g fat (4g sat. fat), 18mg chol., 124mg sod., 26g carb. (25g sugars, 1g fiber), 2g pro.

Test Kitchen Tip: This recipe makes 4¾ cups of strawberry mixture before freezing and yields about 6 cups after freezing. If you have a 1-qt. ice cream maker, you will probably need to make the gelato in two batches.

STRAWBERRY RHUBARB CHEESECAKE BARS

These cheesecake bars layer a buttery pecan shortbread crust with a rich and creamy filling and sweet-tart strawberry rhubarb jam. For larger squares, cut into nine bars instead of 16.
—Amanda Scarlati, Sandy, UT

PREP: 30 MIN. + CHILLING • **BAKE:** 15 MIN. + COOLING • **MAKES:** 16 SERVINGS

- **1 cup all-purpose flour**
- **⅓ cup packed brown sugar**
- **Dash kosher salt**
- **½ cup cold butter, cubed**
- **⅓ cup finely chopped pecans**

FILLING

- **1 pkg. (8 oz.) cream cheese, softened**
- **¼ cup sugar**
- **2 Tbsp. 2% milk**
- **1 Tbsp. lemon juice**
- **½ tsp. vanilla extract**
- **Dash kosher salt**
- **1 large egg, room temperature, lightly beaten**

JAM

- **½ cup sugar**
- **2 Tbsp. cornstarch**
- **1⅓ cups chopped fresh strawberries**
- **1⅓ cups sliced fresh or frozen rhubarb**
- **1 Tbsp. lemon juice**

1. Preheat oven to 350°. Line an 8-in. square baking pan with parchment, letting ends extend up sides. In a small bowl, mix flour, brown sugar and salt; cut in butter until crumbly. Stir in pecans.

2. Press into bottom of prepared pan. Bake until edges just begin to brown, 12-15 minutes. Cool completely on a wire rack.

3. In a large bowl, beat cream cheese and sugar until smooth. Beat in milk, lemon juice, vanilla and salt. Add egg; beat on low speed just until blended. Pour over crust.

4. Bake until filling is set, 15-20 minutes. Cool on a wire rack for 1 hour.

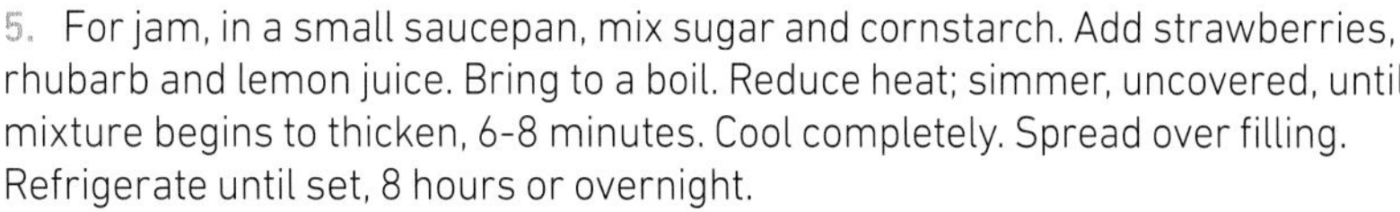

5. For jam, in a small saucepan, mix sugar and cornstarch. Add strawberries, rhubarb and lemon juice. Bring to a boil. Reduce heat; simmer, uncovered, until mixture begins to thicken, 6-8 minutes. Cool completely. Spread over filling. Refrigerate until set, 8 hours or overnight.

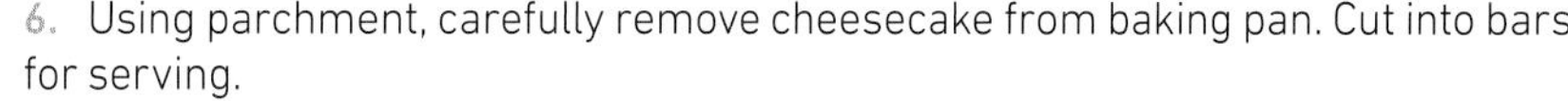

6. Using parchment, carefully remove cheesecake from baking pan. Cut into bars for serving.

1 bar: 215 cal., 13g fat (7g sat. fat), 41mg chol., 113mg sod., 24g carb. (15g sugars, 1g fiber), 3g pro.

STRAWBERRY TARRAGON CHICKEN SALAD

STRAWBERRY TARRAGON CHICKEN SALAD

After thinking about creating this salad for some time, this past spring I used my homegrown strawberries and fresh tarragon to do a little experimenting. It didn't take me very long to come up with a winner! My husband enjoyed my creation as much as I did, and we can't wait for strawberry season to come around again!

—Sue Gronholz, Beaver Dam, WI

TAKES: 30 MIN. • MAKES: 5 SERVINGS

- **½ cup mayonnaise**
- **2 tsp. sugar**
- **2 tsp. minced fresh tarragon or 1 tsp. dried tarragon**
- **¼ tsp. salt**
- **⅛ tsp. pepper**
- **2½ cups cubed cooked chicken breast**
- **2 cups quartered fresh strawberries**
- **1 cup fresh shelled peas or frozen peas, thawed**
- **½ cup chopped celery**
- **2 Tbsp. chopped sweet onion**
- **Torn mixed salad greens**
- **½ cup chopped pecans, toasted**

In a large bowl, whisk the first 5 ingredients until blended. Stir in the chicken, strawberries, peas, celery and onion. Serve over salad greens; sprinkle with pecans.

1 cup: 378 cal., 26g fat (4g sat. fat), 56mg chol., 285mg sod., 13g carb. (7g sugars, 4g fiber), 23g pro.

Test Kitchen Tip: This salad is better when made ahead of time so the flavors can blend. But don't add the strawberries until you're ready to serve, as they tend to turn the salad pink when they sit.

STRAWBERRY BUTTER

There are several farms in our community where families can pick their own strawberries. We usually pick a big bucketful and can't resist sampling some in the car on the way home, but we make sure to save enough for this delicious spread.

—Kim Hammond, Watsonville, CA

PREP: 10 MIN. + CHILLING • MAKES: 2 CUPS

- **1 pkg. (8 oz.) cream cheese, softened**
- **½ cup butter, softened**
- **1 cup confectioners' sugar**
- **1 tsp. vanilla extract**
- **1 cup fresh strawberries, pureed**

In a bowl, beat cream cheese and butter until smooth. Gradually add sugar and vanilla; mix well. Stir in strawberries. Cover tightly and refrigerate for several hours or overnight. May be stored in the refrigerator up to 1 week. Serve with English muffins, toast, waffles or pancakes.

2 Tbsp.: 132 cal., 11g fat (7g sat. fat), 31mg chol., 100mg sod., 8g carb. (8g sugars, 0 fiber), 1g pro.

CHAPTER 7

STONE FRUITS

Fresh, sweet and loaded with juicy appeal, stone fruits are a hallmark of summer. There's plenty of goodness to go around all year, however, with these delightful recipes at your fingertips.

CHERRY-CHICKEN LETTUCE WRAPS

I came up with this amazing recipe when I had a load of cherries on hand. My family polished off these wraps fast, and asked for more. Luckily I had enough fruit to make them again the next day!

—Melissa Barlow, Fruit Heights, UT

TAKES: 25 MIN. • **MAKES:** 4 SERVINGS

- **¾ lb. boneless skinless chicken breasts, cut into ¾-in. cubes**
- **1 tsp. ground ginger**
- **¼ tsp. salt**
- **¼ tsp. pepper**
- **2 tsp. olive oil**
- **1½ cups shredded carrots**
- **1¼ cups coarsely chopped pitted fresh sweet cherries**
- **4 green onions, chopped**
- **⅓ cup coarsely chopped almonds**
- **2 Tbsp. rice vinegar**
- **2 Tbsp. reduced-sodium teriyaki sauce**
- **1 Tbsp. honey**
- **8 Bibb or Boston lettuce leaves**

1. Sprinkle the chicken with ginger, salt and pepper. In a large nonstick skillet, heat oil over medium-high heat. Add chicken; cook and stir 3-5 minutes or until no longer pink.

2. Remove from heat. Stir in carrots, cherries, green onions and almonds. In a small bowl, mix vinegar, teriyaki sauce and honey; stir into chicken mixture. Divide among lettuce leaves; fold lettuce over filling.

2 filled lettuce wraps: 257 cal., 10g fat (1g sat. fat), 47mg chol., 381mg sod., 22g carb. (15g sugars, 4g fiber), 21g pro. **Diabetic exchanges:** 3 lean meat, 1 vegetable, ½ fruit, ½ fat.

CHERRY-ALMOND STREUSEL TART

Brimming with fresh cherries and topped with a crunchy streusel, this tempting tart will end dinner on a sweet note. It is fast to fix, looks elegant and tastes delicious.

—Marion Lee, Mount Hope, ON

PREP: 20 MIN. • **BAKE:** 30 MIN. • **MAKES:** 8 SERVINGS

- **1 sheet refrigerated pie crust**
- **⅔ cup sugar**
- **3 Tbsp. cornstarch**
- **Dash salt**
- **4 cups fresh or frozen pitted tart cherries, thawed**
- **⅛ tsp. almond extract**

TOPPING

- **¼ cup quick-cooking oats**
- **3 Tbsp. all-purpose flour**
- **2 Tbsp. brown sugar**
- **1 Tbsp. slivered almonds**
- **2 Tbsp. cold butter**

1. Unroll crust onto the bottom and up the sides of an ungreased 9-in. fluted tart pan with removable bottom; trim the edges.

2. In a large saucepan, combine the sugar, cornstarch and salt. Stir in the cherries; bring to a boil over medium heat, stirring constantly. Cook and stir for 1-2 minutes or until thickened. Remove from the heat; stir in extract. Pour into crust.

3. For topping, combine the oats, flour, brown sugar and almonds. Cut in butter until mixture resembles coarse crumbs. Sprinkle over filling. Bake at 350° until topping is golden brown, 30-35 minutes. Cool on a wire rack.

1 piece: 298 cal., 11g fat (5g sat. fat), 13mg chol., 143mg sod., 49g carb. (27g sugars, 2g fiber), 3g pro.

CHERRY-CHICKEN
LETTUCE WRAPS

CHERRY CHIP WAFFLES WITH CHERRY SYRUP

❄ CHERRY CHIP WAFFLES WITH CHERRY SYRUP

While on a recent trip to Door County, Wisconsin, for a family reunion, I created this yummy recipe using some freshly picked cherries. It was a hit with all ages and everyone was asking for more.

—Heather Karow, Burnett, WI

PREP: 25 MIN. • COOK: 10 MIN./BATCH • MAKES: 6 SERVINGS

- ½ **cup sugar**
- ½ **cup plus 2 Tbsp. water, divided**
- ½ **cup fresh or frozen pitted dark sweet cherries, thawed and finely chopped**
- 1 **Tbsp. cornstarch**

WAFFLES

- 1¼ **cups all-purpose flour**
- 1 **tsp. baking powder**
- 1 **tsp. ground cinnamon**
- 1 **tsp. baking soda**
- 1½ **cups buttermilk**
- 2 **large eggs, room temperature**
- ⅓ **cup canola oil**
- ½ **tsp. almond extract**
- 1½ **cups fresh or frozen pitted dark sweet cherries, thawed and chopped**
- ½ **cup miniature semisweet chocolate chips**
- **Additional miniature semisweet chocolate chips, optional**

1. Preheat waffle maker. In a small saucepan, cook and stir sugar and ½ cup water over medium heat until sugar is dissolved. Add cherries; cook and stir until cherries are tender, 3-5 minutes. Mix cornstarch and remaining 2 Tbsp. water until smooth; stir into pan. Bring to a boil; cook and stir for 1-2 minutes or until thickened. Remove and keep warm.

2. In a large bowl, whisk the flour, baking powder, cinnamon and baking soda. In another bowl, whisk buttermilk, eggs, oil and extract until blended. Add to dry ingredients; stir just until moistened. Stir in cherries and chocolate chips. Bake waffles according to manufacturer's directions until golden brown. Serve with syrup and, if desired, additional chocolate chips.

Freeze option: Cool waffles on wire racks. Freeze between layers of waxed paper in an airtight container. Freeze cherry syrup in a freezer container. To use, partially thaw cherry syrup in refrigerator overnight. Heat through in a saucepan, stirring occasionally. Reheat waffles in a toaster on medium setting. Or, microwave each waffle on high until heated through, 30-60 seconds.

2 waffles with 2 Tbsp. cherry syrup: 428 cal., 19g fat (4g sat. fat), 64mg chol., 432mg sod., 59g carb. (33g sugars, 2g fiber), 8g pro.

HOW-TO

Buy Cherries

Cherries should be firm and show no blemishes, cuts or bruises. Look for cherries that have their stems attached, as this increases the amount of time they will keep. If you want sweet cherries, choose darker ones. Avoid those that look especially small.

Store Cherries

Store unwashed cherries, with stems intact, in an airtight container in the refrigerator for 4-10 days. To freeze, wash, drain and pit cherries. Arrange in a single layer on a parchment-lined baking sheet. Once frozen, transfer to freezer container. Freeze up to 1 year.

Prep Cherries

Wash cherries and remove the stems before eating or using in a recipe. For a quick way to pit cherries, place one at a time on the lip of an empty soft drink bottle. Use a chopstick to push the pit through the cherry and into the bottle.

JUICY CHERRY PIE

Lucky you! Tart, or sour, cherry season is in the heart of summer. Choose fresh tart cherries that are bright in color, shiny and plump. They should feel relatively firm when pressed lightly.

—Karen Berner, New Canaan, CT

PREP: 35 MIN. + CHILLING • **BAKE:** 55 MIN. • **MAKES:** 8 SERVINGS

- **2½ cups all-purpose flour**
- **½ tsp. salt**
- **⅔ cup cold unsalted butter, cubed**
- **⅓ cup shortening**
- **6 to 10 Tbsp. ice water**

FILLING

- **5 cups fresh tart cherries, pitted**
- **2 tsp. lemon juice**
- **¼ tsp. almond extract**
- **1 cup sugar**
- **⅓ cup all-purpose flour**
- **1 tsp. ground cinnamon**

SUGAR TOPPING

- **1 Tbsp. 2% milk**
- **1 tsp. sugar**

1. In a large bowl, mix the flour and salt; cut in butter and shortening until crumbly. Gradually add ice water, tossing with a fork until dough holds together when pressed. Divide dough in half. Shape each into a disk; wrap. Refrigerate 1 hour or overnight.

2. Preheat oven to 375°. For filling, place cherries in a large bowl; drizzle with lemon juice and almond extract. In a small bowl, mix sugar, flour and cinnamon. Sprinkle over cherries and toss gently to coat.

3. On a lightly floured surface, roll 1 dough portion into a ⅛-in.-thick circle; transfer to a 9-in. pie plate. Trim crust even with rim. Add filling.

4. Roll remaining dough into a ⅛-in.-thick circle; cut out stars or other shapes using cookie cutters. Place top crust over the filling. Trim, seal and flute edge. If desired, decorate top with cutouts.

5. Bake 40 minutes. For topping, brush top of pie with milk; sprinkle with sugar. Bake 15-20 minutes longer or until crust is golden brown and filling is bubbly. Cool on a wire rack.

1 piece: 521 cal., 24g fat (12g sat. fat), 41mg chol., 155mg sod., 72g carb. (34g sugars, 3g fiber), 6g pro.

JUICY
CHERRY PIE

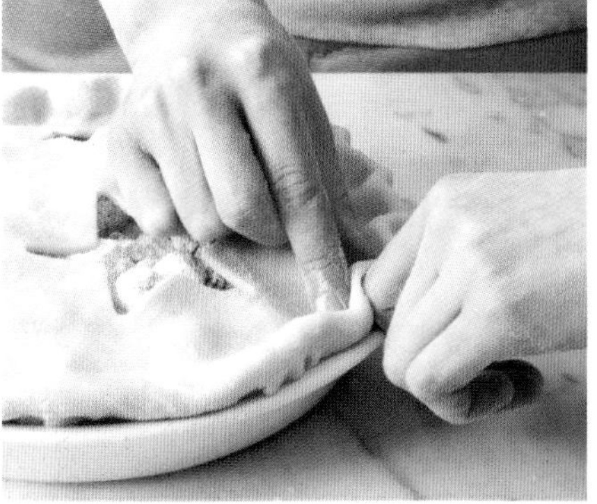

BING CHERRY-AMARETTI FOOL

BING CHERRY-AMARETTI FOOL

When Bing cherries are in season, I make this fruity custard-style fool. The sweet cherries and whipped cream balance perfectly with the sour cream.

—Mary Ann Lee, Clifton Park, NY

PREP: 30 MIN. + CHILLING • **MAKES:** 8 SERVINGS

- **1 envelope unflavored gelatin**
- **⅓ cup cold water**
- **1 cup sour cream**
- **½ cup sugar**
- **1 Tbsp. lemon juice**
- **½ tsp. almond extract**
- **½ tsp. vanilla extract**
- **2 cups coarsely chopped fresh Bing or other dark sweet cherries, divided**
- **1 cup heavy whipping cream**
- **1 cup coarsely crushed amaretti cookies (about 16 cookies)**
- **Optional toppings: Fresh mint leaves, Bing cherries and additional crushed amaretti cookies**

1. In a small saucepan, sprinkle gelatin over cold water; let stand 1 minute. Heat and stir over low heat until gelatin is completely dissolved. Let stand 5 minutes.

2. Place sour cream, sugar, lemon juice, extracts, 1 cup cherries and gelatin mixture in a blender; cover and process until cherries are pureed. Transfer to a large bowl.

3. In a small bowl, beat cream until soft peaks form. Remove ½ cup whipped cream; reserve for topping. Gently fold remaining whipped cream into cherry mixture. Fold in the crushed cookies and the remaining chopped cherries. Divide mixture among 8 dessert dishes. Refrigerate at least 2 hours.

4. Serve with reserved whipped cream and optional toppings as desired.

1 serving: 323 cal., 19g fat (10g sat. fat), 41mg chol., 26mg sod., 36g carb. (32g sugars, 1g fiber), 4g pro.

ALMOND CHERRY COBBLER

This bubbling cherry cobbler is one of my favorite dishes. Serve warm with vanilla ice cream or whipped cream.

—Melissa Wagner, Eden Prairie, MN

PREP: 20 MIN. • **BAKE:** 45 MIN. • **MAKES:** 6 SERVINGS

- **3½ cups fresh dark sweet cherries, pitted**
- **1 cup all-purpose flour**
- **¼ cup plus ½ cup sugar, divided**
- **1 tsp. baking powder**
- **¼ tsp. salt**
- **½ cup fat-free milk**
- **3 Tbsp. butter, melted**
- **1 Tbsp. cornstarch**
- **¼ tsp. ground cinnamon**
- **¾ cup boiling water**
- **1 tsp. almond extract**

1. Preheat oven to 350°. Place cherries in an 8-in. square baking dish coated with cooking spray.

2. In a small bowl, mix flour, ¼ cup sugar, baking powder and salt. Add milk and melted butter; stir in just until moistened. Spread over cherries.

3. In another bowl, mix cornstarch, cinnamon and remaining sugar; sprinkle over batter. Mix boiling water and almond extract; pour slowly over top. Bake, uncovered, 45-50 minutes or until top is golden brown and filling is bubbly. Serve warm.

1 serving: 297 cal., 6g fat (4g sat. fat), 16mg chol., 225mg sod., 59g carb. (36g sugars, 1g fiber), 3g pro.

PEPPER MANGO SALSA

Whenever I make this, the bowl is always left empty! The idea for a homemade mango salsa hit me after I saw a chef on television make something similar. It sounded so good, and it wasn't something I could find in a store at the time. The salsa is especially tasty served with artisan chips—the black bean and roasted garlic types are my favorite. When strawberries are in season, I add them into the mix, too.

—Wendy Rusch, Cameron, WI

PREP: 15 MIN. + CHILLING • MAKES: 6 CUPS

3 Tbsp. lime juice
3 Tbsp. honey
1 tsp. olive oil
Dash salt
Dash coarsely ground pepper
3 medium mangoes, peeled and finely chopped
2 cups finely chopped fresh pineapple
1 large sweet red pepper, finely chopped
1 Anaheim or poblano pepper, seeded and finely chopped
½ cup finely chopped red onion
¼ cup chopped fresh cilantro
Tortilla chips

1. Whisk together first 5 ingredients. In a large bowl, combine fruit, peppers, onion and cilantro; toss with the lime juice mixture.

2. Refrigerate, covered, 1 hour to allow flavors to blend. Stir before serving. Serve with chips.

¼ cup salsa: 47 cal., 0 fat (0 sat. fat), 0 chol., 63mg sod., 11g carb. (10g sugars, 1g fiber), 1g pro. **Diabetic exchanges:** ½ starch.

Test Kitchen Tip: Select plump mangoes with a sweet, fruity aroma. Avoid very soft or bruised fruit. The skin of a ripe mango is green to yellow in color with a tinge of red. It should yield slightly when pressed and have a fruity aroma at the stem end.

HOW-TO

Dice a Mango

- Lay the washed mango on the counter, then turn it so the top and bottom are now the sides. Using a sharp knife, make a lengthwise cut as close to the long, flat seed as possible to remove each side of the fruit. Trim fruit away from the seed.
- Score each side of the fruit lengthwise and widthwise, being careful not to cut through the skin.
- Using your hand, push the skin up, turning the fruit out. Cut fruit off at the skin with a knife.

MANGO CHICKEN THIGHS WITH BASIL-COCONUT SAUCE

This recipe brings the restaurant fare to my home kitchen. And it's easy, too! The meal comes together quickly and fills my home with wonderful aromas. Plus, leftovers are just as spectacular the next day.

—Kathi Jones-DelMonte, Rochester, NY

PREP: 20 MIN. • **COOK:** 30 MIN. • **MAKES:** 4 SERVINGS

- **4 boneless skinless chicken thighs (about 1 lb.)**
- **½ tsp. salt**
- **¼ tsp. pepper**
- **1 Tbsp. olive oil**
- **3 garlic cloves, minced**
- **1 Tbsp. minced fresh gingerroot**
- **1 can (13.66 oz.) coconut milk**
- **1 medium mango, peeled and chopped**
- **4 green onions, sliced**
- **½ cup thinly sliced fresh basil, divided**
- **¼ cup miso paste**
- **2 tsp. Sriracha chili sauce**
- **2 cups cooked jasmine rice**
- **2 medium limes, quartered**

1. Sprinkle chicken with salt and pepper. In a large skillet, heat oil over medium heat. Brown chicken on both sides. Add the garlic and ginger; cook 1 minute longer.

2. Stir in coconut milk, mango, green onions, ¼ cup basil, miso paste and chili sauce. Cook and stir until the sauce is slightly reduced and a thermometer inserted in chicken reads 170°, about 20 minutes. Sprinkle with remaining ¼ cup basil. Serve with rice and limes.

1 serving: 552 cal., 28g fat (18g sat. fat), 76mg chol., 1209mg sod., 46g carb. (17g sugars, 4g fiber), 28g pro.

Test Kitchen Tip: This recipe also works well with seafood, especially shrimp or scallops. It's also great with clams or mussels.

MANGO & HABANERO GUACAMOLE

For the ultimate sweet-spicy combo, pair mango with fresh habanero chili peppers. Depending on your preferred taste, you can control the guac's heat with the number of pepper seeds you use.

—Taste of Home *Test Kitchen*

TAKES: 15 MIN. • **MAKES:** 6 SERVINGS

- **3 medium ripe avocado, peeled and cubed**
- **2 to 3 Tbsp. fresh lime juice**
- **½ to 1 tsp. kosher salt**
- **1 medium mango, peeled and chopped**
- **½ to 1 habanero pepper, seeded and chopped**

In a bowl, mash avocados until almost smooth. Stir in lime juice and ½ tsp. salt. Let stand 10 minutes to allow flavors to blend. Adjust seasoning with additional lime juice and salt if desired. Top with mango and habanero.

¼ cup: 150 cal., 11g fat (2g sat. fat), 0 chol., 166mg sod., 15g carb. (8g sugars, 6g fiber), 2g pro. **Diabetic exchanges:** 2 fat, 1 starch.

PORK CHOPS WITH NECTARINE SALSA

My special pork dish has so much flavor and is a snap to prepare. A sweet, fruity salsa perfectly balances the spicy rub coating the pan-fried chops.

—*Bonnie Bufford, Nicholson, PA*

TAKES: 20 MIN. • MAKES: 4 SERVINGS

- **2 tsp. chili powder**
- **1 tsp. ground coriander**
- **½ tsp. ground cumin**
- **½ tsp. paprika**
- **¼ tsp. salt**
- **¼ tsp. pepper**
- **4 boneless pork loin chops (4 oz. each and ½ in. thick)**
- **1 Tbsp. olive oil**
- **¼ cup salsa**
- **2 Tbsp. apricot spreadable fruit**
- **2 cups sliced peeled nectarines or peaches**
- **2 Tbsp. minced fresh cilantro**
- **1 Tbsp. minced fresh oregano or 1 tsp. dried oregano**

1. In a small bowl, combine the first 6 ingredients. Rub over both sides of pork chops. In a large nonstick skillet, cook pork chops in oil over medium-high heat until juices run clear, 5-6 minutes on each side. Remove to a serving platter and keep warm.

2. In the same skillet, combine salsa and spreadable fruit. Bring to a boil. Reduce heat; cook and stir over medium heat for 1 minute. Stir in nectarines, cilantro and oregano; cook until heated through, 2-3 minutes. Serve with pork.

1 pork chop with ½ cup salsa: 246 cal., 10g fat (3g sat. fat), 55mg chol., 279mg sod., 15g carb. (10g sugars, 2g fiber), 23g pro. **Diabetic exchanges:** 3 lean meat, 1 fruit.

HOW-TO

Buy Nectarines

Select nectarines that are firm but yield a bit to gentle pressure. They should be bright with skin free of discoloration, soft spots or bruises. Choose fruits with defined clefts, as this indicates they are mature and sweeter.

Store Nectarines

Nectarines can be stored unrefrigerated for up to 4 days, depending on how ripe they were when you bought them.

Prep Nectarines

Give the fruit a light rinse; scrubbing will remove its delicate skin. Fully slice the fruit lengthwise. Take the two halves and twist. Remove the pit.

PORK CHOPS WITH NECTARINE SALSA

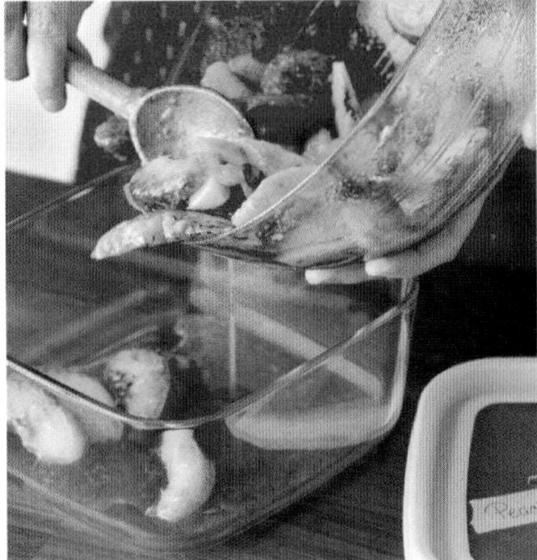

HOW-TO

Use Frozen Nectarines

Frozen nectarines are perfect for smoothies, directly from the freezer, and work great in baked or cooked recipes. However, once thawed, a frozen nectarine's texture is different from fresh. For this reason, they won't do as well in fresh dishes—such as salads—as they do in baked goods, like pastries, pies and cobblers.

CANNED NECTARINES IN HONEY SYRUP

5i CANNED NECTARINES IN HONEY SYRUP

Nectarines are in season for such a short time, you'll want to do whatever you can to extend the season. With this quick method for canning nectarines, you'll have delicious fruit all year long.

—Taste of Home *Test Kitchen*

PREP: 30 MIN. **PROCESS:** 20 MIN./BATCH • **MAKES:** 8 PINT JARS

- **1 gallon water**
- **1 tsp. ascorbic acid powder**
- **5 lbs. nectarines, halved, pitted and sliced into 1-in. slices**
- **2 cups water**
- **⅔ cup sugar**
- **½ cup honey**

1. Combine 1 gallon water and ascorbic acid powder until dissolved; place the nectarines in liquid immediately after cutting each one. In a Dutch oven, combine 2 cups water, sugar and honey. Bring to a boil, stirring to dissolve sugar. Drain nectarines and add to the canning syrup; return just to a boil. Remove from heat.

2. Carefully ladle hot mixture into 8 hot wide-mouth 1-pint jars, leaving ½-in. headspace. Remove air bubbles and, if necessary, adjust headspace by adding hot cooking liquid. Wipe rims. Center lids on jars; screw on bands until fingertip tight.

3. Place jars into canner with simmering water, ensuring they are completely covered with water. Bring to a boil; process for 20 minutes. Remove jars and cool.

½ cup: 64 cal., 0 fat (0 sat. fat), 0 chol., 1mg sod., 17g carb. (17g sugars, 0 fiber), 0 pro.

5i GRILLED STONE FRUITS WITH BALSAMIC SYRUP

Get ready to experience another side of stone fruits. Hot off the grill, this late-summer dessert practically melts in your mouth.

—Sonya Labbe, West Hollywood, CA

TAKES: 20 MIN. • **MAKES:** 4 SERVINGS

- **½ cup balsamic vinegar**
- **2 Tbsp. brown sugar**
- **2 medium peaches, peeled and halved**
- **2 medium nectarines, peeled and halved**
- **2 medium plums, peeled and halved**

1. In a small saucepan, combine vinegar and brown sugar. Bring to a boil; cook until liquid is reduced by half.

2. On a lightly oiled rack, grill peaches, nectarines and plums, covered, over medium heat or broil 4 in. from the heat until tender, 3-4 minutes on each side.

3. Slice fruits; arrange on a serving plate. Drizzle with sauce.

1 serving: 114 cal., 1g fat (0 sat. fat), 0 chol., 10mg sod., 28g carb. (24g sugars, 2g fiber), 2g pro. **Diabetic exchanges:** 1 starch, 1 fruit.

NECTARINE PLUM COBBLER

I live in northern Manitoba, where fresh nectarines and plums are usually available only at summer's end. So I make up the fruit filling and freeze it for use all winter. My family really enjoys this recipe, and it's wonderful topped with vanilla ice cream.

—Darlene Jackson, The Pas, MB

PREP: 30 MIN. • BAKE: 30 MIN. • MAKES: 12 SERVINGS

- **1¼ cups sugar, divided**
- **2 Tbsp. cornstarch**
- **¾ cup unsweetened apple juice**
- **5 cups sliced peeled fresh plums**
- **5 cups sliced peeled nectarines or peaches**
- **2½ cups all-purpose flour**
- **3 tsp. baking powder**
- **½ tsp. baking soda**
- **½ tsp. salt**
- **½ cup cold butter**
- **1½ cups buttermilk**
- **Vanilla ice cream, optional**

1. Preheat oven to 375°. In a large saucepan, combine ¾ cup sugar and cornstarch. Gradually stir in apple juice until smooth. Stir in plums and nectarines. Cook and stir until mixture comes to a boil; cook 1-2 minutes longer or until thickened and bubbly. Reduce heat; simmer, uncovered, for 5 minutes.

2. Remove from heat; cool for 10 minutes. Pour into a greased 13x9-in. baking dish.

3. In a large bowl, whisk flour, baking powder, baking soda, salt and the remaining ½ cup sugar. Cut in butter until crumbly. Make a well in the center; stir in buttermilk just until a soft dough forms. Drop by tablespoonfuls over fruit mixture. Bake until golden brown, 30-35 minutes. Serve warm, with ice cream if desired.

1 serving: 333 cal., 9g fat (5g sat. fat), 22mg chol., 361mg sod., 61g carb. (36g sugars, 3g fiber), 5g pro.

GRILLED NECTARINE KABOBS

Fire up the grill and get out of the kitchen to make these juicy, tasty kabobs. Whether served over pound cake or a scoop of vanilla ice cream, you'll be glad that grilling isn't just for meat and veggies.

—Trisha Kruse, Eagle, ID

TAKES: 20 MIN. • MAKES: 2 KABOBS

- **1 medium peach, cut into wedges**
- **1 medium nectarine, cut into wedges**
- **1 medium plum, cut into wedges**
- **¼ cup peach preserves**
- **2 Tbsp. butter, cubed**
- **Optional: Pound cake and whipped topping**

1. On 2 metal or soaked wooden skewers, alternately thread the fruits. In a small saucepan, heat preserves and butter over medium heat until butter is melted; set aside ¼ cup for dipping.

2. On a lightly oiled rack, grill kabobs, covered, over medium heat or broil 4 in. from the heat for 8-10 minutes or until the fruit is tender, turning and basting with the remaining preserves mixture.

3. Serve with reserved sauce, and, if desired, cake and whipped topping.

1 kabob: 269 cal., 12g fat (7g sat. fat), 30mg chol., 81mg sod., 42g carb. (37g sugars, 2g fiber), 2g pro.

NECTARINE PLUM COBBLER

HOW-TO

Peel Nectarines

Peeling nectarines is easier than you might think. Use this method when you need to peel ripe nectarines or other stone fruits such as peaches or apricots.

- Place nectarines in a large pot of boiling water for 10-20 seconds or until the skin splits.
- Remove nectarines with a slotted spoon. Immediately place in an ice water bath to cool or "shock" the fruit and stop the cooking process.
- Use a paring knife to peel the skin, which should come off easily. If there are stubborn areas of skin that won't peel, return nectarines to the boiling water for a few more seconds.

PEACHY PORK RIBS

PEACHY PORK RIBS

These meaty ribs are great picnic fare. Bake them first to make them tender, then simply finish them off on the grill with a fruity basting sauce.

—Tom Arnold, Milwaukee, WI

PREP: 20 MIN. • **COOK:** 2 HOURS 10 MIN. • **MAKES:** 4 SERVINGS

- 2 racks pork baby back ribs (4 lbs.), cut into serving-size pieces
- ½ cup water
- 3 medium ripe peaches, peeled and cubed
- 2 Tbsp. chopped onion
- 2 Tbsp. butter
- 1 garlic clove, minced
- 3 Tbsp. lemon juice
- 2 Tbsp. orange juice concentrate
- 1 Tbsp. brown sugar
- 2 tsp. soy sauce
- ½ tsp. ground mustard
- ¼ tsp. salt
- ¼ tsp. pepper

1. Place ribs in a shallow roasting pan; add water. Cover and bake at 325° for at least 2 hours.

2. Meanwhile, for sauce, place peaches in a blender; cover and process until blended. In a small saucepan, saute onion in butter until tender. Add garlic; cook 1 minute longer. Stir in the lemon juice, orange juice concentrate, brown sugar, soy sauce, mustard, salt, pepper and peach puree; heat through.

3. Drain ribs. Spoon some of the sauce over ribs. Grill ribs on a lightly oiled rack, covered, over medium heat for 8-10 minutes or until browned, turning occasionally and brushing with sauce.

1 serving: 884 cal., 67g fat (26g sat. fat), 260mg chol., 553mg sod., 16g carb. (13g sugars, 1g fiber), 52g pro.

BUTTERMILK PEACH ICE CREAM

My mother's family owned peach orchards in Missouri. I live in Tennessee, a top consumer of buttermilk. This summery ice cream combines my past and present.

—Kim Higginbotham, Knoxville, TN

PREP: 15 MIN. + CHILLING • **PROCESS:** 30 MIN./BATCH + FREEZING • **MAKES:** 2 QT.

- 2 lbs. ripe peaches (about 7 medium), peeled and quartered
- ½ cup sugar
- ½ cup packed brown sugar
- 1 Tbsp. lemon juice
- 1 tsp. vanilla extract
- Pinch salt
- 2 cups buttermilk
- 1 cup heavy whipping cream

1. Place peaches in a food processor; process until smooth. Add sugars, lemon juice, vanilla and salt; process until blended.

2. In a large bowl, mix buttermilk and cream. Stir in peach mixture. Refrigerate, covered, 1 hour or until cold.

3. Fill cylinder of ice cream maker no more than two-thirds full. Freeze according to manufacturer's directions, refrigerating any remaining mixture to process later. Transfer ice cream to freezer containers, allowing headspace for expansion. Freeze 2-4 hours or until firm. Let the ice cream stand at room temperature for 10 minutes before serving.

½ cup: 137 cal., 6g fat (4g sat. fat), 22mg chol., 75mg sod., 20g carb. (19g sugars, 1g fiber), 2g pro. **Diabetic exchanges:** 1 starch, 1 fat.

QUICK WHITE SANGRIA

Using white instead of red wine makes my version of sangria a bit lighter, yet with the same wonderful sweetness. Frozen fruit allows me to serve this refreshing sipper any time of year.

—Sharon Tipton, Casselberry, FL

TAKES: 15 MIN. • MAKES: 6 SERVINGS

- **¼ cup sugar**
- **¼ cup brandy**
- **1 cup sliced peeled fresh or frozen peaches, thawed**
- **1 cup sliced fresh or frozen sliced strawberries, thawed**
- **1 medium lemon, sliced**
- **1 medium lime, sliced**
- **1 bottle (750 ml) dry white wine, chilled**
- **1 can (12 oz.) lemon-lime soda, chilled**
- **Ice cubes**

In a pitcher, mix sugar and brandy until sugar is dissolved. Add the remaining ingredients; stir gently to combine. Serve over ice.

¾ cup: 196 cal., 0 fat (0 sat. fat), 0 chol., 12mg sod., 23g carb. (19g sugars, 1g fiber), 1g pro.

PEACH BRUSCHETTA

As a starter or light snack, this bruschetta is a wonderful way to savor the season with just a bit of fresh peach amid a medley of lively flavors.

—Nikiko Masumoto, Del Ray, CA

PREP: 35 MIN. • COOK: 15 MIN. • MAKES: 2 DOZEN

- **¼ cup chopped walnuts**
- **1 garlic clove**
- **1½ cups fresh arugula**
- **¼ cup extra virgin olive oil**
- **Salt and pepper to taste**

BRUSCHETTA

- **1 Tbsp. olive oil plus additional for brushing bread, divided**
- **1 large red onion, thinly sliced (1½ cups)**
- **1 tsp. minced fresh rosemary**
- **24 slices French bread baguette (⅜ in. thick)**
- **1 to 2 garlic cloves, halved**
- **2 small ripe peaches, cut into ¼-in. slices**
- **Shaved Parmesan cheese**
- **Coarse salt**

1. For pesto, place walnuts and garlic in a small food processor; pulse until finely chopped. Add arugula; process until blended. Continue processing while gradually adding oil in a steady stream. Season with salt and pepper to taste.

2. For bruschetta, in a large skillet, heat 1 Tbsp. oil over medium heat. Add the onion and rosemary; cook until onion is softened, 15-20 minutes, stirring occasionally.

3. Brush both sides of the bread slices with additional oil. Grill, covered, over medium heat or broil 4 in. from heat until golden brown, 1-2 minutes on each side.

4. Rub garlic halves on both sides of toasts; discard garlic. Spread toasts with pesto. Top with onion mixture, peaches and cheese. If desired, sprinkle with coarse salt. Serve immediately.

1 appetizer: 69 cal., 5g fat (1g sat. fat), 0 chol., 37mg sod., 5g carb. (1g sugars, 0 fiber), 0 pro.

JUST PEACHY PORK TENDERLOIN

I had a pork tenderloin and ripe peaches and decided to put them together. The results proved irresistible! Here's a fresh entree that tastes like summer.
—Julia Gosliga, Addison, VT

TAKES: 20 MIN. • MAKES: 4 SERVINGS

- **1 lb. pork tenderloin, cut into 12 slices**
- **½ tsp. salt**
- **¼ tsp. pepper**
- **2 tsp. olive oil**
- **4 medium peaches, peeled and sliced**
- **1 Tbsp. lemon juice**
- **¼ cup peach preserves**

1. Flatten each tenderloin slice to ¼-in. thickness. Sprinkle with salt and pepper. In a large nonstick skillet over medium heat, cook the pork in oil until tender. Remove and keep warm.

2. Add peaches and lemon juice, stirring to loosen browned bits from pan. Cook and stir 3-4 minutes or until peaches are tender. Stir in the pork and preserves; heat through.

1 serving: 241 cal., 6g fat (2g sat. fat), 63mg chol., 340mg sod., 23g carb. (20g sugars, 2g fiber), 23g pro. **Diabetic exchanges:** 3 lean meat, 1 fruit, ½ starch, ½ fat.

CHICKEN WITH PEACH-CUCUMBER SALSA

To keep our kitchen cool, we grill chicken outdoors and serve it with a minty peach salsa that can easily be made ahead.
—Janie Colle, Hutchinson, KS

TAKES: 25 MIN. • MAKES: 4 SERVINGS

- **1½ cups chopped peeled fresh peaches (about 2 medium)**
- **¾ cup chopped cucumber**
- **4 Tbsp. peach preserves, divided**
- **3 Tbsp. finely chopped red onion**
- **1 tsp. minced fresh mint**
- **¾ tsp. salt, divided**
- **4 boneless skinless chicken breast halves (6 oz. each)**
- **¼ tsp. pepper**

1. For salsa, in a small bowl, combine peaches, cucumber, 2 Tbsp. preserves, onion, mint and ¼ tsp. salt.

2. Sprinkle chicken with pepper and remaining salt. On a lightly oiled grill rack, grill chicken, covered, over medium heat 5 minutes. Turn; grill 7-9 minutes longer or until a thermometer reads 165°, brushing tops occasionally with remaining preserves. Serve with salsa.

1 chicken breast half with ½ cup salsa: 261 cal., 4g fat (1g sat. fat), 94mg chol., 525mg sod., 20g carb. (17g sugars, 1g fiber), 35g pro. **Diabetic exchanges:** 5 lean meat, ½ starch, ½ fruit.

GRILLED PEACH, RICE & ARUGULA SALAD

GRILLED PEACH, RICE & ARUGULA SALAD

This hearty salad was created when I needed to clear out some leftovers from the fridge—and it became an instant hit! I think grilled peaches are the ultimate salad booster.

—Lauren Wyler, Dripping Springs, TX

TAKES: 30 MIN. • MAKES: 6 SERVINGS

- 3 Tbsp. cider vinegar
- 2 Tbsp. Dijon mustard
- 2 Tbsp. canola oil
- 2 Tbsp. maple syrup
- 1 Tbsp. finely chopped shallot
- ¼ tsp. cayenne pepper

SALAD

- 1 pkg. (8.8 oz.) ready-to-serve long grain and wild rice
- 2 medium peaches, quartered
- 6 cups fresh arugula (about 4 oz.)
- 6 bacon strips, cooked and crumbled
- ½ cup crumbled goat cheese

1. For dressing, whisk together first 6 ingredients.

2. Prepare the rice according to package directions; cool slightly. Place peaches on a lightly oiled grill rack over medium heat. Grill, covered, until lightly browned, 6-8 minutes, turning occasionally.

3. To serve, add bacon and ¼ cup dressing to rice. Line a platter with arugula; top with rice mixture and peaches. Drizzle with remaining dressing; top with cheese.

1 serving: 218 cal., 11g fat (3g sat. fat), 20mg chol., 530mg sod., 23g carb. (9g sugars, 2g fiber), 7g pro. **Diabetic exchanges:** 2 fat, 1 starch, 1 vegetable.

IVA'S PEACH COBBLER

My mother received this recipe from a friend of hers many years ago, and fortunately she shared it with me. Boise is situated right between two large fruit-producing areas in our state, so peaches are plentiful in the summer.

—Ruby Ewart, Boise, ID

PREP: 15 MIN. • BAKE: 45 MIN. • MAKES: 12 SERVINGS

- 6 to 8 large ripe peaches, peeled and sliced
- 2½ Tbsp. cornstarch
- ¾ to 1 cup sugar

CRUST

- 1 cup all-purpose flour
- 2 large egg yolks, room temperature
- ¼ cup butter, melted
- 1 tsp. baking powder
- 1 cup sugar
- 2 large egg whites, room temperature, stiffly beaten

Combine peaches, cornstarch and sugar; place in a greased 13x9-in. baking dish. For crust, combine the flour, egg yolks, butter, baking powder and sugar in a bowl. Gently fold in egg whites. Spread over peaches. Bake at 375° until the fruit is bubbling around edges and the top is golden, about 45 minutes.

½ cup: 224 cal., 5g fat (3g sat. fat), 46mg chol., 83mg sod., 44g carb. (33g sugars, 1g fiber), 3g pro.

PEACH CREAM PUFFS

On a sizzling day, we crave something light, airy and cool. Nothing says "yum" like these cream puffs stuffed with peaches and whipped cream.

—Angela Benedict, Dunbar, WV

PREP: 55 MIN. + COOLING • BAKE: 25 MIN. + COOLING • MAKES: 16 SERVINGS

- **1 cup water**
- **½ cup butter, cubed**
- **⅛ tsp. salt**
- **1 cup all-purpose flour**
- **4 large eggs, room temperature**

FILLING

- **4 medium peaches, peeled and cubed (about 3 cups)**
- **½ cup sugar**
- **½ cup water**
- **½ cup peach schnapps liqueur or peach nectar**
- **½ tsp. ground cinnamon**
- **¼ tsp. ground nutmeg**

WHIPPED CREAM

- **2 cups heavy whipping cream**
- **½ cup confectioners' sugar**
- **3 Tbsp. peach schnapps liqueur, optional**
- **Additional confectioners' sugar**

1. Preheat oven to 400°. In a large saucepan, bring water, butter and salt to a rolling boil. Add flour all at once and beat until blended. Cook over medium heat, stirring vigorously until mixture pulls away from sides of pan and forms a ball. Transfer dough to a large bowl; let stand 5 minutes.

2. Add eggs, 1 at a time, beating well after each addition until smooth. Continue beating until mixture is smooth and shiny.

3. Cut a ½-in. hole in tip of a pastry bag. Transfer dough to bag; pipe sixteen 2-in. mounds 3 in. apart onto parchment-lined baking sheets.

4. Bake on a lower oven rack 25-30 minutes or until puffed, very firm and golden brown. Pierce side of each puff with tip of a knife to allow steam to escape. Cool completely on wire racks.

5. Meanwhile, in a large saucepan, combine filling ingredients; bring to a boil, stirring occasionally. Reduce heat; simmer, uncovered, 25-30 minutes or until mixture is slightly thickened and peaches are tender. Cool completely.

6. In a bowl, beat cream until it begins to thicken. Add confectioners' sugar and, if desired, peach schnapps; beat until soft peaks form.

7. Cut top third off each cream puff. Pull out and discard soft dough from inside tops and bottoms.

8. To serve, spoon 2 Tbsp. whipped cream into each bottom; top with 2 Tbsp. filling and 2 Tbsp. additional whipped cream. Replace cream puff tops. Dust with additional confectioners' sugar.

1 cream puff with ¼ cup whipped cream and 2 Tbsp. filling: 256 cal., 18g fat (11g sat. fat), 103mg chol., 94mg sod., 21g carb. (14g sugars, 1g fiber), 3g pro.

Test Kitchen Tip: Dry dough? You boiled the water too long, causing too much liquid to evaporate. Soggy bottoms? Be patient! You filled them too soon. If you can fill just before serving, do so. Don't fill more than 2 hours before serving. Outside not crisp? Bake them longer. They should be golden brown, crisp and dry.

PEACH CREAM PUFFS

PEACH, GREEN CHILE & CHEDDAR PIE

PEACH, GREEN CHILE & CHEDDAR PIE

After tasting a fantastic green chile apple pie in a local restaurant, I knew I would have to try it with peaches. The result was fantastic! The combination of flavors in this unique pie tells you what every New Mexican knows: Green chile goes well with everything!

—Rd Stendel-Freels, Albuquerque, NM

PREP: 40 MIN. + CHILLING • **BAKE:** 45 MIN. • **MAKES:** 8 SERVINGS

- **2½ cups all-purpose flour**
- **3 Tbsp. sugar**
- **14 Tbsp. butter, cubed**
- **½ cup shredded aged cheddar cheese**
- **1 large egg yolk, room temperature**
- **6 to 8 Tbsp. ice water**

FILLING

- **3 Hatch peppers, roasted, peeled, seeded and chopped (about 1 cup)**
- **⅔ cup sugar**
- **¼ cup all-purpose flour**
- **½ tsp. ground cinnamon**
- **¼ tsp. ground nutmeg**
- **¼ tsp. salt**
- **5 cups sliced peeled peaches (about 6 medium peaches)**
- **¼ cup shredded aged cheddar cheese**
- **2 Tbsp. butter**

1. Place flour and sugar in a food processor; pulse until blended. Add butter; pulse until butter is the size of peas. Add ½ cup cheese; pulse 1-2 times. Transfer the flour mixture to a large bowl. Mix together egg yolk and 6 Tbsp. ice water; gradually add to flour mixture. Toss with a fork until dough holds together when pressed, adding more water if needed. Divide the dough in half. Shape each into a disk. Wrap and refrigerate 30 minutes or overnight.

2. Preheat oven to 450°. Wrap chopped green chiles in 3 layers of paper towel and squeeze gently to remove excess moisture. In a large bowl, combine sugar, flour, cinnamon, nutmeg and salt. Add peaches and green chiles; toss to coat.

3. On a lightly floured surface, roll 1 dough portion into a ⅛-in.-thick circle; transfer to a 9-in. pie plate. Trim crust even with rim. Sprinkle bottom with cheese. Add filling; dot with butter. Roll out remaining dough; make a lattice crust. Place over the filling. Trim, seal and flute edge.

4. Bake on lower rack for 10 minutes. Reduce the oven setting to 350°. Bake 35-40 minutes longer or until crust is golden brown and filling is bubbly. Cool on a wire rack.

1 piece: 525 cal., 27g fat (16g sat. fat), 91mg chol., 308mg sod., 65g carb. (30g sugars, 4g fiber), 8g pro.

5i PEACH-BASIL COOLER

A combo of peaches, basil and lemon make the starter for this lovely beverage. Mix with club soda for a cool and refreshing mocktail!

—Dana Hinck, Pensacola, FL

PREP: 25 MIN. + CHILLING • **MAKES:** 12 SERVINGS

- **2 cups sugar**
- **4 cups chopped peeled fresh peaches or 1 lb. frozen unsweetened sliced peaches**
- **1 pkg. (¾ oz.) fresh basil leaves**
- **2 cups cold water**
- **1½ cups fresh lemon juice**
- **Additional cold water**
- **Ice cubes**
- **Club soda or champagne**
- **Additional fresh basil leaves**

1. In a large saucepan, combine sugar, peaches, basil and water; bring to a boil. Reduce the heat; simmer, uncovered, 5 minutes. Remove from heat; let stand for 30 minutes. Discard basil; stir in lemon juice. Refrigerate until cooled completely.

2. Place peach mixture in a blender; cover and process until blended. Strain into a pitcher; add additional cold water to reach desired consistency. To serve, fill glasses with ice. Pour peach mixture halfway up glass; top with club soda or, if desired, champagne. Serve with additional basil.

1 cup: 157 cal., 0 fat (0 sat. fat), 0 chol., 1mg sod., 41g carb. (38g sugars, 1g fiber), 1g pro.

FRESH PLUM CRUMB DESSERT

Talk about comfort food! This old-fashioned dessert has the perfect sweet-tart balance with its fresh-plum tang and sweet, crispy topping. Imagine it warm from the oven, served with a scoop of ice cream...yum.

—Janet Fahrenbruck-Lynch, Cincinnati, OH

PREP: 25 MIN. • BAKE: 40 MIN. + COOLING • MAKES: 8 SERVINGS

- **7 large plums, pitted and quartered**
- **½ cup packed brown sugar**
- **3 Tbsp. plus 1 cup all-purpose flour, divided**
- **1 tsp. ground cinnamon**
- **1 cup sugar**
- **1 tsp. baking powder**
- **¼ tsp. salt**
- **¼ tsp. ground mace**
- **1 large egg, room temperature, lightly beaten**
- **½ cup butter, melted**

1. In a large bowl, combine the plums, brown sugar, 3 Tbsp. flour and cinnamon. Spoon into a greased 2-qt. baking dish.

2. In a small bowl, combine the sugar, baking powder, salt, mace and remaining flour. Add egg; stir with a fork until crumbly. Sprinkle over plum mixture. Drizzle with butter.

3. Bake at 375° for 40-45 minutes or until plums are tender and top is golden brown. Cool for 10 minutes before serving. Serve warm or at room temperature.

1 piece: 358 cal., 13g fat (7g sat. fat), 57mg chol., 253mg sod., 60g carb. (44g sugars, 2g fiber), 3g pro.

PLUM STREUSEL KUCHEN

This recipe is actually called platz (flat) in German, and has been in my family since before I was born. The fresh fruits make it a favorite.

—Lisa Warkentin, Winnipeg, MB

PREP: 25 MIN. • BAKE: 35 MIN. • MAKES: 15 SERVINGS

- **2 cups all-purpose flour**
- **¼ cup sugar**
- **2 tsp. baking powder**
- **¼ tsp. salt**
- **2 Tbsp. shortening**
- **1 large egg, room temperature**
- **1 cup heavy whipping cream**
- **6 fresh plums, sliced**

TOPPING

- **⅔ cup all-purpose flour**
- **⅔ cup sugar**
- **2 Tbsp. cold butter**
- **2 Tbsp. heavy whipping cream**

1. Preheat oven to 350°. In a large bowl, combine the flour, sugar, baking powder and salt; cut in shortening until mixture resembles fine crumbs. In another bowl, whisk the egg and cream; add to crumb mixture, tossing gently with a fork until mixture forms a ball.

2. Press dough into a greased 13x9-in. baking dish. Arrange plums over crust.

3. For topping, in a small bowl, combine the flour and sugar; cut in butter until mixture resembles fine crumbs. Add cream, mixing gently with a fork until moist crumbs form. Sprinkle over plums.

4. Bake until a toothpick inserted in center comes out clean, 35-40 minutes. Cool on wire rack.

1 piece: 235 cal., 10g fat (6g sat. fat), 37mg chol., 126mg sod., 33g carb. (15g sugars, 1g fiber), 3g pro.

FRESH PLUM CRUMB DESSERT

CHAPTER 8

FABULOUS FRUITS & MELONS

You'll take a bite out of summer every time you prepare these finger-licking favorites. From apples to watermelon and everything in between, these popular pieces of produce always deliver satisfaction, particularly when prepared in these exciting new ways.

SKILLET PORK CHOPS WITH APPLES & ONION

Simple recipes that land on the table fast are a lifesaver. I serve these skillet pork chops with veggies and, when there's time, cornbread stuffing.

—Tracey Karst, Ponderay, ID

TAKES: 20 MIN. • MAKES: 4 SERVINGS

- **4 boneless pork loin chops (6 oz. each)**
- **3 medium apples, cut into wedges**
- **1 large onion, cut into thin wedges**
- **¼ cup water**
- **⅓ cup balsamic vinaigrette**
- **½ tsp. salt**
- **¼ tsp. pepper**

1. Place a large nonstick skillet over medium heat; brown pork chops on both sides, about 4 minutes. Remove from pan.

2. In same skillet, combine apples, onion and water. Place pork chops over apple mixture; drizzle chops with vinaigrette. Sprinkle with salt and pepper. Reduce heat; simmer, covered, until a thermometer inserted in chops reads 145°, 3-5 minutes.

1 pork chop with ¾ cup apple mixture: 360 cal., 15g fat (4g sat. fat), 82mg chol., 545mg sod., 22g carb. (15g sugars, 3g fiber), 33g pro. **Diabetic exchanges:** 5 lean meat, 1 fruit, 1 fat.

NUTTY APPLE BUTTER

Being a New England native, I love apple-picking season. Grab some apples and peanut butter to make this creamy PB&J riff. Use it for dunking sliced fruit or graham crackers, or spread it on a sandwich.

—Brandie Cranshaw, Rapid City, SD

PREP: 20 MIN. • COOK: 8 HOURS • MAKES: 5 CUPS

- **4 lbs. apples (about 8 large), peeled and chopped**
- **¾ to 1 cup sugar**
- **¼ cup water**
- **3 tsp. ground cinnamon**
- **¼ tsp. ground nutmeg**
- **¼ tsp. ground cloves**
- **¼ tsp. ground allspice**
- **¼ cup creamy peanut butter**

1. In a greased 5-qt. slow cooker, combine the first 7 ingredients. Cook, covered, on low 8-10 hours or until apples are tender.

2. Whisk in peanut butter until apple mixture is smooth. Cool to room temperature. Store in an airtight container in the refrigerator.

2 Tbsp.: 43 cal., 1g fat (0 sat. fat), 0 chol., 7mg sod., 9g carb. (8g sugars, 1g fiber), 0 pro. **Diabetic exchanges:** ½ starch.

SKILLET PORK CHOPS
WITH APPLES & ONION

EASY APPLE STRUDEL

EASY APPLE STRUDEL

My family always loves it when I make this wonderful dessert. Old-fashioned strudel was too fattening and time-consuming, but this revised classic is just as good. It's best served warm from the oven.

—Joanie Fuson, Indianapolis, IN

PREP: 30 MIN. • **BAKE:** 35 MIN. • **MAKES:** 6 SERVINGS

- **⅓ cup raisins**
- **2 Tbsp. water**
- **¼ tsp. almond extract**
- **3 cups coarsely chopped peeled apples**
- **⅓ cup plus 2 tsp. sugar, divided**
- **3 Tbsp. all-purpose flour**
- **¼ tsp. ground cinnamon**
- **2 Tbsp. butter, melted**
- **2 Tbsp. canola oil**
- **8 sheets phyllo dough (14x9-in. size)**
- **Confectioners' sugar, optional**

FARMERS MARKET FIND

Apples range in flavor from sweet to tart, depending on the variety, so get creative with them. Try apples in things such as salads and sauces as well as in pies and breads.

1. Preheat oven to 350°. Place raisins, water and extract in a large microwave-save bowl; microwave, uncovered, on high for 1½ minutes. Let stand 5 minutes. Drain. Add apples, ⅓ cup sugar, flour and cinnamon; toss to combine.

2. In a small bowl, mix melted butter and oil; remove 2 tsp. mixture for brushing top. Place 1 sheet of the phyllo dough on a work surface; brush lightly with some of the butter mixture. (Keep remaining phyllo covered with a damp towel to prevent it from drying out.) Layer with 7 additional phyllo sheets, brushing each layer with some of the butter mixture. Spread apple mixture over phyllo to within 2 in. of 1 long side.

3. Fold the short edges over filling. Roll up jelly-roll style, starting from the side with a 2-in. border. Transfer to a baking sheet coated with cooking spray. Brush with the reserved butter mixture; sprinkle with the remaining sugar. With a sharp knife, cut diagonal slits in top of strudel.

4. Bake until golden brown, 35-40 minutes. Cool on a wire rack. If desired, dust with confectioners' sugar before serving.

1 slice: 229 cal., 9g fat (3g sat. fat), 10mg chol., 92mg sod., 37g carb. (24g sugars, 2g fiber), 2g pro.

HOW-TO

Buy Apples

Look for apples with deep colors, as that indicates when apples have absorbed a lot of sunlight. Give apples a squeeze; they should be firm with no give. Also inspect them for blemishes or dents, as these can accelerate decay.

Store Apples

Store apples in a cool place. If storing in the refrigerator, place apples in a bag with holes in it in the crisper bin. Remove any damaged apples so rot does not spread. Don't store other fruits or vegetables in the same drawer; apples give off ethylene gas, which causes produce to rot faster.

Prep Apples

Always wash apples (especially nonorganic apples) before eating or prepping for use in a recipe. Use 1 tsp. of baking soda to 2 cups of water as a wash; this has been shown to remove the majority of trace pesticides from apple skin.

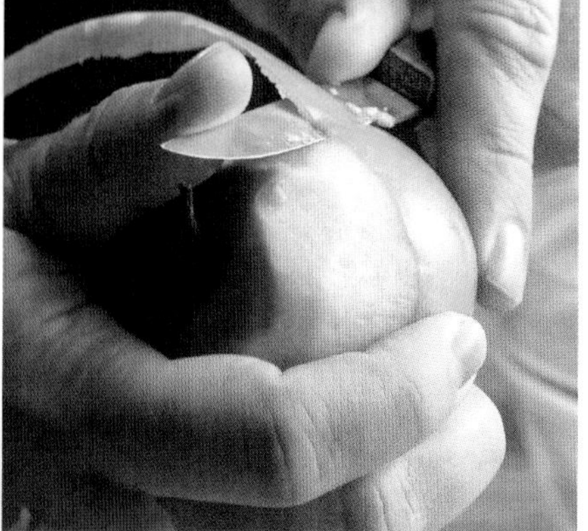

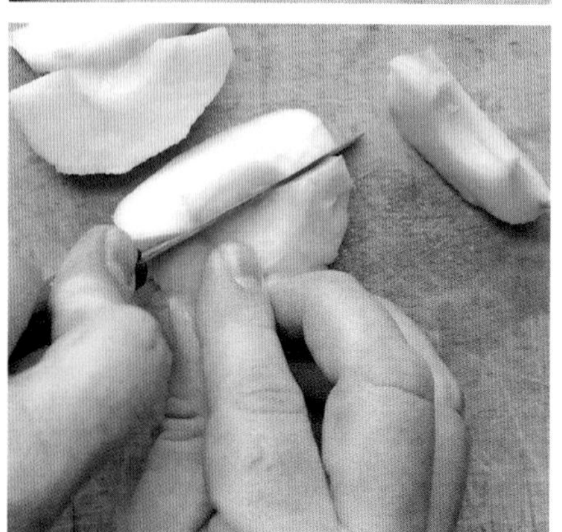

HOW-TO

Peel, Scoop & Slice Apples
Using a sharp knife, peel a washed apple and cut in half. Use a spoon or small scoop to remove the center seeds and membranes. Slice each apple half into wedges or as desired. You can also core a whole apple using an apple corer.

APPLE COMFORT

Years ago, we were without electricity for nine days during an ice storm, but I was able to run the slow cooker from our generator. The situation called for dessert, and I pulled it off with this recipe. It has been a favorite ever since.
—Awynne Thurstenson, Siloam Springs, AR

PREP: 30 MIN. • COOK: 4 HOURS • MAKES: 8 SERVINGS

- **8 medium tart apples, peeled and sliced**
- **1 cup sugar**
- **¼ cup all-purpose flour**
- **2 tsp. ground cinnamon**
- **2 large eggs**
- **1 cup heavy whipping cream**
- **1 tsp. vanilla extract**
- **1 cup graham cracker crumbs**
- **½ cup chopped pecans**
- **¼ cup butter, melted**
- **Optional: Vanilla or cinnamon ice cream**

1. In a large bowl, combine the apples, sugar, flour and cinnamon. Spoon into a greased 3-qt. slow cooker. Whisk the eggs, cream and vanilla; pour over apple mixture. Combine the cracker crumbs, pecans and butter; sprinkle over top.

2. Cover and cook on low for 4-5 hours or until apples are tender. Serve warm, with ice cream if desired.

¾ cup: 443 cal., 25g fat (12g sat. fat), 109mg chol., 133mg sod., 55g carb. (42g sugars, 4g fiber), 4g pro.

Test Kitchen Tip: Choose an apple that will hold up to cooking. Granny Smith, Honeycrisp or Jonagold are good options.

"THIS WAS A BIG HIT WITH THE FAMILY AT CHRISTMAS. IT IS NOW REQUESTED FOR EVERY FAMILY GATHERING WE HAVE—BIG OR SMALL."

—NANNY51, TASTEOFHOME.COM

APPLE COMFORT

BLUE-RIBBON APPLE PIE

BLUE-RIBBON APPLE PIE

With its hidden layer of walnuts, this pie is special to me because I won a blue ribbon for it at the local fair, which allowed me to enter it in the state farm show.

—Collette Gaugler, Fogelsville, PA

PREP: 45 MIN. • **BAKE:** 55 MINUTES • **MAKES:** 8 SERVINGS

Pastry for double-crust pie

WALNUT LAYER

- **¾ cup ground walnuts**
- **2 Tbsp. brown sugar**
- **2 Tbsp. lightly beaten egg**
- **1 Tbsp. butter, melted**
- **1 Tbsp. 2% milk**
- **¼ tsp. lemon juice**
- **¼ tsp. vanilla extract**

FILLING

- **6 cups sliced peeled tart apples (4-5 medium)**
- **2 tsp. lemon juice**
- **½ tsp. vanilla extract**
- **¾ cup sugar**
- **3 Tbsp. all-purpose flour**
- **1¼ tsp. ground cinnamon**
- **¼ tsp. ground nutmeg**
- **⅛ tsp. salt**
- **3 Tbsp. butter, cubed**

TOPPING

- **1 tsp. 2% milk**
- **2 tsp. sugar**

1. Preheat the oven to 375°. On a lightly floured surface, roll half of dough to a ⅛-in.-thick circle; transfer to a 9-in. pie plate. Trim crust even with rim.

2. In a small bowl, mix walnut layer ingredients until blended. Spread onto bottom of crust. Refrigerate while preparing filling.

3. For filling, in a large bowl, toss apples with lemon juice and vanilla. In a small bowl, mix the sugar, flour, cinnamon, nutmeg and salt; add to apple mixture and toss to coat.

4. Pour filling over walnut layer; dot with butter. Roll the remaining dough to a ⅛-in.-thick circle. Place over filling. Trim, seal and flute edge. Brush top with milk; sprinkle with sugar. Cut slits in crust.

5. Place pie on a baking sheet. Bake 55-65 minutes or until crust is golden brown and filling is bubbly. Cover edge loosely with foil during the last 10 minutes if needed to prevent overbrowning. Remove foil. Cool on a wire rack.

1 piece: 611 cal., 36g fat (10g sat. fat), 31mg chol., 234mg sod., 67g carb. (33g sugars, 3g fiber), 6g pro.

Pastry for double-crust pie (9 in.): Combine 2½ cups all-purpose flour and ½ tsp. salt; cut in 1 cup shortening until crumbly. Gradually add 4 to 5 Tbsp. ice water, tossing with a fork until dough holds together when pressed. Divide dough in half and shape into disks; wrap and refrigerate 1 hour.

HOW-TO

Buy Cantaloupe

Select melons that are heavy for their size and have no cracks or dents in the skin. A ripe melon should have a fruity, pleasant aroma. Avoid melons that are bruised or have a strong aroma, which indicates they are overripe.

Store Cantaloupe

Store underripe melons at room temperature for 2-3 days. Store ripe melons in the refrigerator for 1 week. Store cut melon in an airtight container in the refrigerator.

Prep Cantaloupe

Cut the melon in half and remove the seeds. Cut into cubes or wedges, or use a melon baller or ice cream scoop to shape fruit into balls. Serve chilled if desired. Note that chilling sometimes diminishes the flavor.

TANDOORI-STYLE CHICKEN WITH CANTALOUPE RELISH

We all need those quick meals that are deliciously healthy. At our house, I marinate chicken before leaving for work, and when I get home, I grill it and make this relish. My husband loves the spicy flavor. If more heat is desired, add more crushed red pepper flakes.

—Naylet LaRochelle, Miami, FL

PREP: 20 MIN. + MARINATING • GRILL: 15 MIN. • MAKES: 4 SERVINGS

- **1½ cups reduced-fat plain yogurt**
- **2 Tbsp. lemon juice, divided**
- **1½ tsp. garam masala or curry powder**
- **½ tsp. salt**
- **¼ to ½ tsp. crushed red pepper flakes**
- **4 boneless skinless chicken breast halves (6 oz. each)**
- **1½ cups chopped cantaloupe**
- **½ cup chopped seeded peeled cucumber**
- **2 green onions, finely chopped**
- **2 Tbsp. minced fresh cilantro**
- **1 Tbsp. minced fresh mint**
- **¼ cup toasted sliced almonds, optional**

1. In a small bowl, whisk yogurt, 1 Tbsp. lemon juice, garam masala, salt and pepper flakes until blended. Pour 1 cup marinade into a large bowl. Add chicken; turn to coat. Cover; refrigerate up to 6 hours. Cover and refrigerate remaining marinade.

2. For the relish, in a small bowl, mix the cantaloupe, cucumber, green onions, cilantro, mint and remaining lemon juice.

3. Drain chicken, discarding marinade in bowl. Grill chicken, covered, on a lightly oiled rack over medium heat or broil 4 in. from heat until a thermometer reads 165°, 6-8 minutes on each side. Serve with relish and reserved marinade. If desired, sprinkle with almonds.

1 serving: 247 cal., 5g fat (2g sat. fat), 98mg chol., 332mg sod., 10g carb. (9g sugars, 1g fiber), 38g pro. **Diabetic exchanges:** 5 lean meat, ½ starch.

TANDOORI-STYLE CHICKEN WITH CANTALOUPE RELISH

MOJITO MARINATED FRUIT

MOJITO MARINATED FRUIT

All the flavors of the popular mojito cocktail are featured in this fantastic salad. After you eat the fruit, you'll want to sip the luscious syrup!

—Marcy Griffith, Excelsior, MN

PREP: 20 MIN. + CHILLING • MAKES: 8 SERVINGS

- **⅔ cup sugar**
- **⅓ cup water**
- **½ cup light rum**
- **2 Tbsp. lime juice**
- **1 tsp. grated lime zest**
- **2 cups each cantaloupe, honeydew and seedless watermelon balls or chunks**
- **2 cups cubed fresh pineapple**
- **3 mint sprigs**
- **Fresh mint leaves, optional**

1. In a small saucepan, combine sugar and water; cook and stir over medium heat until the sugar is dissolved. Remove from heat. Stir in the rum, lime juice and zest. Cool completely.

2. In a large bowl, combine melons, pineapple and mint sprigs. Add rum mixture; toss to coat. Refrigerate, covered, overnight.

3. Discard mint sprigs. Spoon fruit with syrup into serving dishes. If desired, top with mint.

1 cup: 128 cal., 0 fat (0 sat. fat), 0 chol., 8mg sod., 26g carb. (24g sugars, 1g fiber), 1g pro.

CANTALOUPE CHICKEN SALAD WITH YOGURT CHIVE DRESSING

It's hard to find recipes that all four children and my husband love. That's why this refreshing combo of melon and chicken is so special to our family.

—Elizabeth King, Duluth, MN

TAKES: 30 MIN. • MAKES: 5 SERVINGS

- **½ cup plain yogurt**
- **½ cup reduced-fat mayonnaise**
- **1 Tbsp. minced chives**
- **1 Tbsp. lime juice**
- **¼ tsp. salt**
- **5 cups cubed cantaloupe**
- **2½ cups cubed cooked chicken breast**
- **1 medium cucumber, seeded and chopped**
- **1 cup green grapes, halved**

In a large bowl, combine the first 5 ingredients. Add the cantaloupe, chicken, cucumber and grapes; toss gently to combine. Serve immediately.

2 cups: 290 cal., 11g fat (2g sat. fat), 65mg chol., 380mg sod., 24g carb. (21g sugars, 2g fiber), 24g pro. **Diabetic exchanges:** 3 lean meat, 1½ fruit, 1 fat.

Curried Chicken Fruit Salad: Cut dressing in half; substitute ¼ to ½ tsp. curry powder for chives. Add the chicken, green grapes, and a drained 8-oz. can of pineapple tidbits.

GINGER-GLAZED GRILLED HONEYDEW

If you've never grilled fruit like this before, you're in for a real treat! I love the idea of cooking everything from appetizers to desserts on the grill, and this dinner finale is sweet and light!

—Jacqueline Correa, Landing, NJ

TAKES: 25 MIN. • MAKES: 6 SERVINGS

- **¼ cup peach preserves**
- **1 Tbsp. lemon juice**
- **1 Tbsp. finely chopped crystallized ginger**
- **2 tsp. grated lemon zest**
- **⅛ tsp. ground cloves**
- **1 medium honeydew melon, cut into 2-in. cubes**

1. In a small bowl, combine the first 5 ingredients. Thread honeydew onto 6 metal or soaked wooden skewers; brush with half the glaze.

2. On a lightly oiled rack, grill honeydew, covered, over medium-high heat or broil 4 in. from the heat just until the melon begins to soften and brown, 4-6 minutes, turning and basting frequently with the remaining glaze.

1 skewer: 101 cal., 0 fat (0 sat. fat), 0 chol., 18mg sod., 26g carb. (23g sugars, 1g fiber), 1g pro. **Diabetic exchanges:** 1 fruit, ½ starch.

Test Kitchen Tip: These honeydew skewers are a sweet (and delicious) way to get a healthy dose of vitamin C and potassium.

HONEYDEW GRANITA

Make this refreshing summer treat when melons are ripe and flavorful. I like to garnish each serving with a sprig of mint or a small slice of honeydew.

—Bonnie Hawkins, Elkhorn, WI

PREP: 10 MIN. • COOK: 5 MIN. + FREEZING • MAKES: 5½ CUPS

- **1 cup sugar**
- **1 cup water**
- **6 cups cubed honeydew melon**
- **2 Tbsp. sweet white wine**

1. In a small saucepan, bring sugar and water to a boil over medium-high heat. Cook and stir until sugar is dissolved. Cool.

2. Pulse the honeydew, sugar syrup and wine in batches in a food processor until smooth, 1-2 minutes. Transfer to an 8-in. square dish. Freeze 1 hour. Stir with a fork. Freeze mixture, stirring every 30 minutes, until frozen, 2-3 hours longer. Stir with a fork just before serving.

½ cup: 107 cal., 0 fat (0 sat. fat), 0 chol., 17mg sod., 27g carb. (26g sugars, 1g fiber), 1g pro. **Diabetic exchanges:** 1½ starch, ½ fruit.

Test Kitchen Tip: Instead of cubing the melon, try using an ice cream scoop to remove the fruit from the rind.

HONEYDEW GRANITA

HONEYDEW, CUCUMBER
& STRAWBERRY SALAD

HONEYDEW, CUCUMBER & STRAWBERRY SALAD

Strawberries and cucumbers together—I just love this combination! We used to eat a lot of cucumbers growing up in upstate New York. We'd get them, along with strawberries and melons, from fruit and veggie stands to make this sweet and tangy salad.
—Melissa McCabe, Victor, NY

TAKES: 20 MIN. • **MAKES:** 8 SERVINGS

- **1 container (16 oz.) fresh strawberries, halved**
- **1 English cucumber, halved lengthwise and cut into ¼-in. slices**
- **1 cup cubed honeydew melon (½-in. pieces)**
- **3 Tbsp. honey**
- **2 Tbsp. lime juice**
- **1 tsp. grated lime zest**

1. In a large bowl, combine strawberries, cucumber and honeydew. Chill until serving.

2. In a small bowl, whisk the remaining ingredients. Just before serving, drizzle over strawberry mixture; toss gently to coat.

¾ cup: 56 cal., 0 fat (0 sat. fat), 0 chol., 6mg sod., 15g carb. (12g sugars, 2g fiber), 1g pro. **Diabetic exchanges:** 1 fruit.

ICED HONEYDEW MINT TEA

I grow mint in the garden on my balcony. In this minty tea, I blend two of my favorite beverages—Moroccan mint tea and honeydew agua fresca.
—Sarah Batt Throne, El Cerrito, CA

TAKES: 20 MIN. • **MAKES:** 10 SERVINGS (2½ QT.)

- **4 cups water**
- **24 fresh mint leaves**
- **8 green tea bags**
- **⅔ cup sugar**
- **5 cups diced honeydew melon**
- **3 cups ice cubes**
- **Additional ice cubes**

1. In a large saucepan, bring water to a boil; remove from heat. Add the mint leaves and tea bags; steep, covered, 3-5 minutes according to taste, stirring occasionally. Discard mint and tea bags. Stir in sugar.

2. Place 2½ cups honeydew, 2 cups tea and 1½ cups ice in a blender; cover and process until blended. Serve over additional ice. Repeat with remaining ingredients.

1 cup: 83 cal., 0 fat (0 sat. fat), 0 chol., 15mg sod., 21g carb. (20g sugars, 1g fiber), 0 pro. **Diabetic exchanges:** 1 starch, ½ fruit.

MIMOSA ROASTED CHICKEN

This aromatic seasoned chicken with a rich and buttery champagne gravy will delight all who taste it.

—Taste of Home *Test Kitchen*

PREP: 15 MIN. • BAKE: 2¼ HOURS + STANDING • MAKES: 6 SERVINGS

- **2 medium navel oranges**
- **1 roasting chicken (6 to 7 lbs.)**
- **¾ tsp. pepper, divided**
- **¼ cup butter, softened**
- **4 garlic cloves, minced**
- **1 Tbsp. dried basil**
- **1 tsp. salt**
- **½ tsp. onion powder**
- **½ tsp. dried marjoram**
- **2 cups brut champagne**
- **2 medium onions, cut into wedges**
- **½ cup chicken broth**
- **½ cup orange juice**

GRAVY

- **Chicken broth or water**
- **1 Tbsp. butter**
- **2 Tbsp. all-purpose flour**

1. Cut 1 orange into slices; cut remaining orange into wedges. With fingers, carefully loosen the skin from both sides of chicken breast. Place orange slices under the skin. Place orange wedges inside cavity and sprinkle chicken with ¼ tsp. pepper.

2. Tuck wings under chicken. Place breast side up on a rack in a shallow roasting pan. Combine the butter, garlic, basil, salt, onion powder, marjoram and remaining pepper; rub over chicken.

3. Bake, uncovered, at 350° for 30 minutes. Meanwhile, in a large bowl, combine the champagne, onions, broth and orange juice; pour into pan. Bake until a thermometer reads 175°, 1½-2 hours longer, basting occasionally with pan juices. Cover loosely with foil if chicken browns too quickly. Cover and let stand for 15 minutes before slicing chicken.

4. For gravy, pour drippings and loosened browned bits into a measuring cup. Skim fat, reserving 1 Tbsp. Add enough broth to the drippings to measure 1 cup. In a small saucepan, melt butter and reserved fat. Stir in the flour until smooth, gradually add broth mixture. Bring to a boil; cook and stir until thickened, about 2 minutes. Serve with the chicken.

6 oz. cooked chicken with 2 Tbsp. gravy: 731 cal., 41g fat (15g sat. fat), 204mg chol., 798mg sod., 17g carb. (9g sugars, 2g fiber), 58g pro.

"THIS IS VERY MOIST, AND IT'S EVEN GOOD COLD THE NEXT DAY."

—EILEENSDELITES, TASTEOFHOME.COM

MIMOSA
ROASTED CHICKEN

SOUTH-OF-THE-BORDER
CITRUS SALAD

SOUTH-OF-THE-BORDER CITRUS SALAD

Orange, grapefruit and jicama add color and texture to this out-of-the-ordinary fruit salad. Sometimes I'll toss in slices of mango and cucumber for extra flair.

—Mary Fuller, SeaTac, WA

TAKES: 20 MIN. • MAKES: 6 SERVINGS

- **3 medium pink grapefruit**
- **3 medium oranges**
- **1 cup julienned peeled jicama**
- **2 Tbsp. minced fresh cilantro**
- **2 Tbsp. lime juice**
- **¼ tsp. ground cinnamon**

1. Cut a thin slice from the top and bottom of each grapefruit and orange; stand fruit upright on a cutting board. With a knife, cut peel and outer membrane from fruit. Cut fruit crosswise into slices; place in a large bowl.

2. Add remaining ingredients; toss to combine. Transfer to a platter; refrigerate, covered, until serving.

¾ cup: 70 cal., 0 fat (0 sat. fat), 0 chol., 2mg sod., 17g carb. (13g sugars, 3g fiber), 1g pro. **Diabetic exchanges:** 1 fruit.

HAPPY ORANGE TURKEY

Champagne and oranges flavor this special bird—this will become one of your favorite turkey recipes ever.

—Tara Baier, Menomonie, WI

PREP: 30 MIN. • BAKE: 3¾ HOURS + STANDING • MAKES: 24 SERVINGS

- **3 medium oranges**
- **½ cup butter, softened**
- **1 turkey (14 to 16 lbs.)**
- **1 Tbsp. garlic powder**
- **1 tsp. salt**
- **½ tsp. pepper**
- **2 Tbsp. butter, melted**
- **1 small onion, cut into wedges**
- **4 fresh rosemary sprigs**
- **2 fresh thyme sprigs**
- **2 Tbsp. all-purpose flour**
- **Turkey-size oven roasting bag**
- **1½ cups Champagne**
- **½ cup orange juice**

1. Finely grate zest from oranges. Cut the fruit into wedges. Combine softened butter and orange zest. With fingers, carefully loosen skin from the turkey; rub butter mixture under the skin.

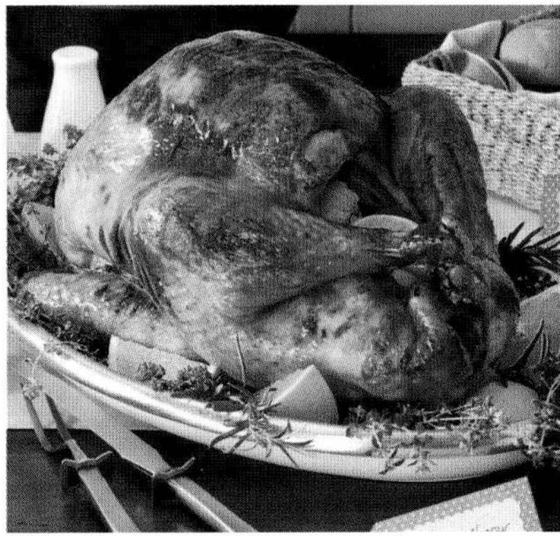

2. Pat turkey dry. Combine the garlic powder, salt and pepper; rub over the outside and inside of turkey. Drizzle with melted butter. Place the oranges, onion, rosemary and thyme inside the cavity. Skewer the turkey openings; tie the drumsticks together.

3. Place flour in oven bag and shake to coat. Place oven bag in a roasting pan. Place the turkey, breast side up, in bag. Pour Champagne and orange juice over turkey. Cut six ½-in. slits in top of bag; close bag with tie provided.

4. Bake at 325° for 3¾-4¼ hours or until a thermometer inserted in thickest part of thigh reads 170°-175°. Remove turkey to a serving platter and keep warm. Let stand for 20 minutes before carving. If desired, thicken pan drippings for gravy.

6 oz. cooked turkey: 374 cal., 19 fat (7 sat. fat), 156 chol., 238 sod.,3g carb. 2g sugar, 0 fiber), 43g pro.

CITRUS-SPICE GLAZED HAM

My dad gave me this recipe. With its Chinese-inspired glaze, it's a fun twist on traditional ham.
—Amanda Lambert, Bethel, OH

PREP: 10 MIN. • BAKE: 2¾ HOURS • MAKES: 12 SERVINGS

1 fully cooked bone-in ham (7 to 9 lbs.)

GLAZE

½ cup orange juice, divided
1 tsp. Chinese five-spice powder
⅓ cup packed brown sugar
1 Tbsp. honey
4 tsp. cornstarch
2 medium oranges, peeled and sectioned
1 can (20 oz.) unsweetened pineapple tidbits, drained

1. Preheat oven to 325°. Place ham on a rack in a shallow roasting pan. Cover and bake until a thermometer reads 130°, 2½-3 hours.

2. Meanwhile, in a small saucepan, combine ¼ cup orange juice and the Chinese five-spice powder; bring to a boil. Reduce heat; simmer, uncovered, until thickened, 1-2 minutes. Stir in brown sugar and honey. In a small bowl, mix the cornstarch and remaining orange juice until smooth; stir into brown sugar mixture. Return to a boil, stirring constantly; cook and stir until thickened, 1-2 minutes.

3. Remove ham from oven. Brush with half of the glaze. Bake the ham, uncovered, until a thermometer reads 140°, 15-20 minutes. Just before serving, stir fruit into the remaining glaze; heat through. Serve with ham.

5 oz. cooked ham: 293 cal., 7g fat (2g sat. fat), 116mg chol., 1392mg sod., 19g carb. (17g sugars, 1g fiber), 39g pro.

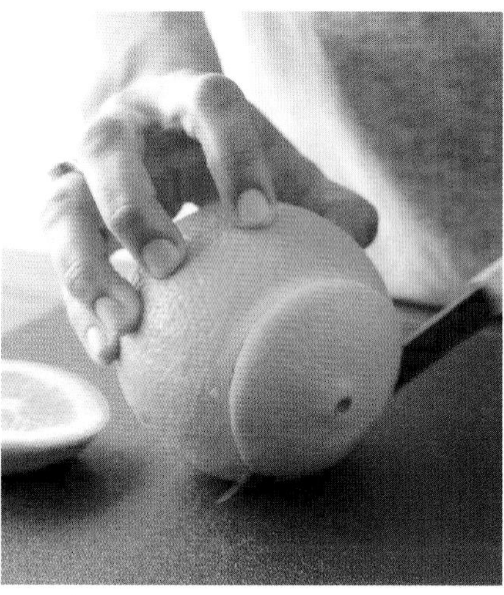

HOW-TO

Segment Oranges

- Slice off both ends of citrus, then stand fruit on one end.
- Using a paring knife, carefully cut away the peel and white pith, following the curve of the fruit.
- Working over a bowl, cut against the membrane on either side to release the orange segments.

CITRUS-SPICE GLAZED HAM

WATERMELON PIZZA

WATERMELON PIZZA

Start with grilled melon slices and layer on the tangy, salty and sweet toppings for a summer-fresh appetizer.

—Ellen Riley, Murfreesboro, TN

PREP: 25 MIN. • GRILL: 10 MIN. + CHILLING • MAKES: 8 SERVINGS

- **8 wedges seedless watermelon, about 1 in. thick**
- **1 cup heirloom cherry tomatoes, sliced**
- **1 cup fresh baby arugula**
- **½ cup fresh blueberries**
- **⅓ cup crumbled feta cheese**
- **⅓ cup pitted Greek olives, halved**
- **1 Tbsp. olive oil**
- **⅛ tsp. kosher salt**
- **⅛ tsp. coarsely ground pepper**
- **Balsamic glaze, optional**

1. Grill watermelon, covered, on a greased grill rack over medium-high direct heat until seared, 5-6 minutes on each side. Remove from heat; transfer to a platter. Chill.

2. To serve, top chilled watermelon with the tomatoes, arugula, blueberries, feta and olives. Drizzle with olive oil; season with salt and pepper. If desired, drizzle with balsamic glaze.

1 wedge: 91 cal., 4g fat (1g sat. fat), 3mg chol., 169mg sod., 13g carb. (11g sugars, 1g fiber), 2g pro. **Diabetic exchanges:** 1 fruit, 1 fat.

5i WATERMELON SHERBET

My family has been harvesting watermelons for generations. Our church group often serves this refreshing treat at the town's watermelon festival.

—Lisa McAdoo, Rush Springs, OK

PREP: 10 MIN. + CHILLING • COOK: 5 MIN. + FREEZING • MAKES: ½ GALLON

- **8 cups seeded chopped watermelon**
- **1½ cups sugar**
- **½ cup lemon juice**
- **2 envelopes unflavored gelatin**
- **½ cup cold water**
- **2 cups whole milk**

1. In a large bowl, combine watermelon, sugar and lemon juice. Chill mixture for 30 minutes; place half in a blender. Blend until smooth; pour into a large bowl. Repeat with the other half; set aside.

2. In a saucepan, cook and stir gelatin and water over low heat until gelatin dissolves. Add to the watermelon mixture; mix well. Stir in the milk until well blended.

3. Freeze in an ice cream freezer according to the manufacturer's directions. Serve immediately or freeze and allow to thaw about 20 minutes before serving.

½ cup: 120 cal., 1g fat (1g sat. fat), 4mg chol., 18mg sod., 26g carb. (25g sugars, 0 fiber), 2g pro.

MINT WATERMELON SALAD

I invented this refreshing fruit salad one sultry afternoon while my friends were gathered around my pool. It was quick to prepare and disappeared from their plates even quicker. Even the kids loved it!

—Antoinette DuBeck, Huntingdon Valley, PA

TAKES: 20 MIN. • MAKES: 8 SERVINGS

- **6 cups cubed seedless watermelon**
- **2 Tbsp. minced fresh mint**
- **1 Tbsp. lemon juice**
- **1 Tbsp. olive oil**
- **2 tsp. sugar**

Place watermelon and mint in a large bowl. In a small bowl, whisk lemon juice, oil and sugar until sugar is dissolved. Drizzle over salad; toss gently to combine.

¾ cup: 56 cal., 2g fat (0 sat. fat), 0 chol., 2mg sod., 9g carb. (9g sugars, 1g fiber), 1g pro. **Diabetic exchanges:** ½ fruit.

FRUIT & MELON SALAD

For picnics, cookouts and showers, we make a sweet salad of watermelon, cherries, blueberries and microgreens. No matter where I take it, it always delivers on wow factor.

—Kaliska Russell, Talkeetna, AK

TAKES: 15 MIN. • MAKES: 6 SERVINGS

- **2 cups watermelon balls**
- **2 cups fresh sweet cherries, pitted and halved**
- **1 cup fresh blueberries**
- **½ cup cubed English cucumber**
- **½ cup microgreens or torn mixed salad greens**
- **½ cup crumbled feta cheese**
- **3 fresh mint leaves, thinly sliced**
- **¼ cup honey**
- **1 Tbsp. lemon juice**
- **1 tsp. grated lemon zest**

Combine the first 7 ingredients. In a small bowl, whisk together the remaining ingredients. Drizzle over the salad; toss.

¾ cup: 131 cal., 2g fat (1g sat. fat), 5mg chol., 94mg sod., 28g carb. (24g sugars, 2g fiber), 3g pro. **Diabetic exchanges:** 1 starch, 1 fruit.

MINT WATERMELON SALAD

HOW-TO

Buy Watermelon

Look for a watermelon that is round, dark green and feels heavy for its size. Also, be sure there's a yellow spot on the fruit's underside. This "ground spot" indicates that the melon was ripe when it was picked, ensuring sweetness.

Store Watermelon

Store in a cool, dark place or in the refrigerator, if possible. Store cut melon in an airtight container in the refrigerator for up to 1 week.

Prep Watermelon

Wash the outside of the melon to remove any dirt, then slice the melon lengthwise. Continue slicing to get the desired number of pieces. Remove the rind by slicing along the edge where the white of the rind meets the red flesh of the melon.

WATERMELON CUPS

QUICK WATERMELON SALSA

On hot days, this sweet salsa with watermelon, pineapple and fresh cilantro is sure to satisfy. Best of all, you can toss it together in a matter of minutes.

—Betsy Hanson, Tiverton, RI

PREP: 15 MIN. + CHILLING • MAKES: 3 CUPS

- **2 cups chopped seedless watermelon**
- **1 can (8 oz.) unsweetened crushed pineapple, drained**
- **¼ cup chopped sweet onion**
- **¼ cup minced fresh cilantro**
- **3 Tbsp. orange juice**
- **⅛ tsp. hot pepper sauce**
- **Tortilla chips**

In a large bowl, combine the first 6 ingredients. Cover and refrigerate for at least 1 hour. Serve salsa with tortilla chips.

¼ cup: 23 cal., 0 fat (0 sat. fat), 0 chol., 1mg sod., 5g carb. (5g sugars, 0 fiber), 0 pro. **Diabetic exchanges:** ½ fruit.

WATERMELON CUPS

This lovely appetizer is almost too pretty to eat! Sweet watermelon cubes hold a refreshing topping that showcases cucumber, red onion and fresh herbs.

—Taste of Home *Test Kitchen*

TAKES: 25 MIN. • MAKES: 16 APPETIZERS

- **16 seedless watermelon cubes (1 in.)**
- **⅓ cup finely chopped cucumber**
- **5 tsp. finely chopped red onion**
- **2 tsp. minced fresh mint**
- **2 tsp. minced fresh cilantro**
- **½ to 1 tsp. lime juice**

1. Using a small melon baller or measuring spoon, scoop out the center of each watermelon cube, leaving a ¼-in. shell (save flesh for another use).

2. In a small bowl, combine the remaining ingredients; carefully spoon into the watermelon cubes.

1 appetizer: 7 cal., 0 fat (0 sat. fat), 0 chol., 1mg sod., 2g carb. (2g sugars, 0 fiber), 0 pro.

CHAPTER 9

DIY DELICIOUS

Make the most of farm-fresh produce with finger-licking preserves, pickled specialties and the sweet frosty treats everyone craves. Follow these easy recipes and enjoy your garden bounty for months.

Note: The processing time listed for the following canning/jarring is for altitudes of 1,000 feet or less. For altitudes up to 3,000 feet, add 5 minutes; 6,000 feet, add 10 minutes; 8,000 feet, add 15 minutes; 10,000 feet, add 20 minutes.

HOW-TO

Make Freezer Jam

- Bring all ingredients to a full rolling boil.
- Remove pan from heat and skim off foam.
- Use a canning funnel to ladle jam into freezer containers, leaving ½ in. headspace.

STRAWBERRY FREEZER JAM

5i ❄ STRAWBERRY FREEZER JAM

Strawberry season is in early June here in Indiana, and I try to take advantage of it. A dear friend gave me this recipe when we lived in Germany. We even like it on ice cream!

—Mary Jean Ellis, Indianapolis, IN

PREP: 40 MIN. + FREEZING • **MAKES:** 9 HALF-PINTS

- **2 qt. fresh strawberries**
- **5½ cups sugar**
- **1 cup light corn syrup**
- **¼ cup lemon juice**
- **¾ cup water**
- **1 pkg. (1¾ oz.) powdered fruit pectin**

1. Rinse 9 half-pint plastic or freezer-safe containers and lids with boiling water. Dry thoroughly.

2. Wash and mash berries, measuring out enough mashed berries to make 4 cups; place in a large bowl. Stir in sugar, corn syrup and lemon juice. Let stand 10 minutes.

3. In a Dutch oven, combine strawberry mixture and water. Stir in pectin. Bring to a full rolling boil over high heat, stirring constantly. Boil 1 minute, stirring constantly. Remove from heat; skim off foam.

4. Ladle into containers, leaving ½ in. headspace. Cover and let stand overnight or until set, but not longer than 24 hours. Refrigerate up to 3 weeks or freeze up to 12 months.

2 Tbsp.: 79 cal., 0 fat (0 sat. fat), 0 chol., 3mg sod., 20g carb. (20g sugars, 0 fiber), 0 pro.

❄ HONEY BLUEBERRY COBBLER JAM

I work at a farmers market, and honey blueberry jam is my top seller. You've gotta taste it with fresh goat cheese and toasted candied pecans.

—Krystal Wertman, Humble, TX

PREP: 20 MIN. + STANDING • **MAKES:** 5 CUPS

- **5 cups fresh or frozen blueberries, thawed**
- **1 cup apple juice**
- **1 pkg. (1¾ oz.) pectin for lower sugar recipes**
- **1 cup honey**
- **½ tsp. ground nutmeg**
- **¼ tsp. ground cinnamon**
- **1 tsp. vanilla extract**

1. Rinse five 1-cup plastic or freezer-safe containers and lids with boiling water. Dry thoroughly.

2. Place blueberries in a large saucepan; mash blueberries. Stir in the juice and pectin. Bring to a full rolling boil over high heat, stirring constantly. Stir in the honey, nutmeg and cinnamon; return to a full rolling boil. Boil and stir 1 minute. Remove from heat; stir in vanilla.

3. Immediately fill all containers to within ½ in. of tops. Wipe off top edges of containers; immediately cover with lids. Let stand at room temperature 24 hours. Refrigerate up to 2 weeks.

Freeze option: Freeze jam for up to 12 months. To use, thaw in the refrigerator overnight before serving.

2 Tbsp.: 39 cal., 0 fat (0 sat. fat), 0 chol., 12mg sod., 10g carb. (9g sugars, 0 fiber), 0 pro.
Diabetic exchanges: ½ starch.

CARROT CAKE JAM

For a change of pace from berry jams, try this unique option. Spread on a bagel with cream cheese, it tastes almost as good as real carrot cake!

—Rachelle Stratton, Rock Springs, WY

PREP: 45 MIN. • PROCESS: 5 MIN. • MAKES: 8 HALF-PINTS

- **1 can (20 oz.) unsweetened crushed pineapple, undrained**
- **1½ cups shredded carrots**
- **1½ cups chopped peeled ripe pears**
- **3 Tbsp. lemon juice**
- **1 tsp. ground cinnamon**
- **¼ tsp. ground cloves**
- **¼ tsp. ground nutmeg**
- **1 pkg. (1¾ oz.) powdered fruit pectin**
- **6½ cups sugar**

1. Place first 7 ingredients in a large saucepan; bring to a boil. Reduce heat; simmer, covered, until pears are tender, 15-20 minutes, stirring occasionally. Stir in pectin. Bring to a full rolling boil over high heat, stirring constantly. Stir in sugar; return to a full rolling boil. Boil and stir 1 minute.

2. Remove from heat; skim off foam. Ladle hot mixture into 8 hot sterilized half-pint jars, leaving ¼-in. headspace. Remove the air bubbles and adjust headspace, if necessary, by adding hot mixture. Wipe rims. Center lids on jars; screw on bands until fingertip tight.

3. Place jars into canner with simmering water, ensuring that they are completely covered with water. Bring to a boil; process for 5 minutes. Remove jars and cool.

2 Tbsp.: 88 cal., 0 fat (0 sat. fat), 0 chol., 2mg sod., 23g carb. (22g sugars, 0 fiber), 0 pro.

5i RHUBARB JELLY

To be honest, I don't especially like cooking. My husband, however, loves it! Now that he's retired, Bob's taken up making jelly. I help him with the pouring and skimming for this one—my own personal favorite. It's nice as both a breakfast spread and a topping for pork or other meat.

—Jean Coleman, Ottawa, ON

PREP: 20 MIN. + STANDING • PROCESS: 10 MIN. • MAKES: 8 HALF-PINTS

- **4½ to 5 lbs. rhubarb (4½ to 5 qt.), cut into 1-in. pieces**
- **7 cups sugar**
- **1 to 2 drops red food coloring, optional**
- **2 pouches (3 oz. each) liquid fruit pectin**

1. Grind the rhubarb in a food processor or grinder. Line a strainer with 4 layers of cheesecloth and place over a bowl. Place rhubarb in strainer; cover with edges of cheesecloth. Let stand for 30 minutes or until liquid measures 3½ cups. Pour juice into a Dutch oven; add sugar and, if desired, food coloring.

2. Bring to a boil over high heat, stirring constantly. Add pectin; bring to a full rolling boil. Boil for 1 minute, stirring constantly. Remove from the heat; let stand a few minutes. Skim off foam. Carefully ladle hot mixture into hot half-pint jars, leaving ¼-in. headspace. Remove air bubbles; wipe rims. Center lids on jars; screw on bands until fingertip tight. Place jars into canner with hot water, ensuring that they are completely covered with water. Bring to a boil; process for 10 minutes. Remove jars and cool.

2 Tbsp.: 92 cal., 0 fat (0 sat. fat), 0 chol., 2mg sod., 24g carb. (22g sugars, 1g fiber), 0 pro.

CARROT CAKE JAM

TEXAS JALAPENO JELLY

TEXAS JALAPENO JELLY

A jar of this jelly is always warmly received. When I give it as a gift, I like to add a little southwestern accent by trimming the lid with a bandanna.

—Lori McMullen, Victoria, TX

PREP: 20 MIN. • PROCESS: 10 MIN. • MAKES: 7 HALF-PINTS

- **2 jalapeno peppers, seeded and chopped**
- **3 medium green peppers, cut into 1-in. pieces, divided**
- **1½ cups white vinegar, divided**
- **6½ cups sugar**
- **½ to 1 tsp. cayenne pepper**
- **2 pouches (3 oz. each) liquid fruit pectin**
- **About 6 drops green food coloring, optional**
- **Cream cheese and crackers, optional**

1. In a blender or food processor, place the jalapenos, half of the green peppers and ½ cup vinegar; cover and process until pureed. Transfer to a large Dutch oven.

2. Repeat with the remaining green peppers and another ½ cup vinegar. Add the sugar, cayenne and remaining vinegar to pan. Bring to a rolling boil over high heat, stirring constantly. Quickly stir in pectin. Return to a rolling boil; boil for 1 minute, stirring constantly.

3. Remove from the heat; skim off foam. Add food coloring if desired. Carefully ladle hot mixture into hot half-pint jars, leaving ¼-in. headspace. Remove air bubbles; wipe rims and adjust lids.

4. Process for 10 minutes in a boiling-water canner. Serve over cream cheese with crackers if desired.

2 Tbsp.: 92 cal., 0 fat (0 sat. fat), 0 chol., 1mg sod., 24g carb. (23g sugars, 0 fiber), 0 pro.

5I WATERMELON JELLY

With its beautiful color and intense watermelon flavor, this jelly preserves summer to enjoy long after the cool weather arrives.

—Taste of Home *Test Kitchen*

PREP: 25 MIN. + STANDING • PROCESS: 10 MIN. • MAKES: 5 HALF-PINTS

- **6 cups seeded chopped watermelon**
- **5 cups sugar**
- **⅓ cup white wine vinegar or white balsamic vinegar**
- **¼ cup lemon juice**
- **2 to 3 drops red food coloring, optional**
- **2 pouches (3 oz. each) liquid fruit pectin**

1. Place watermelon in a food processor; cover and process until pureed. Line a strainer with 4 layers of cheesecloth and place over a bowl. Place the pureed watermelon in prepared strainer; cover with edges of cheesecloth. Let stand 10 minutes or until liquid measures 2 cups.

2. Discard watermelon pulp from cheesecloth; place liquid in a large saucepan. Stir in sugar, vinegar, lemon juice and, if desired, red food coloring. Bring to a full rolling boil over high heat, stirring constantly. Stir in pectin. Continue to boil for 1 minute, stirring constantly.

3. Remove from heat; skim off foam. Ladle hot mixture into 5 hot half-pint jars, leaving ¼-in. headspace. Wipe rims. Center lids on jars; screw on bands until fingertip tight.

4. Place jars into canner with simmering water, ensuring that they are completely covered with water. Bring to a boil; process for 10 minutes. Remove jars and cool.

2 Tbsp.: 106 cal., 0 fat (0 sat. fat), 0 chol., 1mg sod., 27g carb. (27g sugars, 0 fiber), 0 pro.

OVER-THE-TOP CHERRY JAM

We adore the wonderful flavor and color of tart cherries, particularly in this sweet jam. Brilliant jars make lovely gifts for friends, neighbors and family.

—Karen Haen, Sturgeon Bay, WI

PREP: 35 MIN. • PROCESS: 5 MIN. • MAKES: 6 HALF-PINTS

2½ lbs. fresh tart cherries, pitted
1 pkg. (1¾ oz.) powdered fruit pectin
½ tsp. butter
4¾ cups sugar

1. In a food processor, cover and process cherries in batches until finely chopped. Transfer to a Dutch oven; stir in pectin and butter. Bring to a full rolling boil over high heat, stirring constantly. Stir in the sugar; return to a full rolling boil. Boil and stir 1 minute.

2. Remove from heat; skim off foam. Ladle the hot mixture into 6 hot sterilized half-pint jars, leaving ¼-in. headspace. Remove air bubbles and adjust headspace, if necessary, by adding hot mixture. Wipe rims. Center lids on jars; screw on bands until fingertip tight.

3. Place jars into canner with simmering water, ensuring that they are completely covered with water. Bring to a boil; process for 5 minutes. Remove jars and cool.

2 Tbsp.: 89 cal., 0 fat (0 sat. fat), 0 chol., 1mg sod., 23g carb. (22g sugars, 0 fiber), 0 pro.

LUSCIOUS BLUEBERRY JAM

This perfectly spreadable blueberry jam boasts a beautiful dark color with a sweet, seasonal flavor.

—Karen Haen, Sturgeon Bay, WI

PREP: 20 MIN. • COOK: 20 MIN. + STANDING • MAKES: 8 CUPS

8 cups fresh blueberries
2 Tbsp. lemon juice
1 pkg. (1¾ oz.) powdered fruit pectin
7 cups sugar

1. Rinse eight 1-cup plastic or freezer-safe containers and lids with boiling water. Dry thoroughly.

2. Mash blueberries; transfer to a Dutch oven. Add lemon juice; stir in pectin. Bring to a full rolling boil over high heat, stirring constantly.

3. Stir in sugar; return to a full rolling boil. Boil for 1 minute, stirring constantly. Remove from the heat; skim off foam. Ladle into containers and cool to room temperature, about 1 hour.

4. Cover and let stand overnight or until set, but not longer than 24 hours. Refrigerate for up to 3 weeks or freeze for up to 12 months.

2 Tbsp.: 95 cal., 0 fat (0 sat. fat), 0 chol., 0 sod., 25g carb. (24g sugars, 0 fiber), 0 pro.

LUSCIOUS
BLUEBERRY JAM

HOW-TO

Use a Steam Canner

- Fill the bottom of the steam canner with water.
- Place jars into canner with simmering water; place dome on base.
- Slowly increase stove temperature until a column of steam appears at the base of the dome. Process 10 minutes. Turn off heat. Let rest 2-3 minutes, then remove the dome. Let the jars cool completely.

BEST EVER SWEET PICKLES

BEST EVER SWEET PICKLES

Our urban backyard doesn't have room for a garden, so we use a trellis to grow cucumbers. Every summer I use up our bounty by packing away these sweet pickles.

—Ellie Martin Cliffe, Milwaukee, WI

PREP: 1 HOUR + STANDING • PROCESS: 10 MIN. • MAKES: 4 PINTS

- **9 cups sliced pickling cucumbers**
- **1 large sweet onion, halved and thinly sliced**
- **¼ cup canning salt**
- **1 cup sugar**
- **1 cup water**
- **1 cup white vinegar**
- **½ cup cider vinegar**
- **2 Tbsp. mustard seed**
- **1 tsp. celery seed**
- **½ tsp. whole peppercorns**
- **4 bay leaves**
- **12 garlic cloves, crushed**

1. In a large nonreactive bowl, combine cucumbers, onion and salt. Cover with crushed ice and mix well. Let stand 3 hours. Drain; rinse and drain thoroughly.

2. In a Dutch oven, combine sugar, water, vinegars, mustard seed, celery seed and peppercorns. Bring to a boil, stirring to dissolve sugar. Add cucumber mixture; return to a boil, stirring occasionally. Reduce heat; simmer, uncovered, 4-5 minutes or until heated through.

3. Carefully the ladle hot mixture into 4 hot wide-mouth 1-pint jars, leaving ½-in. headspace. Add 3 garlic cloves and 1 bay leaf to each jar. Remove air bubbles and, if necessary, adjust headspace by adding hot pickling liquid. Wipe rims. Center lids on jars; screw on bands until fingertip tight.

4. Place jars into canner with simmering water, ensuring that they are completely covered with water. Bring to a boil; process for 10 minutes. Remove jars and cool.

¼ cup: 35 cal., 0 fat (0 sat. fat), 0 chol., 175mg sod., 8g carb. (7g sugars, 0 fiber), 0 pro.

MOM'S PICKLED CARROTS

My mother is the only other person I've known to make this recipe. In fact, when I take it to a potluck or picnic, no one has ever heard of pickled carrots. But once they try them, they are hooked.

—Robin Koble, Fairview, PA

PREP: 15 MIN. + CHILLING • COOK: 20 MIN. • MAKES: 6 CUPS

- **2 lbs. carrots, cut lengthwise into ¼-in.-thick strips**
- **1½ cups sugar**
- **1½ cups water**
- **1½ cups cider vinegar**
- **¼ cup mustard seed**
- **3 cinnamon sticks (3 in.)**
- **3 whole cloves**

1. Place carrots in a large saucepan; add enough water to cover. Bring to a boil. Cook, covered, until crisp-tender, 3-5 minutes. Drain. Transfer carrots to a large bowl. In another large saucepan, combine remaining ingredients. Bring to a boil. Reduce heat; simmer, uncovered, for 20 minutes. Pour the mixture over carrots. Refrigerate, covered, overnight to allow flavors to blend.

2. Transfer mixture to jars. Cover and refrigerate up to 1 month.

¼ cup: 30 cal., 0 fat (0 sat. fat), 0 chol., 170mg sod., 7g carb. (6g sugars, 1g fiber), 1g pro.

5i BEST BEET PICKLES

Even though these luscious, sweet-spicy beets stand out like jewels at meals throughout the year, the flavor always takes me back to summer days.

—Marla Fogderud, Mason, MI

PREP: 1¼ HOURS • **PROCESS:** 35 MIN. • **MAKES:** 6 PINTS

- **3 lbs. fresh beets**
- **4 cups water**
- **2 cups sugar**
- **2 cups white vinegar**
- **2 Tbsp. mixed pickling spices**
- **12 whole cloves**

1. Scrub beets and trim tops to 1 in. Place in a Dutch oven and cover with water. Bring to a boil. Reduce heat; cover and simmer for 30-60 minutes or until tender. Remove from the water; cool. Peel beets and cut into 1-in. pieces.

2. Place beets in a Dutch oven. Add the water, sugar and vinegar. Place pickling spices on a double thickness of cheesecloth; bring up corners of cloth and tie with string to form a bag. Add to the beet mixture. Bring to a boil. Reduce heat; cover and simmer for 20 minutes. Discard spice bag.

3. Divide cloves among 6 hot pint jars; carefully pack beets into jars to within ½ in. of the top. Carefully ladle hot liquid over beets, leaving ½-in. headspace. Remove air bubbles; wipe rims and adjust lids. Process for 35 minutes in a boiling-water canner.

¼ cup: 40 cal., 0 fat (0 sat. fat), 0 chol., 52mg sod., 9g carb. (8g sugars, 1g fiber), 1g pro.

CHICAGO-STYLE HOT GIARDINIERA

I've lived in Chicago for the last 12 years and have grown to love the spicy giardiniera served at local restaurants, so I developed my own to use at home. We love it on everything from eggs to pizza!

—Andrea Quiroz, Chicago, IL

PREP: 30 MIN. + CHILLING • **MAKES:** 8 CUPS

- **1 small head cauliflower, broken into small florets (about 5 cups)**
- **2 celery ribs, chopped**
- **1 medium carrot, chopped**
- **4 jalapeno peppers, sliced**
- **4 serrano peppers, sliced**
- **½ cup salt**
- **1 cup white vinegar**
- **3 garlic cloves, minced**
- **2 tsp. dried oregano**
- **1 tsp. crushed red pepper flakes**
- **1 cup canola oil**
- **1 jar (10 oz.) small pimiento-stuffed olives, drained**

1. In a large bowl, toss cauliflower, celery, carrot and peppers with salt. Add cold water to cover. Refrigerate, covered, overnight.

2. Drain vegetables; rinse with cold water and drain again. In a large nonreactive bowl, whisk vinegar, garlic, oregano and pepper flakes. Gradually whisk in oil until blended. Add olives and drained vegetables; toss to coat. Refrigerate, covered, overnight to allow flavors to blend.

3. Transfer mixture to jars. Cover and refrigerate up to 3 weeks.

¼ cup: 80 cal., 8g fat (1g sat. fat), 0 chol., 174mg sod., 2g carb. (0 sugars, 0 fiber), 0 pro.

Test Kitchen Tip: Wear disposable gloves when cutting hot peppers; the oils can burn skin. Avoid touching your face.

"THIS IS AMAZING ON SANDWICHES!"

—KBIORDI, TASTEOFHOME.COM

CHICAGO-STYLE HOT GIARDINIERA

HOW-TO

Quick-Pickle Any Veggie

Quick pickles have three components: vegetables, brine and flavoring.

- *The Vegetables*. You can pickle just about any vegetable, but you'll get the best results using naturally firm, crisp produce. Leave slim vegetables, like green beans or asparagus, whole. Cut larger veggies into smaller pieces so they absorb the brine and flavorings better. You can cut veggies into coins, slices or spears, but always cut off the ends and stems, which contain an enzyme that can make pickles soggy.

- *The Brine*. A basic pickling brine contains vinegar, water and salt. This mixture preserves the vegetables and adds flavor. For quick-pickling, the brine is heated, allowing the salt to dissolve and the other ingredients to come together. Simply pour it over the veggies. As the vegetables soak, they soften slightly and take on flavor.

- *The Flavoring*. There are several ways to experiment with flavoring.
  Herbs: Add one type of herb. Adding more can muddy the flavor. Use dried or fresh, whole sprigs or chopped. After pouring the brine over the veggies, add dill,bay leaves, basil, cilantro, oregano, thyme, rosemary or tarragon.
  Spices: You can flavor with a spice or two. A hot spice and a fragrant spice often work well together. Toss them into the brine so the heat can bring out flavors and then pour over the veggies. Consider red pepper flakes, peppercorns, cumin, coriander, cayenne pepper or fennel seeds.
  Aromatics: Use as many aromatics as desired, knowing that the flavor will intensify over time. Slice aromatics with the veggies. Pour the brine over all. Try garlic, sliced onions, and spicy peppers such as jalapenos or bird's eye chiles.

REFRIGERATOR
JALAPENO
DILL PICKLES

REFRIGERATOR JALAPENO DILL PICKLES

I'm passionate about making pickles. My husband is passionate about eating them. He's too impatient to let them cure on the shelf, so I found this quick recipe to make him happy. Add hotter peppers if you'd like.

—Annie Jensen, Roseau, MN

PREP: 20 MIN. + CHILLING • MAKES: ABOUT 4 DOZEN PICKLE SPEARS

- **3 lbs. pickling cucumbers (about 12)**
- **1 small onion, halved and sliced**
- **¼ cup snipped fresh dill**
- **1 to 2 jalapeno peppers, sliced**
- **3 garlic cloves, minced**
- **2½ cups water**
- **2½ cups cider vinegar**
- **⅓ cup canning salt**
- **⅓ cup sugar**

1. Cut each cucumber lengthwise into 4 spears. In a very large bowl, combine cucumbers, onion, dill, jalapenos and garlic. In a large saucepan, combine water, vinegar, salt and sugar. Bring to a boil; cook and stir just until salt and sugar are dissolved. Pour over cucumber mixture; cool.

2. Cover tightly and refrigerate for at least 24 hours. Store in the refrigerator for up to 2 months.

1 pickle: 4 cal., 0 fat (0 sat. fat), 0 chol., 222mg sod., 1g carb. (0 sugars, 0 fiber), 0 pro.

Test Kitchen Tip: The garlic might turn a greenish hue due to a reaction between enzymes and the vinegar, but the overall flavor won't be affected.

QUICK PICKLED RADISHES

These pickled radishes are the perfect addition to tacos, barbecue or just about any sandwich you can dream of. Each sliced radish is a little bit sweet, slightly crunchy and has an amazing amount of zing.

—Colleen Delawder, Herndon, VA

PREP: 25 MIN. + CHILLING • MAKES: 3 CUPS

- **1 lb. radishes**
- **½ cup water**
- **½ cup cider vinegar**
- **¼ cup sugar**
- **¼ cup packed light brown sugar**
- **1 Tbsp. mustard seed**
- **1 tsp. kosher salt**
- **1 tsp. whole peppercorns**
- **1 to 2 bay leaves**

With a mandoline or vegetable peeler, cut radishes into very thin slices. Place radishes in a 1-qt. jar. In a large saucepan, bring remaining ingredients to a boil. Carefully ladle hot liquid over radishes. Cover and refrigerate overnight.

¼ cup: 11 cal., 0 fat (0 sat. fat), 0 chol., 296mg sod., 2g carb. (1g sugars, 1g fiber), 0 pro.

WATERMELON RIND PICKLES

Waste not, want not has always been smart advice—especially when it produces results that are so refreshing.
—Taste of Home *Test Kitchen*

PREP: 45 MIN. + CHILLING • PROCESS: 10 MIN. • MAKES: 4 PINTS

- **8 cups sliced peeled watermelon rind (2x1-in. pieces)**
- **6 cups water**
- **1 cup canning salt**
- **4 cups sugar**
- **2 cups white vinegar**
- **6 cinnamon sticks (3 in.), divided**
- **1 tsp. whole cloves**
- **1 tsp. whole peppercorns**

1. Place rind in a large nonreactive bowl; stir in water and salt. Refrigerate for several hours or overnight. Rinse and drain well.

2. In a Dutch oven, mix sugar, vinegar, 2 cinnamon sticks, cloves and whole peppercorns. Bring to a boil. Add rinds; return to a boil. Reduce heat; simmer, uncovered, 10 minutes or until tender. Discard cinnamon sticks.

3. Carefully ladle hot mixture into 4 hot 1-pint jars, leaving ½-in. headspace. Add a remaining cinnamon stick to each jar. Remove air bubbles and adjust headspace, if necessary, by adding hot mixture. Wipe rims. Center lids on jars; screw on bands until fingertip tight.

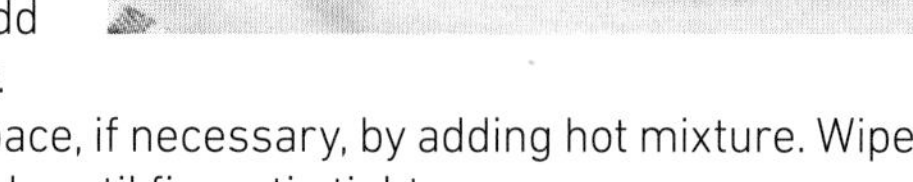

4. Place jars into canner with simmering water, ensuring that they are completely covered with water. Bring to a boil; process for 10 minutes. Remove jars and cool.

¼ cup: 16 cal., 0 fat (0 sat. fat), 0 chol., 96mg sod., 5g carb. (5g sugars, 0 fiber), 0 pro.

PICKLED PEACHES

Fresh peach quarters soaked in vinegar, sugar and warm spices is a classic southern treat. Serve with ice cream, pound cake, roasted meat and veggies, or mix into your favorite salad greens.
—Nick Iverson, Denver, CO

PREP: 20 MIN. • PROCESS: 15 MIN. • MAKES: 12 SERVINGS

- **6 cinnamon sticks (3 in.)**
- **24 whole peppercorns**
- **18 whole cloves**
- **2 tsp. thinly sliced fresh gingerroot**
- **12 medium peaches, peeled, pitted and quartered**
- **3 cups sugar**
- **1 cup white vinegar**
- **1 cup water**

1. Divide cinnamon sticks, peppercorns, cloves and ginger slices among 6 hot pint jars; add peaches.

2. In a large saucepan, bring sugar, vinegar and water to a boil. Carefully ladle hot liquid over the peaches, leaving ½-in. headspace. Remove air bubbles and adjust headspace, if necessary, by adding hot mixture. Wipe rims. Center lids on jars; screw on bands until fingertip tight.

3. Place jars into canner with simmering water, ensuring that they are completely covered with water. Bring to a boil; process for 15 minutes. Remove jars and cool.

4 pieces: 78 cal., 0 fat (0 sat. fat), 0 chol., 0 sod., 19g carb. (17g sugars, 2g fiber), 1g pro.

PICKLED PEACHES

THE BEST
MARINARA SAUCE

THE BEST MARINARA SAUCE

I developed this recipe with a friend to make the most of a bumper crop of tomatoes. Now we like to make huge batches—we're talking 220 pounds of tomatoes—and then give jars along with a pound of pasta as gifts around the holidays.

—Shannon Norris, Cudahy, WI

PREP: 1 HOUR + SIMMERING • PROCESS: 40 MIN. • MAKES: 9 CUPS

- **3 Tbsp. olive oil**
- **1 cup chopped onion**
- **⅓ cup minced garlic, divided**
- **12 lbs. plum tomatoes, quartered**
- **2 cups water**
- **1¼ cups minced fresh basil, divided**
- **¼ cup minced fresh oregano**
- **¼ cup tomato paste**
- **2 tsp. kosher salt**
- **1 tsp. coarsely ground pepper**
- **¼ cup plus 1½ tsp. lemon juice**

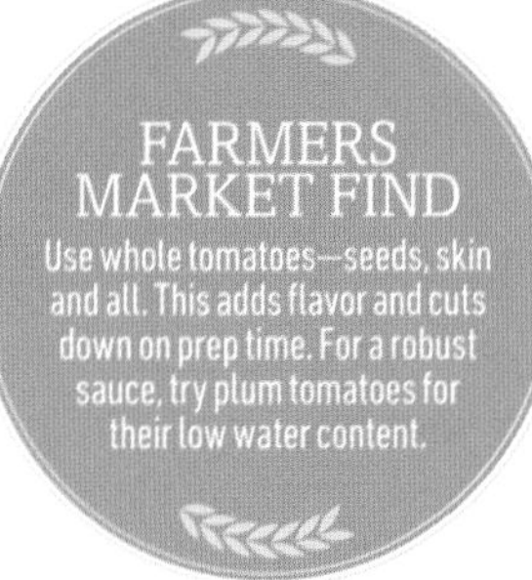

FARMERS MARKET FIND

Use whole tomatoes—seeds, skin and all. This adds flavor and cuts down on prep time. For a robust sauce, try plum tomatoes for their low water content.

1. In a stockpot, heat oil over medium heat. Add onion; cook and stir until softened, 3-4 minutes. Add 2 Tbsp. garlic; cook 1 minute longer. Add tomatoes, water and ½ cup basil; bring to a boil. Reduce heat; simmer, covered, until tomatoes are completely broken down and soft, about 1 hour, stirring occasionally.

2. Press tomato mixture through a food mill into a large bowl; discard the skins and seeds. Return tomato mixture to stockpot; add ½ cup of remaining basil, oregano and remaining garlic. Bring to a boil. Reduce the heat; simmer, uncovered, until thickened, 3½-4 hours, stirring occasionally. Add tomato paste and remaining ¼ cup of basil; season with salt and pepper.

3. Add 1 Tbsp. plus 1½ tsp. lemon juice to each of 3 hot 1½-pint jars. Ladle the hot mixture into jars, leaving ½-in. headspace. Remove air bubbles and adjust headspace, if necessary, by adding hot mixture. Wipe rims. Center lids on jars; screw on bands until fingertip tight.

4. Place jars into canner with simmering water, ensuring that they are completely covered with water. Bring to a boil; process for 40 minutes. Remove jars and cool.

¾ cup: 131 cal., 4g fat (1g sat. fat), 0 chol., 348mg sod., 22g carb. (13g sugars, 6g fiber), 5g pro. **Diabetic exchanges:** 1½ starch, 1 fat.

DR PEPPER BBQ SAUCE

My family is stationed in Italy with my husband. He grew up in Tennessee, and I'm from Texas, so this sauce reminds us of weekend barbecues with our families.

—Tina Blackman, Naples, AE

PREP: 5 MIN. • COOK: 35 MIN. • MAKES: 1 CUP

- **1 can (12 oz.) Dr Pepper**
- **1 cup crushed tomatoes**
- **¼ cup packed brown sugar**
- **2 Tbsp. spicy brown mustard**
- **1 Tbsp. orange juice**
- **1 Tbsp. Worcestershire sauce**
- **1 garlic clove, minced**
- **¼ tsp. salt**
- **⅛ tsp. pepper**

In a small saucepan, combine all ingredients; bring to a boil. Reduce heat; simmer, uncovered, 30-35 minutes or until slightly thickened, stirring occasionally. Refrigerate leftovers.

2 Tbsp.: 60 cal., 0 fat (0 sat. fat), 0 chol., 193mg sod., 15g carb. (12g sugars, 1g fiber), 1g pro.

END-OF-GARDEN RELISH

We dollop this tangy relish on burgers, hot dogs and salads. It's a cool way to use up garden produce and is always appreciated at picnics and potlucks.

—Karen Stucky, Freeman, SD

PREP: 45 MIN. + STANDING • PROCESS: 20 MIN. • MAKES: 6 PINTS

- **7 large cucumbers, shredded**
- **3 large onions, finely chopped**
- **3 cups shredded carrots**
- **2 medium sweet red peppers, finely chopped**
- **5 Tbsp. salt**
- **5 cups sugar**
- **3 cups white vinegar**
- **1 Tbsp. celery seed**
- **1 Tbsp. mustard seed**

1. Toss first 5 ingredients; let stand for 3 hours. Drain; squeeze and blot dry with paper towels.

2. In a Dutch oven, mix sugar, vinegar, celery seed and mustard seed; bring to a boil. Reduce heat; simmer, uncovered, 5 minutes. Add the vegetables; bring to a boil. Reduce heat; simmer, uncovered, 20 minutes.

3. Ladle hot mixture into hot 1-pint jars, leaving ½-in. headspace. Remove air bubbles and adjust headspace, if necessary, by adding hot mixture. Wipe rims. Center lids on jars; screw on bands until fingertip tight.

4. Place jars into canner with simmering water, ensuring that they are completely covered with water. Bring to a boil; process for 20 minutes. Remove jars and cool.

2 Tbsp.: 8 cal., 0 fat (0 sat. fat), 0 chol., 7mg sod., 2g carb. (1g sugars, 0 fiber), 0 pro.

BERRY-CHERRY PEACH SAUCE

Fresh peaches and berries shine in this pretty, refreshing sauce. It's terrific on ice cream, but also adds a sweet and tangy touch to pancakes, waffles or French toast at brunch.

—Sandra Gould, Verndale, MN

TAKES: 20 MIN. • MAKES: 2 CUPS

- **2 cups fresh or frozen sliced peeled peaches**
- **½ cup fresh or frozen blueberries**
- **6 fresh or frozen pitted dark sweet cherries, halved**
- **1 cup plus 1 Tbsp. orange juice, divided**
- **⅓ cup sugar**
- **1 Tbsp. cornstarch**
- **Vanilla ice cream**

1. In a large saucepan, combine the peaches, blueberries, cherries, 1 cup orange juice and sugar; cook and stir over low heat until sugar is dissolved. Bring to a boil. Reduce heat; simmer, uncovered, for 7 minutes or until peaches are tender.

2. Combine cornstarch and remaining orange juice until smooth; stir into hot fruit mixture. Bring to a boil; cook and stir for 2 minutes or until thickened. Remove from the heat. Serve with ice cream.

¼ cup: 76 cal., 0 fat (0 sat. fat), 0 chol., 0 sod., 19g carb. (16g sugars, 1g fiber), 1g pro.

SPICY BEET RELISH

We love the flavor of this ruby red relish with any type of meat or bean dish. It's also yummy as an appetizer spread. You can adjust the amount of cayenne and horseradish to suit your taste.

—Norma Leatherwood, Sevierville, TN

PREP: 1 HOUR • PROCESS: 15 MIN. • MAKES: 3 PINTS

4 lbs. fresh beets
1 cup sugar
1 cup cider vinegar
2 Tbsp. grated peeled horseradish
2 tsp. canning salt
½ tsp. cayenne pepper
¼ tsp. pepper
Optional: Sliced baguette and grated lemon zest

1. Scrub beets and trim tops to 1 in. Place in a Dutch oven; add water to cover. Bring to a boil. Reduce heat; simmer, covered, 45-60 minutes or until tender. Remove from water; cool. Peel and shred beets.

2. In a Dutch oven, combine sugar and vinegar; cook and stir over medium heat until sugar is dissolved. Stir in shredded beets, horseradish, salt, cayenne and pepper; bring to a boil.

3. Ladle hot mixture into hot 1-pint jars, leaving ½-in. headspace. Remove air bubbles and adjust headspace, if necessary, by adding hot relish. Wipe rims. Center lids on jars; screw on bands until fingertip tight.

4. Place jars into canner, ensuring that they are completely covered with water. Bring to a boil; process for 15 minutes. Remove jars and cool. If desired, serve on baguette and sprinkle with lemon zest.

¼ cup: 70 cal., 0 fat (0 sat. fat), 0 chol., 256mg sod., 17g carb. (15g sugars, 2g fiber), 1g pro.

COLORFUL CORN SALSA

This bright salsa is worth the extra time it takes to grill the ears of corn. The flavor goes well with barbecued meats, but it's also tasty served with chips.

—Nancy Horsburgh, Everett, ON

PREP: 30 MIN. • GRILL: 20 MIN. + COOLING • MAKES: ABOUT 2½ CUPS

2 medium ears sweet corn in husks
2 medium tomatoes, chopped
1 small onion, chopped
2 Tbsp. minced fresh cilantro
1 Tbsp. lime juice
1 Tbsp. finely chopped green pepper
1 Tbsp. finely chopped sweet red pepper
1 tsp. minced seeded jalapeno pepper
¼ tsp. salt
Dash pepper
Tortilla chips

1. Peel back husks of corn but don't remove; remove silk. Replace husks and tie with kitchen string. Place corn in a bowl and cover with water; soak for 20 minutes. Drain. Grill corn, covered, over medium-high heat until husks are blackened and corn is tender, turning several times, 20-35 minutes. Cool.

2. Remove corn from cobs and place in a bowl. Add tomatoes, onion, cilantro, lime juice, peppers, salt and pepper. Serve with tortilla chips.

¼ cup: 24 cal., 0 fat (0 sat. fat), 0 chol., 64mg sod., 5g carb. (0 sugars, 1g fiber), 1g pro. **Diabetic exchanges:** 1 vegetable.

AUTUMN PEPPER RELISH

I serve this colorful relish over cream cheese or a block of sharp cheddar cheese along with crackers or French baguette slices.

—Barbara Pletzke, Herndon, VA

PREP: 1 HOUR 20 MIN. + STANDING • **PROCESS:** 20 MIN./BATCH • **MAKES:** 8 HALF-PINTS

- **8 medium sweet red peppers (about 3 lbs.)**
- **6 jalapeno peppers**
- **4 medium Granny Smith apples (about 1¼ lbs.)**
- **2 medium pears (about 1 lb.)**
- **1 medium onion**
- **3 Tbsp. canning salt**
- **2 cups white vinegar**
- **2 cups sugar**
- **1 cup packed brown sugar**
- **¾ tsp. fennel seed**

1. Seed and coarsely chop peppers. Peel and cut apples, pears and onion into 1-in. pieces. Pulse in batches in a food processor until finely chopped. Transfer to a large bowl; sprinkle with salt and toss. Let stand 6 hours. Rinse and drain well; blot dry with paper towels.

2. In a Dutch oven, combine the drained pepper mixture, vinegar, sugars and fennel seed; bring to a boil. Reduce heat; simmer, uncovered, 40-45 minutes or until mixture is slightly thickened.

3. Carefully ladle the hot mixture into 8 hot half-pint jars, leaving ½-in. headspace. Remove air bubbles and adjust headspace, if necessary, by adding hot mixture. Wipe rims. Center lids on jars; screw on bands until fingertip tight.

4. Place jars into canner with simmering water, ensuring that they are completely covered with water. Bring to a boil; process for 20 minutes. Remove jars and cool.

2 Tbsp.: 13 cal., 0 fat (0 sat. fat), 0 chol., 4mg sod., 3g carb. (2g sugars, 1g fiber), 0 pro.

5i CHUNKY PEACH SPREAD

Here's a fruit spread that captures the best tastes of late summer. I like that it's low in sugar and not overly sweet.

—Rebecca Baird, Salt Lake City, UT

PREP: 20 MIN. • **COOK:** 10 MIN. + COOLING • **MAKES:** ABOUT 3½ CUPS

- **7 medium peaches (2 to 2½ lbs.)**
- **1 envelope unflavored gelatin**
- **¼ cup cold water**
- **⅓ cup sugar**
- **1 Tbsp. lemon juice**

1. Fill a large saucepan two-thirds full with water; bring to a boil. Cut a shallow "X" on the bottom of each peach. Using tongs, place peaches, a few at a time, in boiling water 30-60 seconds or just until skin at the "X" begins to loosen. Carefully remove the peaches and immediately drop into ice water. Pull off the skins with tip of a knife; discard skins. Chop peaches.

2. In a small bowl, sprinkle gelatin over cold water; let stand 1 minute. Meanwhile, in a large saucepan, combine peaches, sugar and lemon juice; bring to a boil. Mash peaches. Reduce heat; simmer, uncovered, 5 minutes. Add gelatin mixture; cook 1 minute longer, stirring until gelatin is completely dissolved. Cool 10 minutes.

3. Pour into jars. Refrigerate, covered, up to 3 weeks.

2 Tbsp.: 25 cal., 0 fat (0 sat. fat), 0 chol., 1mg sod., 6g carb. (5g sugars, 1g fiber), 1g pro.

CHUNKY
PEACH SPREAD

ROASTED EGGPLANT SPREAD

ROASTED EGGPLANT SPREAD

Black pepper and garlic perk up this out-of-the-ordinary spread that hits the spot on a crisp cracker or toasted bread slice.

—Barbara McCalley, Allison Park, PA

PREP: 20 MIN. • BAKE: 45 MIN. • MAKES: 2 CUPS

- **3 Tbsp. olive oil**
- **3 garlic cloves, minced**
- **½ tsp. salt**
- **½ tsp. pepper**
- **2 large sweet red peppers, cut into 1-in. pieces**
- **1 medium eggplant, cut into 1-in. pieces**
- **1 medium red onion, cut into 1-in. pieces**
- **1 Tbsp. tomato paste**
- **Toasted baguette slices or assorted crackers**

1. Preheat oven to 400°. Mix first 4 ingredients. Place the vegetables in a large bowl; toss with oil mixture. Transfer to a 15x10x1-in. pan coated with cooking spray. Roast vegetables until softened and lightly browned, 45-50 minutes, stirring once.

2. Transfer to a food processor; cool slightly. Add tomato paste; pulse just until blended (mixture should be chunky).

3. Transfer to a bowl; cool completely. Serve with toasted baguette.

¼ cup spread: 84 cal., 5g fat (1g sat. fat), 0 chol., 153mg sod., 9g carb. (5g sugars, 3g fiber), 1g pro. **Diabetic exchanges:** 1 vegetable, 1 fat.

SPICY KETCHUP

When this zesty ketchup is bubbling on the stove, the aroma takes me back to my childhood. One taste and I'm home again.

—Karen Naihe, Kamuela, HI

PREP: 30 MIN. • COOK: 1½ HOURS + CHILLING • MAKES: 1 CUP

- **1 Tbsp. olive oil**
- **1 medium onion, chopped**
- **3 lbs. tomatoes (about 11 medium), coarsely chopped**
- **1 cinnamon stick (3 in.)**
- **¾ tsp. celery seed**
- **½ tsp. mustard seed**
- **¼ tsp. whole allspice**
- **⅓ cup sugar**
- **1 tsp. salt**
- **¾ cup red wine vinegar**
- **1½ tsp. smoked paprika**
- **1½ tsp. Sriracha chili sauce, optional**

1. In a large saucepan, heat oil over medium-high heat. Add onion; cook and stir until tender. Stir in tomatoes; cook, uncovered, over medium heat 25-30 minutes or until tomatoes are softened.

2. Press tomato mixture through a fine-mesh strainer; discard solids. Return mixture to pot; bring to a boil. Cook, uncovered, until liquid is reduced to 1½ cups, about 10 minutes.

3. Place cinnamon, celery seed, mustard seed and allspice on a double thickness of cheesecloth. Gather corners of cloth to enclose spices; tie securely with string. Add to tomatoes. Stir in sugar and salt; return to a boil. Reduce heat; simmer, uncovered, 20-25 minutes or until thickened.

4. Stir in the vinegar, paprika and, if desired, chili sauce; bring to a boil. Simmer, uncovered, 10-15 minutes longer or until desired consistency is reached, stirring occasionally. Discard the spice bag.

5. Transfer to a covered container; cool slightly. Refrigerate until cold. Store in refrigerator for up to 1 week.

1 Tbsp.: 46 cal., 1g fat (0 sat. fat), 0 chol., 152mg sod., 9g carb. (7g sugars, 1g fiber), 1g pro. **Diabetic exchanges:** ½ starch.

HOW-TO

Make Freezer Pops With or Without a Mold

- Choose your mold. If you don't have a specialty freezer mold for pops, you can simply use an ice cube tray, small disposable cups or muffin tins lined with foil cupcake wrappers.
- Pour the ingredients into the mold, cover with aluminum foil and spear a wooden pop stick through the foil into the center of the mold. The foil will help the stick stay upright.
- Place the filled mold in the freezer. It should take about 2 hours for the treats to fully set.
- Check to see if the pops are firm before attempting to remove them from the mold.

BLUEBERRY CREAM POPS

5i ❄ BLUEBERRY CREAM POPS

Blueberries and cream make such a fun afternoon snack. These simple frosty treats star that combo of flavors.

—Cindy Reams, Philipsburg, PA

PREP: 15 MIN. + FREEZING • MAKES: 8 POPS

- **⅔ cup sugar**
- **⅔ cup water**
- **2 cups fresh or frozen blueberries, thawed**
- **¼ cup heavy whipping cream**
- **8 freezer pop molds or 8 paper cups (3 oz. each) and wooden pop sticks**

1. For sugar syrup, in a small saucepan, combine sugar and water; bring to a boil, stirring to dissolve sugar. Cool completely.

2. Meanwhile, in a bowl, coarsely mash blueberries; stir in cream and sugar syrup. Spoon into molds or paper cups. Top molds with holders. If using cups, top with foil and insert sticks through foil. Freeze until firm. To serve, let pops stand at room temperature 10 minutes before unmolding.

1 pop: 112 cal., 3g fat (2g sat. fat), 10mg chol., 3mg sod., 22g carb. (21g sugars, 1g fiber), 0 pro.

5i ❄ CANTALOUPE ICE POPS

Your reminders to eat your fruit will finally stick once kids take a lick of these snacks. A perfect use for overripe cantaloupe, these pops make a light dessert or healthy between-meal refresher.

—Susan Hein, Burlington, WI

PREP: 10 MIN. + FREEZING • MAKES: 1 DOZEN

- **4 cups cubed cantaloupe**
- **¼ cup sugar**
- **2 Tbsp. lemon juice**
- **1 Tbsp. chopped fresh mint or 1 tsp. dried mint**
- **½ tsp. grated lemon zest**
- **12 plastic cups or ice pop molds (3 oz. each)**
- **12 wooden pop sticks**

In a blender or food processor, combine the first 5 ingredients; cover and process until smooth. Pour ¼ cup into each cup or mold; insert the pop sticks. Freeze until firm.

1 pop: 35 cal., 0 fat (0 sat. fat), 0 chol., 9mg sod., 9g carb. (8g sugars, 0 fiber), 0 pro. **Diabetic exchanges:** ½ starch.

"THE FRESH MINT I USED, STRAIGHT FROM MY PARENTS' GARDEN, MADE ALL THE DIFFERENCE!"

—VICKYGR, TASTEOFHOME.COM

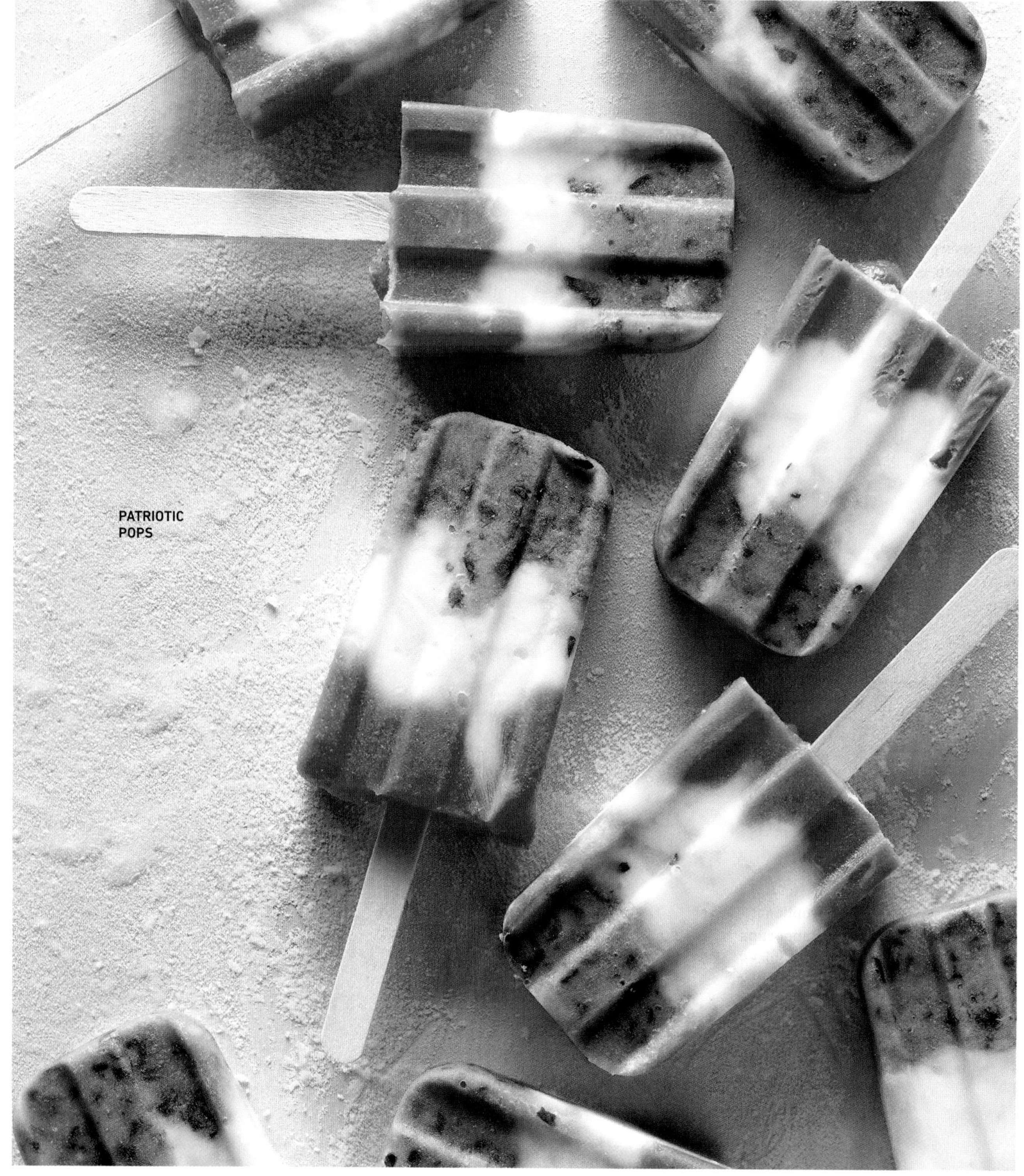

PATRIOTIC POPS

5i ❄ PATRIOTIC POPS

My kids love homemade ice pops, and I love knowing that the ones we make are good for them. We whip up a big batch with multiple flavors so they have many choices, but these patriotic red, white and blue ones are always a favorite!

—Shannon Carino, Frisco, TX

PREP: 15 MIN. + FREEZING • MAKES: 1 DOZEN

- **1¾ cups vanilla yogurt, divided**
- **2 Tbsp. honey, divided**
- **1¼ cups sliced fresh strawberries, divided**
- **1¼ cups fresh or frozen blueberries, thawed, divided**
- **12 freezer pop molds or 12 paper cups (3 oz. each) and wooden pop sticks**

1. Place 2 Tbsp. yogurt, 1 Tbsp. honey and 1 cup strawberries in a blender; cover and process until blended. Remove to a small bowl. Chop remaining strawberries; stir into strawberry mixture.

2. In blender, process 2 Tbsp. yogurt, remaining honey and 1 cup blueberries until blended; remove to another bowl. Stir in remaining blueberries.

3. In each mold, layer 1 Tbsp. strawberry mixture, 2 Tbsp. yogurt and 1 Tbsp. blueberry mixture. Top with holders. (If using paper cups, top with foil and insert sticks through the foil.) Freeze until firm.

1 pop: 55 cal., 1g fat (0 sat. fat), 2mg chol., 24mg sod., 11g carb. (10g sugars, 1g fiber), 2g pro. **Diabetic exchanges:** 1 starch.

5i ❄ STRAWBERRY-RHUBARB ICE POPS

These cool, creamy pops are a deliciously different way to use up the bounty from your rhubarb patch.

—Donna Linihan, Moncton, NB

PREP: 10 MIN. + FREEZING • COOK: 15 MIN. + COOLING • MAKES: 8 POPS

- **3 cups chopped fresh or frozen rhubarb (½ in.)**
- **¼ cup sugar**
- **3 Tbsp. water**
- **1 cup strawberry yogurt**
- **½ cup unsweetened applesauce**
- **¼ cup finely chopped fresh strawberries**
- **2 drops red food coloring, optional**
- **8 freezer pop molds or 8 paper cups (3 oz. each) and wooden pop sticks**

1. Place rhubarb, sugar and water in a large saucepan; bring to a boil. Reduce heat; simmer, uncovered, until thick and blended, 10-15 minutes. Remove ¾ cup mixture to a bowl; cool completely. (Save remaining rhubarb for another use.)

2. Add the yogurt, applesauce and strawberries to bowl; stir until blended. If desired, tint with food coloring. Fill each mold or cup with about ¼ cup rhubarb mixture. Top molds with holders; top cups with foil and insert sticks through foil. Freeze until firm.

1 pop: 72 cal., 0 fat (0 sat. fat), 2mg chol., 18mg sod., 16g carb. (14g sugars, 1g fiber), 2g pro. **Diabetic exchanges:** 1 starch.

RECIPE INDEX

Turn here for an alphabetical listing of the recipes in this book. If you are looking for recipes that call for a specific piece of produce, see page 5 for a detailed table of contents.

D

E

F

G

H

I

J

K

L

M

N

O

P

Q

R

S

T

V

W

Y

Z